CABIN FEVER

Notes from a Part-Time Pioneer

At a certain season of our life, we are accustomed to consider every spot as the possible site of a house.

—Henry David Thoreau, Walden, 1854

CABIN FEVER

Notes from a Part-Time Pioneer

by William L. Sullivan

Illustrated by Janell E. Sorensen

Navillus Press

Eugene, Oregon

For Ian and Karen

Published by the Navillus Press
1958 Onyx Street
Eugene, Oregon 97403
www.oregonhiking.com
Printed in USA

This book is a memoir based on the author's journals.
Place names and characters have been fictionalized to protect privacy.

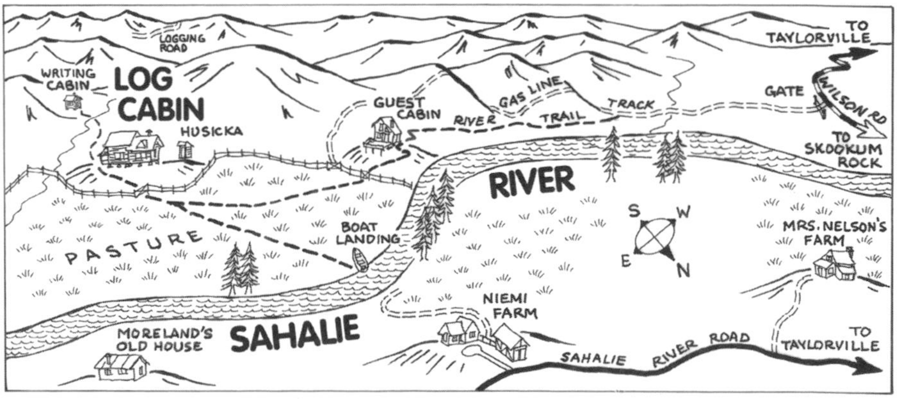

Contents

1

A Castle in the Air

(June 1977)

> If you have built castles in the air, your work need not be lost. That is where they should be. Now put the foundations under them.
>
> —Henry David Thoreau, Walden, 1854

The muddy green Sahalie River writhes through the rainforest canyons of Oregon's Coast Range like an angry bull snake. It hisses past the remnants of the old Sahalie Indian Reservation and coils around the forgotten farms at tidewater. But then look: For the final fifteen brackish miles it will fool you, this great green river. Suddenly it plays old and sleepy, lazing backwards almost as often as it slithers toward the sea. Giant Sitka spruce stand 200 feet tall on either bank, gangly limbs reaching out as if to shake hands in triumph over the silenced stream. Only gradually do you learn the truth, that the river has owned this valley all along. Whether you set down roots or pull them up, whether you build fences or dream of bridges, the Sahalie owns everything in its misty, moss-draped world.

"Say that again?" Janell looked up from her university homework.

"Do you want to build a log cabin out in the woods this summer?" I slid my notebook across the kitchen table of our Eugene, Oregon apartment to show her the doodle I had sketched of a one-room log house.

"A log cabin," she repeated slowly. But she did not laugh—and this is one of the reasons I love her. Although she serves as a voice of caution to my impetuousness, she has joined me on wildly improbable adventures more than once. The previous summer we bought student-standby tickets on the Queen Elizabeth II, sailed to France, and bicycled a thousand miles across Europe. This year we were out of money, desperately studying for teaching jobs. We both needed a summer escape, but could hardly afford tickets to the movies.

"It might be interesting to go camping for a while," she ventured. "When you say 'out in the woods' do you have some particular forest in mind?"

"On the Sahalie River. My parents still have property over there, remember?"

"The Sahalie?" She wrinkled her brow. "That place is awfully remote. I'll never forget the time you took me in there."

"I thought you kind of liked it."

She looked at me sideways. "We had to slog in a mile. The mud almost sucked off my rubber boots. It rained buckets all day."

"It doesn't rain all the time."

"Look, there wasn't even a trail—just some sort of bulldozer track that went straight up and down the hills."

Would I ever be able to explain the spell of the Sahalie? When I had first seen the valley on a family boat trip I was fifteen. On that trip I had felt like Meriwether Lewis on an expedition into a hidden green world.

The memory gave me an idea. "This time we wouldn't have to hike in along the old gas pipeline. We could take a boat. There's a dairy farm across the river. From there we can ferry in everything we need for the summer. My parents have a big wall tent we could borrow, and a Dutch oven for baking in the campfire too. You could bring your plant press and wildflower books. We'd be as snug over there as Robinson Crusoe on a jungle island."

She gave me a wry smile. "Just how snug *was* Robinson Crusoe?"

"Well, he escaped with his life at the end of the book, didn't he?"

We both laughed. I went to refill her coffee cup from the stove, thinking her cautious response might be right after all. When my parents bought the Sahalie property ten years ago they had been caught up by a dream of escaping there too. But the picnic table they built there washed away in a flood. The little travel trailer they tried to bring in slipped and crashed on the steep hill. Later a bear hunter hauled the wreck away. Although Mr. Niemi, the dairy farmer across the river, steadfastly rented our property's twenty-acre pasture, he paid only in beef, so the income didn't even pay the taxes. Finally my parents had written the whole thing off as a foolish investment. Last year they had put the property up for sale. The funny thing was, I think they were secretly glad there weren't yet any buyers.

When I turned to bring Janell her coffee I noticed she was gazing out our apartment window, her eyes focused somewhere beyond the telephone poles and asphalt rooftops of the city. My heart sped up a tick. Maybe I had cast the spell of the Sahalie better than I thought. "So what are you thinking?" I asked.

"I was wondering about the original homestead on that property."

"What you saw is all that's left. Just a pasture and a collapsed barn."

She shook her head. "No, I meant the old homesteader himself. Clyde somebody. Clyde Moreland. Wasn't he murdered over there?"

I handed her the coffee cup and sat down. "That's the rumor, but I'm not sure I believe it. I heard it from one of the farmer's boys, back when he was maybe ten years old. Kids that age have a thing about ghost stories. You don't really think our jungle island would have ghosts, do you?"

"I suppose not." She sipped her coffee, still obviously not quite at ease. The lure of an affordable summer getaway hung there before her. I could sense she was edging closer, sizing up the obstacles to my plan one at a time. "How would we bring enough food for a whole summer?"

"We'll use a boat to carry in things like rice and flour and canned goods," I said with renewed enthusiasm. "Then we can get fresh milk and eggs from the farm across the river."

Janell tilted her head. "Three months is an awful long time to get by without a hot shower or a real bathroom."

"We get by on backpacking trips, and this will be a lot more civilized. We'll bring a big washtub to heat water for baths. For fun, we can even go swimming in the river."

"Now about this cabin thing. How hard would that be, actually? I mean, just the two of us, and we don't have a car, or any money— "

"It would be a *log* cabin," I explained. "Everything we need is right there for free. My parents bought the place a few years after it was logged, and it's grown up crowded with little trees. They're just the right size for a little log cabin. I can notch the logs together like the cabins we saw in Europe, so we wouldn't even need nails."

I took out our photo album and showed her the log huts we had photographed while trekking through the Swiss Alps and the Norwegian uplands. The snapshots brought back memories of the mountain passes we had scaled together, the thundershowers we had waited out in haylofts, and the hardships we had toasted with a bottle of farmer's wine. She looked at me with a smile and a shrug. I knew then we were almost on our way.

"Maybe," she said. "Why not?"

And so that June when school was out Janell and I found ourselves headed a hundred miles west across the Coast Range toward a remote piece of real estate my parents weren't sure they still wanted. I was driving a growling Plymouth borrowed for the day, with an empty boat trailer and a trunk full of food, hand tools, sleeping bags, and tents. My unspoken agreement with Janell was that I had the summer to put foundations under the castle I had built in the air. My agreement with my parents was that we would only cut trees that needed to be thinned anyway from the crowded young forest. I think they expected our summer dreams to drift away like Oregon's coastal fog in the fall. "How much harm can they do?" my mother had asked. I recall my father opening his mouth to answer, but then he closed it without speaking.

Our first task was to tangle with the building permit bureaucracy in Seaview, a sleepy coastal burg that serves as the seat of Taylor County. As we drove into town, fog was rolling in from the gray void of the Pacific Ocean, burying the town's abandoned lighthouse and piling up behind the airy arch of the Harbor Bridge. The edge of the fog hovered over Highway 101, dappling with sun breaks the rust-streaked motel signs and roadside crab stands. We found our way to the courthouse's cement block basement. A weary-looking woman at an old wooden desk was stamping a stack of papers that read, "Mobile Home Application." Finally two young men in ill-fitting suits emerged from an office to see what Janell and I might want.

I laid my drawings on a table and explained, "We'd like to build this log cabin on my parent's property, and we need a permit."

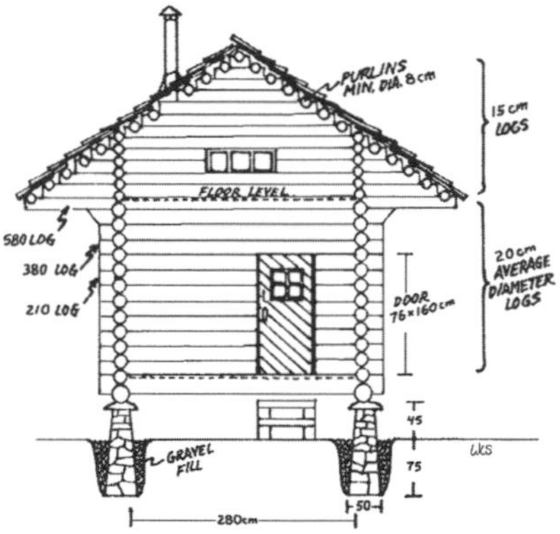

The men studied my sketch, frowning. "What kind of property?" one asked.

"Half timberland and half pasture." I pointed it out on a wall map. "Fifty-three acres on the Sahalie River."

The other man examined the location on the map. "Isn't that the place where the old man was murdered?"

Janell glared at me. "You told me that was just a rumor."

"I thought it was. I heard it from one of the farmer's boys. He made it sound like the homesteader died ages ago."

The first planner shrugged. "It's probably been ten or fifteen years. And I think they finally ruled it a suicide, anyway."

Janell did not look entirely reassured. I wished the incident had been a hundred years in the past, but I wasn't about to back out now. "What about our log cabin?"

"Well, what you've drawn here looks like an accessory building," the second man said.

“No,” I said, “the old homestead that used to be there rotted away.”

“Then we’re talking about a new main dwelling.”

“I suppose.” I looked to Janell for help.

“There’s no road or electricity,” she put in. “It’s really just a place to camp in the summer.”

“Yes, while we take care of the place,” I added.

“Ah, a forest or agricultural shed,” the first planner announced.

The other shook his head. “But this drawing shows a stovepipe. It’s clearly a dwelling. That means we’ll need running water, electricity, and a road for emergency vehicle access. What’s the square footage here?”

“It would be just one room, 280 by 380 centimeters inside,” I said, pointing out the dimension on the drawing.

“Centimeters?” The man pronounced the word slowly, as if he were repeating it from a learn-to-speak Swahili tape.

“Well yes, I drew it up in metric. It’s based on a traditional Norwegian design.”

The planners looked at each other. One scratched his head.

“That’s about ten by twelve feet,” I offered.

The second planner humphed. “A hundred and twenty square feet? Minimum size for a dwelling is five hundred.”

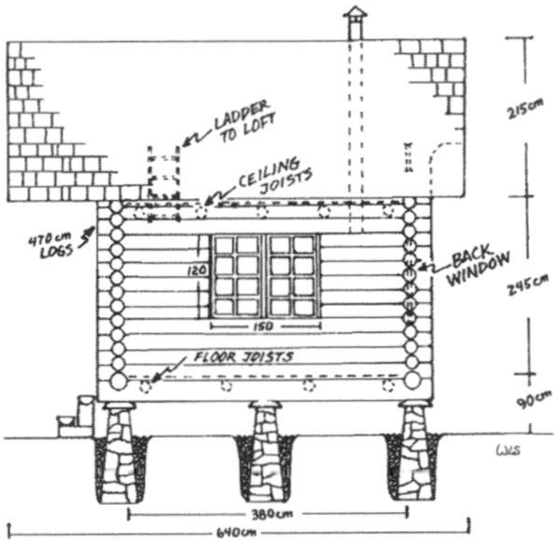

I groaned. “You mean it has to be four times larger or we can’t build it at all?”

He wrinkled his brow. “That does sound a bit stringent. But it’s not our job to make the rules.”

I shook my head. “I think you’d have thrown out Lewis and Clark for substandard housing.”

“Probably,” the first planner said. “The pioneers of yesterday are the shiftless hippies of today.”

Janell crossed her arms at this barb. “College students on summer vacation are *not* shiftless hippies.”

The forcefulness of her response seemed to set the man back. “No?”

“No. We’re—“ she groped for the right word—“We’re part-time pioneers.”

”I see.” He pursed his lips. “Well, hang on and maybe we can find something in the code books that will work.” He pulled several weighty tomes from a shelf and began leafing through them.

Minutes passed. Finally I asked, “Well?”

The second planner scoffed, “He’s just stalling, waiting for a bribe.”

"I am not," the first retorted. Then he glared at me. "Why did you come in here anyway? This is the sort of thing people build out in the woods without bothering about permits."

"I wanted to do it right. My father works for the newspaper, and I don't want to get him in trouble."

The first planner drummed his fingers on the book. "All right, here we have it." He read off a code and section number. "We'll call it a rustic storage facility. Mark, fill out a permit for our pioneers." He slapped the book shut and stalked off to his office.

Mark pulled out a triplicate form and began filling the blanks. "Frontage direction?" he asked.

"Pardon?"

He translated. "Which side of the building faces the road?"

"There isn't a road."

"Right. Well, then the river."

"It bends."

He rolled his eyes. "I'll put down 'east'." Then he asked, "Setback?"

Again I hesitated.

"How many feet is the building set back from the edge of the lot?"

"Oh. Again, that depends. Between an eighth and a quarter mile, I'd say."

Finally he used a felt pen to fill out a stiff yellow cardboard sign. "This will have to be posted conspicuously on the premises until completion."

I read the sign's list of mandatory on-site inspections: Frame. Lath. Wallboard. I asked skeptically, "You do understand that this is a log cabin, and not a frame building?"

Mark shrugged. "We don't have guidelines for log construction."

"And so the inspections—?" I began.

He shook his head. "Don't call. I don't like boat rides."

Janell quickly put in, "Weren't we supposed to get some kind of sewer permit for an outhouse, too?"

Mark looked at her a little sadly. "I didn't hear that question. Goodbye and good luck."

Bright yellow building permit in hand, we drove back along Highway 101 and turned inland along the Sahalie River Road in search of a boat. Janell had agreed that our best approach to my parents' remote property would be rowing across the river from the Niemi dairy farm. My father had noticed a classified advertisement in his newspaper that said Bartola Landing, an old marina along the river, was getting rid of its rowboats for $75 apiece. He suggested offering $50. My mother recommended starting at $35.

When we actually saw the fleet—a row of ancient green wooden rowboats rotting in the tall grass behind the marina's run-down trailer park, I offered $25.

"Those ones over there would be excellent for planters," suggested Barry Bartola, the marina owner. He was a big man with an enormous paunch and a gray stubble beard. Apparently he traveled everywhere on a riding lawn mower—even across his yard to sell a boat. "But this one here's worth every penny of $40. No leaks."

I wiggled the front seat and it came off in my hand. Rusted screws hung from the support slat.

"All right, $25 as is," Bartola grumbled. "Where are you kids planning on launching, anyway? It's an extra $5 to use my boat ramp."

"We're driving to the Niemi dairy farm," I said. "My parents bought some property across the river from them."

Bartola stared at me. Then he chuckled until his paunch jiggled. "Clyde Moreland's place?"

"Why? What's the matter with that?" Everyone we met in this county seemed to know more about our property than we did.

"Nothing, nothing."

Janell asked, "Did you know the old homesteader?"

"Oh yeah. Clyde and me went way back." Bartola's smile faded. He shifted his lawn mower into reverse. "Now let's see your $25."

After we had paid him and he had driven away, Janell and I dragged the heavy twelve-foot boat onto our trailer.

"I hope this thing floats," she sighed.

Something in her voice told me it was not just the boat that worried her. The closer we came to launching our grand adventure, the leakier the entire plan seemed. We were packing into a wilderness rainforest to play at being pioneers, but what did we really know about that lifestyle? We had both grown up in the city. Suddenly the dangers of our back-to-the-earth scheme swelled before us, a frightening tide of doubts.

What would it mean if our predecessor Clyde Moreland really had been murdered? Who would have killed such an isolated settler, and why? Was the killer still in the valley? Would we be targets as well? How much did Barry Bartola know about the whole affair?

And what about wild animals? We knew almost nothing about the bears and cougars that lived in these woods. Were there rattlesnakes or water moccasins too? If a snake bit us, how would we know if it was poisonous? Did the mosquitoes here carry spotted fever? Who knew what leeches and parasites infested the water of this rainforest?

Even if we avoided wildlife attack, we might easily injure ourselves building a house of logs. How would we get help if a tree fell on us, or if we broke a leg, or got food poisoning, or appendicitis? Suppose drunken hunters shot us, or robbers found our camp? Our side of the river had no telephone, and we didn't have a radio transmitter. If we couldn't get across the river to the dairy farm in an emergency, no one would know we needed help.

Before the summer was out we were likely to face torrential rains, lightning, and windstorms. Any of them could destroy our tent camp and leave us shivering in the cold. Even a house would not be a sure refuge in this valley. Because the Sahalie River had no dams, sudden floods roared through, sweeping buildings and cattle before them. If the rains stopped for long, forest fires could flash through the woods.

This daunting list of hazards was topped by one gigantic red warning flag, something any practical observer would have pointed out long ago: Janell and I didn't know if we could build a log cabin at all! For crying out loud, we had never even felled a tree! Sure, we had checked out books on log buildings, and we had been swept up by the "back-to-the-earth" craze of the 1970s. But we were going to need a lot more than macrame skills and whole-grain recipe books to get by.

My parents were scheduled to come pick up our borrowed car that evening. After that we would be marooned out here until they came again with a car later in summer.

"Let's call it *Earnest*," I said.

"Call what?" Janell looked up flustered, as if she too had just surfaced from murky waters.

"Our new boat. It needs a name."

"But why *Earnest*?"

"That way, when we row across the river to start our log cabin, we'll be going in *Earnest*."

She couldn't help laughing. She tilted her head at me and the sun shone as rich as honey on her shoulder-length hair. It was as if we both had needed to laugh at the worries we had brought along. Ahead lay an adventure, and even if we knew less about pioneering than most of the young couples on the Oregon Trail, as long as we had each other, we would get by.

We leaned together into a hug, and I kissed her hair.

2

A Visit to the Niemis

(June 1977)

> Erect your own shelter! Something about building a wilderness home takes you close to the beginning of things. An atavism it is; but none the less vital for all that.
>
> —Bradford Angier, How to Build Your Home in the Woods, 1952

The farther we drove up the Sahalie River Road, towing *Earnest* toward its launch, the fewer mailboxes we passed. When the winding road narrowed and turned to gravel, the occasional farm fields seemed to have given way entirely to forest.

"Do the dairy farmers know we're coming?" Janell asked.

"My father said he'd call ahead."

Janell didn't seem reassured. "I wish I knew more about them, especially if we're going to be neighbors all summer."

"Didn't you read my father's article?"

She nodded. My father wrote a weekly column for the Salem newspaper. The previous month, inspired perhaps by our talk of log cabins, he had done a piece about the challenges faced by the people who live along the Sahalie River. The George Niemi family, he wrote, was carrying on the self-reliant traditions of the area's pioneers from the early 1900s. Many of the first white settlers had been Finnish—including George's father Gus, a man still remembered for his resourcefulness. Together with Waino Paaki, the pioneering Niemi had rescued settlers from starvation in the stormy winter of 1909 by rafting a one-ton box of supplies down the flooded river against great odds.

"Your Dad's column didn't say much about the Niemis now," Janell said. "How many children they have, for example."

"Two boys," I said.

"No daughters?"

"I don't think so. I met the boys when my parents first bought the place. Jack and Joe, I think, or maybe Jerry. I remember being amazed that they could run around barefoot in a field full of thistles and cow pies. They must be out of high school by now. I wonder if they still live at home?"

While we had been talking the rainforest had gradually closed out the sky, turning our road into a dark green tunnel. I was beginning to worry that we had driven too far. Finally I spotted the Niemis' mailbox. I turned down a long driveway through a sunny field.

We drove past a red barn where the heads of curious calves peered out between planks. Across the lane, rusty barbed wire sagged between thick wooden fenceposts. At the end of the driveway a one-story green shake farmhouse overlooked a riverbend. On the far shore in the distance glinted the emerald green of our pioneer pasture.

A large farm dog of uncertain breed had been nipping at our tires as we drove down the lane, perhaps trying to herd us along. Now he parked before us and growled through the window.

Janell has a way with animals. She got out slowly, murmuring assurances, and soon had us up at the farmhouse door, with the giant dog's tail sweeping the walk behind us.

I pushed the doorbell. Although the button didn't seem to activate any device inside, it did set the dog to barking, and this in turn made the kitchen curtain flutter. A moment later the door opened to frame a large, smiling woman in a loose print dress. She was shaped something like an apple, or perhaps I was so strongly reminded of apples because of her rosy cheeks and the magic aroma of pie.

"Mrs. Niemi? I'm Bill Sullivan and—"

She cut me off with a friendly wave that ushered us inside. "Well, and this must be Janell. Yes, we've heard all about you from your father, the newspaperman. That was something, him writing the story about George's father. Call me Dolores, won't you? I'll see if I can get one of the boys to find George."

Inside, the house was so dark it took me a moment to adjust my eyes. Somewhere a television show blared laughter. A bare light bulb hanging in the entryway gradually revealed that the walls and ceiling were made of ordinary four-by-eight-foot sheets of fir plywood, darkened with age. In the living room beyond—where shabby sofas lurked—a brown lampshade was printed with lassos, cattle brands, and other cowboy motifs. Ahead on a wall hung a small plaster cast of praying hands. Toward the kitchen, a decoupage plaque had a picture of a wife clobbering a man with a rolling pin, and a caption about who is boss in the kitchen. The gray carpets of the living room were worn entirely through to the unfinished floorboards. But the *Ruralite* magazines on the coffee table had been arranged as neatly as shingles, and the dirt of the farm boots had been confined to an arc near the door. This was a homemade house that told me it was doing daily battle with the forces of dirt, chaos, and poverty outside. It was holding its own against long odds.

"Hullo." A young man in flopping socks shuffled up sleepily from a corridor I had overlooked. His blue-striped work shirt bulged over a paunch that was surprisingly large for so young a man. I searched the round face, tousled hair, and sheepish grin for a reflection of the Niemi sons I had met on the riverbank years before.

"You must be—Jack?"

"No, uh-uh. I'm Joe." He stooped to pull on a pair of knee-high rubber boots from a row of similar boots just inside the door. "Pa's out in the milking parlor. I'll show you there."

I turned for Janell, but discovered she had slipped into the kitchen with Dolores. In fact, the two women were sitting over coffee mugs at the kitchen table, already talking about which brand of pectin to use when canning strawberry jam. I sensed that walking across the linoleum to join them would be crossing an invisible barrier—breaking a rule that divides this farm by gender.

"Sure. Let's go see the milking parlor," I said. "You probably have to work there a lot?"

Joe shook his head as he pushed out the door. "Naw. No way. I'm too busy with my own stuff." He slowed down a bit as he walked the length of the Plymouth and the boat trailer. His eyes took in everything from the wire hubcaps to the boat's rotten seat. When he had passed it all by, he proudly held out his hand toward a car parked behind a fence. "*This* is mine."

It took me a moment to realize that his vehicle must once have been a Volkswagen beetle. The doors and most of the roof were missing, and the inside had been gutted. A tractor seat had been bolted behind the steering wheel for the driver. But the oddest features of the vehicle were two large metal blades welded onto either side of the chassis with metal struts. The car looked like it was trying to sprout wings.

"Is it—is it going to be an airplane?"

He laughed, and I saw that nearly half of his teeth were missing. "No, uh-uh. It's a skunk cabbage whacker."

"Oh?" I knew a little about skunk cabbage. It grows in damp areas along the coast, sprouting spectacular, three-foot-long, boat-shaped leaves and huge yellow flowers. Tourists sometimes stop along Highway 101 to gather the impressive blooms, only to toss them out the car window moments later when the smell takes hold. Skunk cabbage is pollinated by flies instead of bees, so it strives to smell like something dead.

I could see why a dairy farmer might think of it as a weed.

I looked back to Joe's contraption. "How does it work?"

"You gun the engine across the pasture," he said, flattening his hand like a plane coming in for a landing, "and you hit those suckers at forty miles an hour."

"Joe?" a voice interrupted from the door of a low building by the barn.

Joe scowled. "I'll show you how it works later."

Joe's father, George, leaned out of the shed's doorway. A galvanized milk can dangled from his lanky arm. When he caught sight of us his face shifted visibly through a variety of emotions, from surprise, to consternation, to curiosity. Finally it settled on a half-embarrassed, friendly sort of laugh, which seemed to be its natural state. "Well, why didn't you say we had visitors?"

I strode forward and held out my hand to shake. "Hi, I'm Bill Sullivan."

George pushed the door open wider with his foot, causing the door-closure spring to boing and creak. He pulled out his other hand as if to shake, but it was already holding a piece of stainless steel milking machinery with dangly rubber hoses. He looked from one hand to the other, until he finally set down the milk can and offered me his left hand. As we shook hands I marveled that his fingers were twice the size of mine—callused, bony things capped with immense yellow nails.

"My parents own the pasture across the river," I explained. "My wife and I plan to spend the summer over there, and we're hoping you'll let us launch our boat from your farm."

"Oh—so you bought one of those old boats from Barry Bartola?" This was apparently the only real news in my introductory speech. He craned his neck to see the wooden vessel on our trailer. His face ran through several new expressions—worry, interest, alarm. "How much did he ask?"

"Forty dollars, but I only gave him twenty-five."

George's eyebrows went up and down once. Then he guffawed. "Well, you're sure welcome to use our road, as long as you close the gate behind you. Starts right by the house there. Joe'll show you the way."

"Pa!" Joe objected. "You know I don't—"

George cut him short. "Now a boy's got to do something to earn his keep around here, even if it's just checking on the heifers across the river."

Joe scowled and shuffled off toward his skunk cabbage cutter. George replied with a helpless shrug. Then he picked up the milk can and nodded for me to follow him inside.

The peeling paint on the outside of this unassuming shed did not prepare me for what I found on the interior. The room was immaculately whitewashed, outfitted with gleaming stainless steel tanks, sinks, and pipes. A powerful, sweet smell of warm milk mingled with the sharp tang of chlorine in the humid air. George turned to continue washing milking machinery in a steaming sink. He starting talking to me again, but a pump above his head suddenly turned on, gushing milk through clear plastic tubes toward the steel tank, and drowned him out. When the pump finally churned to a halt, leaving a froth of milk in the transparent hose, George was pointing a dripping finger at a clipboard beside the sink. "Point zero zero one," he chuckled, with a note of genuine pride. "That's the bacteria count the milk driver got on his run here last night. Second lowest in the whole dang Tillamook Creamery. Highest butterfat, too. I'm partial to Jerseys."

Although I hadn't caught much of his talk, I could tell we were close to the next subject I wanted to broach. "Janell and I won't have a lot of fresh food over there this summer, so I was wondering if we could buy milk and eggs from you?"

"Eggs? We've never had chickens, but we've got fifty-eight milk cows. Takes most of the forenoon to milk 'em. There's five or eight folks from up and down the valley that come by to get milk at a dollar a gallon. We don't encourage 'em."

"Would you encourage me?"

He smiled. "Well, sure. Just as long as you bring your own container." He stooped and lifted the metal lid off the little one-gallon milk can with a clang. Thick cream dripped off from the lid's rim to the concrete floor. "It's not homogenized, you know, so most folks ladle off the top two inches. Course my boys like it whole."

While he was talking a black-and-white cat squeezed under an inner door and shot forward to the spilled cream.

"Shoo!" he said. The cat ignored him. George looked up at me. "Inspector says the milking parlor cats can't come in here."

"I'd think they would help keep down the mice," I said.

"Well, they do." He stroked the cat on its neck with his huge, rough fingers, and then gave it a gentle push. It shot back under the door. Beyond, I could hear a radio and a long, low moo.

"Can I take a look?" I asked, pointing to the door.

"Sure."

The door was counterbalanced with a dangling collection of scrap metal that rode up on a pulley as I pushed it open. The first thing I saw inside was a gigantic, snorting Holstein, scraping her hooves on the concrete. She crashed against an iron railing like a wrestler thrown against the ropes.

"God damn it, Twenty-Three, you've had your turn! Now git!" The younger of the two Niemi sons stood on rubber mats in a trough between two railed walkways, poking a stick into the hindquarters of the cow. Finally she tossed her head and pushed through a swinging gate to the barnyard. Promptly the cow behind her stepped up to the stanchion.

The young man nodded briefly to me. Then he hosed off the cow's udder and attached the milking machine cups.

The crackling din of a radio's country music made talk difficult. "Hi, Jack. I'm Bill!" I shouted. If the other son was Joe, this one had to be Jack.

"I call him Mr. Dependable," George told me proudly. "He was up this morning at five, rounding up the cows from the lower field with a flashlight." He ran his big thumbs behind the striped red suspenders across his blue work shirt. Then he stepped forward to inspect a swelling beside the cow's eye.

I wondered at the way Jack and Joe seemed to have changed in the years since I had first met them. I would have thought that Joe, the older son, would have taken up the serious farm work with an eye toward one day inheriting the farm. But instead it was the younger brother, Jack, who sweated in the milking parlor, praised by his farther as "Mr. Dependable." The older boy apparently slept in until noon, scorned the trivial tasks his father assigned him, and spent his time on bizarre skunk cabbage whacking contraptions. I knew all too well that siblings try to be different from each other—my brother Pete and I had likewise each tried to stake out roles the other had overlooked—but I was still surprised that Joe and Jack had changed so much in only a few years.

George spoke a few soothing words to the cow and gently applied a salve from a can on a shelf. Meanwhile the Holstein in the opposite stanchion had begun pawing the concrete walkway there. Jack swung about to take off its milking machine. He dipped its teats in a cup of red disinfectant and prodded the cow onward to make room for the next one to be milked.

Suddenly I felt self-conscious about everything I had planned for the summer. Jack was perhaps seventeen years old. Already he was putting in six hours of hard work per milking, twice a day, from five in the morning until probably long after dark. Building a log cabin without power tools must seem like a lark to Jack. Even my clothes suddenly felt stiff and pretentious: New Sears work boots that had never touched mud. Clean blue jeans without a single hole, while Jack's were threadbare.

With a start I realized that I might not be the same after three months of pioneering in this corner of Oregon. Would the experience harden me, like Jack, or soften me, like Joe? I had come intending to leave my mark on the wilderness. But was I prepared for the mark it would leave on me?

"Don't forget your milk," George said, startling me from my reverie. "And good luck with your log cabin." He chuckled and exchanged a glance with Jack that silently added the words, "You'll need it."

3

Setting Out in Earnest

(June 1977)

> I determined, therefore, to proceed down the river on the east side in search of an eligible place for our winter's residence, and accordingly set out early this morning in the small canoe.
> —Meriwether Lewis, The Journals of Lewis and Clark, 1805

When I returned from the milking parlor to the Niemi farmhouse in search of Janell, I found she had exchanged a dozen of the rolls she had baked the previous night for a jar of Dolores's homemade blueberry jam. Joe was waiting by the open gate with a bored expression and the wagging farm dog. As we drove the Plymouth past I asked if the dog was good at herding cows.

"You mean Laddie?" Joe looked down at the dog as if he had just discovered it. "No, uh-uh. They ignore him. Haven't found any use for him yet."

At the bottom of the little hill the road petered out in a broad pasture of closely cropped grass and a few tall weeds. I backed up toward the bank and got out to take a look. The pasture crumbled twenty feet down to the beachless river. The Niemis' boat lay half-sunk at the water's edge. It was an aluminum husk without seats. For some reason its front deck had been removed with an ax in jagged hacks, leaving the boat with the look of a crudely opened tin can.

Joe and Laddie ambled up to share the view.

"How on earth do you get the cows from our pasture across the river to milk them?" I asked.

"There aren't any cows on your pasture," Joe said. "No way."

"But your father's renting it from us. I thought he had nineteen head over there."

"Nineteen *heifers*, sure," Joe said. "No cows."

I considered this distinction. "So the ones on our side are too young to milk?"

"Yeah. They got to be about two years old and have a calf first. Then we bring 'em back to milk."

By now Janell had joined us. "But how did you get them across the river in the first place? Not in that boat?"

"No, uh-uh. We swum 'em. Then after about five days they all swum back." His eyes narrowed. "I went over there and found bear sign. I figure that's what spooked 'em. But Pa swum 'em back anyway." He looked across the river nervously. "Bears aren't the only dangers over there."

"No? What else?" Janell asked, a new tone of worry in her voice.

Joe shook his head and went to pull an old pair of hand-hewn oars from the blackberry bramble where they had been hidden. "Maybe you'll see."

I mouthed the word "ghosts" to Janell. Joe had always been keen on ghost stories.

She raised an eyebrow. "Come on. I want to get our camp set up. We've got a ton of stuff to move."

"Right. My folks should be here soon with the wheelbarrow. In the meantime, let's just get everything across the river."

This proved to be more difficult than I had imagined. I had forgotten about the effect of tides on this river. Eight miles from the ocean, the water here still rose and fell six feet, twice a day. The river now was at its lowest ebb, leaving four yards of steep, soft mud between the grass and the murky green water.

We let *Earnest* clear a path by pointing him down the bank and giving him a good push. Once he was afloat, and I determined that he didn't leak too badly, we staggered down through the ankle-deep mud with the first load of gear. We loaded the rowboat with two forty-pound wall tents borrowed from our families' camping supplies, a cast-iron Dutch oven, and a three-foot-tall can packed with nearly a hundred pounds of flour and beans.

Anticipating that we would need to guard our food from mice and moisture, we had acquired three of these green metal cans from my parents' church. The cans had been designed to store water in the event of a nuclear attack. They still bore labels with bright yellow instructions from the Civil Defense department. In the late 1950s the basement of my family's church had been identified as one of dozens of bomb shelters where Salem citizens could hunker if the big one fell. In those early days even grade schools held nuclear bomb drills. My family developed a plan to stack books on top of our basement ping pong table and wait down there during an attack, shielded from the radiation outside. But gradually people learned that the fallout from a genuine nuclear attack would leave deadly radiation for centuries, rather than just for a few days, and the bomb shelter craze waned. By then the church was more than willing to clear the storage cans out of its basement.

The boat rode perilously low in the water. Janell and I sat atop our gear, rowing across in *Earnest*. Joe, meanwhile, had bailed and launched his seatless, ax-trimmed vessel. He swung an oar menacingly, trying to keep the muddy farm dog from leaping in after him. When Laddie realized he really was not going to get a ride, he splashed into the river on his own, dog-paddled past us, and was already waiting on the far shore, shaking water like a lawn sprinkler, when we nudged the muddy bank.

Now the real work began, because there was no boat landing on our side of the river. We had to waddle up through the mud with the unwieldy cans and tents, hack a route through the willow brush, and clamber up another thirty feet to the edge of the pasture. After our third boat trip, my parents finally arrived to pick up the borrowed car. By then Janell and I were streaked with mud and sweat, our hands scratched, and our hair awry.

"Are you all right?" My father asked.

My mother sized us up and evidently determined that we should not yet be ready to admit defeat. "Of course they're all right. They just need help." With that she began manhandling a wooden wheelbarrow out of the car and down the bank in her street shoes. Dad followed cautiously with some of the ungainly logging tools we had asked them to bring.

The wheelbarrow and the tools had been the legacy of my grandfather, John Harley Sullivan. He had been a millwright before the Great Depression, building and repairing sawmills in the Portland area. He was the millworkers' union president in the 1930s, when the chief requirement for the job was that you had to be able to beat any man on the crew in a fistfight. With a name like John H. Sullivan—tauntingly close to the prizefighter John L. Sullivan—he had been tested all his life. When he passed away at the age of 82 that spring, the family had gathered at his Portland house to divide up his few possessions.

My oldest brother Mark, who had long since moved away from home and set up his own household, took a carpet. My sister Susan took an antique end table and some china bowls. Peter, my other brother, is only fourteen months older than I am, but is unlike me in many ways. He chose to take a massive ten-horsepower table saw—the same weapon that had once sliced off an inch of Grandpa's ring finger. Pete rolled his eyes when I said I wanted the rotten wooden wheelbarrow behind Grandpa's garage. It had an iron wheel and plank sideboards. I vowed to replace the wood and paint it white.

Perhaps because I was the youngest, I was sent to crawl into Grandpa's attic to see if he had stashed any valuables there. I suppose the family hoped to find a coffee can full of gold coins or silverware. Instead I found three ancient, wood-handled tools. They included a massive timber ax, a five-foot crosscut saw—with handles for two people—, and a strange tool that looked like an ax with its blade turned sideways. I later learned this was an adze, used to flatten the sides of logs. Together, the three tools were the basic equipment needed to build a log cabin.

Why had Grandpa stored such tools in his attic? Had he hidden them up there because he knew they had become useless in the modern world? Or was he secretly concerned that civilization might be a shaky facade over the bedrock of the pioneer landscape? When Grandpa lost his job at the start of the Depression, he had not joined the desperate throngs lining up for soup in the cities. Instead he had moved his family to a rural berry farm to scavenge on their own. Forty years later, the newspapers were once again full of ominous headlines: riots in the inner cities, atomic bomb tests, and Vietnam. Perhaps the ax, saw, and adze in Grandpa's attic were the final insurance policy of a self-reliant man. If the cities should crumble, a millwright could hew a home from the woods with such tools. I wondered: Could I?

I ferried the wheelbarrow across the river and wrestled it up onto the pasture beside the pile of our other gear. Next we had to cart the stuff nearly a quarter mile through the tall grass and thistles to the cabin site. I had decided to build our house beside a dappled green alder grove on an overgrown logging road that curved around the far end of the pasture. It was a spot that had caught my fancy ten years ago, when my family had first visited the Sahalie. My father still called the grove "Bill's Alders."

"Will the cows be a problem?" my mother asked Joe. "You know, chasing us?"

"Heifers? No, uh-uh. No way. They're just gentle dairy cattle. They won't bother your camp none."

Mother looked relieved. "Good. I was afraid there might be a bull."

"Oh, well sure there's a bull," Joe said.

Mother stopped. She picked up a long, stout stick from beneath one of the riverside trees. "Maybe it's safest if we go in a group."

"I'll take the wheelbarrow," I suggested. Everyone else except Joe packed what they could into backpacks. Then I sallied forward. Weeds promptly wrapped around the hub and snarled the wheel. By putting all my weight into the handles, I broke free. But the grass was even deeper farther out in the field. Soon seven- and even eight-foot stalks stood over my head. The heifers had burrowed tunnels through the greenery, but their routes meandered in confusing directions. Green puddles of manure littered the maze of tracks like land mines. When my wheel snarled again, I dropped the handles in frustration.

"Which way's the campsite?" my father asked, bringing up the rear of our group.

"I can't see anything over this grass. Where's Joe?"

"He went off to count the cows," Janell said. "Look, if the sun's ahead of us, we must still be headed the right way." She plowed on ahead, parting the grass with her hands. My parents took her lead. I followed as best I could with my grass-tangled wheel. I had already decided this was the only trip the wheelbarrow would make across the pasture.

For the second trip across the field I marked our route with ten-foot alder poles. Gradually we beat down a trail. It was six o'clock before we had assembled everything at our campsite. The two tents stood facing each other across a patch of sourgrass and ferns on the ancient roadbed. One tent had our sleeping bags and air mattresses. The other held our tools and the cans of food. Two lawn chairs and a hammock completed our furnishings.

"Look at the time!" Dad exclaimed. "We've got to get back home."

My mother handed us a bag of Bing cherries. "A housewarming present. We'll write the Niemis to let you know when we'll drop by again. I'll be curious to see how things go."

Joe looked nervously at the lengthening shadows across the pasture. "Come on, Laddie. We'd better get back on the right side of the river too. I wouldn't be caught dead over here after dark. Too many bears and stuff."

My parents said their farewells. Janell and I thanked them all profusely. Then they left, led by Joe and the farm dog.

As soon as they were gone I could feel the silence of the rainforest closing in around us. Janell looked at me, perhaps with the same thought. There was no wind to rustle the leaves that arched above us like a speckled green roof. I could hear her breath and the beating of my heart.

She cocked her head. "I hear water."

Without another word I took a bucket and followed her through the alder grove to the lazy, foot-wide creek that ran among the ferns. Where it spilled over a fallen log we filled the bucket and took long drinks. On the way back to camp I paused at the grassy corner where I had paced off the dimensions of the future cabin.

"We'll have a view across the whole pasture," I said.

"We already do," she replied. I held her close, glad that our pioneer adventure would give us time to be alone together. Then we carried the bucket between us to the tents, washed up with a damp towel, and collapsed into our sleeping bags, exhausted.

When we finally awoke the next morning the sun was high in the sky. I stumbled out of the tent, pulling on my shirt, and blinked at the green jungle surrounding our primitive camp. My first thought was: Breakfast. We hadn't really eaten dinner the night before—just a few rolls dipped in blueberry jam. We had a three months' supply of oatmeal and flour for porridge or pancakes, but we lacked a place to cook.

"I guess our first order of business is getting rocks for a fireplace," I said.

Janell pushed out past the tent flap. "Well, I don't see any rocks here. Besides, most rocks in the Coast Range are sedimentary."

"What's wrong with sedimentary rocks?" I knew she had spent a year studying geology. She had switched her college major after she learned most job openings for geologists were with oil companies.

"Sedimentary rocks usually have water in them, so they explode when they get hot. I think there's some good basalt back by the old barn."

Years before, when the gas line crews built their steep construction track over the hills past the barn, they had left the hillside strewn with boulders and gravel. "That old barn's a long ways from here. Do you think it's OK to leave our camp?"

She shrugged. "Joe said the dairy cows won't bother anything."

So we hauled a backbreaking load of rocks from the gas line road in backpacks. Then I stacked the rocks into two small, parallel walls, capped them with an iron plate we had brought for the purpose, lit a fire underneath, and soon had breakfast simmering on our impromptu wood stove.

The trouble came after we had cleaned up the dishes and returned to the collapsed barn to scavenge lumber for a picnic table. We were gone only half an hour. But when we returned with the boards I saw we had visitors.

The Niemis' "harmless" heifers stood about the flattened tents, gazing at us with innocent eyes, flicking their ears guiltlessly. One had put a hoof through a lawn chair, ruining the seat. Another was idly munching the bag of cherries my mother had given us.

"Get out!" I shouted. A startled Holstein stumbled over our smoking fireplace, scattering the rocks and the iron plate. The resulting clang sent the rest stampeding. They kicked their heels and raced out across the cabin site to the pasture.

Janell and I surveyed the damage. The supply tent had fared the worst, in part because I had tied one of its ropes to a dead tree, and this had fallen across it lengthwise. All the pegs had pulled out, and one of the grommets was torn. One corner of our sleeping tent still stood, and the rest had hoofprints across it.

Obviously our next order of business would be felling some of the pole-like alder trees near the cabin site for a fence. Irritably I set to righting our damaged tents. When two of the cows began nosing back toward our camp I shouted, "Shoo!" They flinched a little, but did not run.

"They're just curious," Janell said, her voice softening. "They didn't mean any harm." With some grass in her outstretched hand, she advanced toward the lead heifer, a mostly white Holstein. Soon Janell was petting its nose.

"See?" she said to me with a touch of reproach. "This one's tame."

I sighed. "Next you'll start giving them names."

She must not have heard the irony in my voice because she replied, "Well, why not? Look, there's a plastic tag in her ear that says '67'." That's not much of a name. I think I'll call you Elizabeth."

There was nothing for me to do but give in. If these young cows were going to be our nearest neighbors, we might as well try to be friends. I picked a handful of grass and began advancing toward the second heifer. Unlike the Holstein, it was black with a brownish sheen. When I was almost within arm's reach it stomped backwards a pace and tossed its head.

"Yours is shy," Janell laughed.

"Either that or I don't have your knack."

"You'll probably name her Devastation," Janell chided.

I knew what she was thinking. After rowing across the river in *Earnest,* I would want to claim our camp was visited by Devastation. "Actually, I think she looks more like a Tootsie."

And so it was that two of our closest friends that summer became Tootsie and Lizzie. In some ways, we had a lot in common. Like them, we were there for the summer, exploring the great green world along the wilderness side of the Sahalie. Like us, they were still too young to worry much about the grimmer, serious business of life—even though daily milkings eventually awaited them on the far side of the river.

Lizzie, Tootsie, and the others watched all that afternoon as we felled little alder trees and built a makeshift fence around our camp. I fashioned a wooden gate that led to the cabin site. On the gate I nailed up the yellow cardboard building permit the county officials insisted should be "posted in a conspicuous place."

The next morning, when we awoke to the disorienting sound of crunching footsteps and heavy breathing, I rolled over and squinted out the tent's screen window. Tootsie and Elizabeth were at the new gate, taking turns chewing on the last of the little yellow sign. I knew then that they had decided to accept us. A Holstein and a part-Jersey, they had taken over for the absent county building inspectors, and had both signed off on our conspicuous permit.

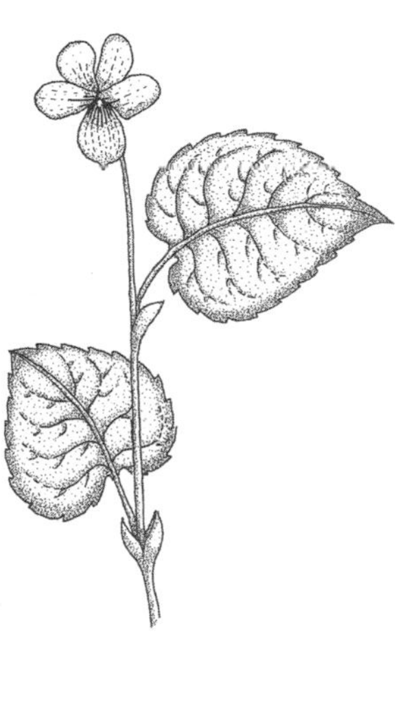

4

The Butcher

(July 1977)

> Obviously you still have a lot of underbrush in your head!
> —Chuang Tzu, Free and Easy Wandering, circa 320 BC

Some nights later—I can't say just when, because even now the memory spooks up more like a dream than reality—an unearthly light began jerking about through the dark trees on the far side of the pasture. Janell and I were sitting in folding chairs behind the campfire holding mugs of peppermint tea. The iron plate we had set over the fire to heat pots of water kept our faces in the shadow, but tongues of flame crept up from the sides, sending shivering ghosts up through the cavern of white alder trunks. An occasional pop launched a frantic column of sparks up into the starless night.

We were both so tired from a long day of hauling foundation rocks that we didn't speak until the faint alien light climbed down from the distant riverside trees and began jerking its way unmistakably across the pasture toward us.

"What the devil is that?" I set my tea on a stump and stood up, thinking in confused alarm what kind of weapon I might use to defend us if the weird light should attack. An ax? A stick? A flashlight? One of the tools of my Swiss army knife?

"Or who?" Janell said, her voice rising uneasily. "It sounds a little like a car."

We looked at each other in the dark. I knew she was thinking how crazy her words sounded. We had spent much of the day lugging fifty-pound rocks from the ruins of the ancient cat road that climbed over the steep hills of the gas pipeline. What kind of car could cross that hellacious road at night, leap over the barricade of logs and brush that kept the cows in the pasture, and then crawl through the six-foot-tall jungle of grass?

"Or a helicopter?" I ventured. As the light neared, the growl of its engine grew louder. Just as I was about to get the ax, the light caught the bare spot we had cleared for the future log cabin. Suddenly the engine noise stopped. The spotlight swiveled toward us. We froze in place, like deer caught in the beams of highway traffic. Behind us the tent canvas glowed, the silver screen of our theater of operations. The only movement was the billowing white fog of campfire smoke. Then the light went out.

The sudden darkness left me so blind that I really couldn't go get the ax, even when I heard footsteps creeping up through the grass toward our camp. Janell began moving the pots around on the cooking plate, although I couldn't understand why. I reached down and grabbed a stick of firewood—the only thing that came to hand.

At that moment a man's white face appeared in the firelight, his eyes sunken to red shadows, his long black hair trailing in disarray down the camouflage green of an old Army coat.

"Who are you?" I demanded.

The man smiled slowly, a possibly maniacal grin that exposed teeth so white I could see his skin actually wore a weathered tan.

"I'm the *butcher*," he said.

"Oh!" Janell exclaimed. Then, almost in the same breath, she added, "Would you care for some peppermint tea?"

The man raised his eyebrows. "Uh, yeah, actually that sounds really good, thanks."

My heart was still beating much too fast, stuck in creature confrontation mode. Awkwardly I used the stick of firewood in my hand to motion our guest toward one of the stumps on the far side of the fire. "Have a seat. I'm Bill and this is Janell."

There was a pause.

To break the ice I added, as casually as I could, "So you say you're the butcher?"

The man waved the comment away with a deprecating hand. "Just his apprentice, actually, but people call me Butch. You see my real name's Boucher. When I served in 'Nam everybody called me the Butcher, so when I got back I figured I might as well learn the trade."

"I see." This was not making me feel more at ease. Here we had a Vietnam veteran with a nickname earned no doubt through violence. The man had stumbled onto our camp while piloting some kind of jungle vehicle. He could be a shell-shocked lunatic for all we knew.

Janell handed him a steaming mug. "Careful, it's hot."

"Thanks." He held the mug in his hands as if it were a wounded bird. "Man, your hands get cold riding an ATV at night."

Janell glanced to me, then back to Butch. "You drove in over the gas line road on an all-terrain vehicle?"

He grunted affirmatively and hunkered down to sip the tea. We waited while he slurped.

Finally I ventured, "So as an apprentice, what kinds of things do you—uh, butcher?"

"Oh, everything." He looked up at me with enthusiasm. "Pigs, cows, elk, bear. I'm learning to make this truly excellent pastrami. You'd never know it was raccoon."

"Really?" I nodded encouragingly.

"Yeah, so that's what I'm doing here tonight, you know, hunting 'coons. You just drive around the edge of the pasture and they climb up the trees along the river. Then it's easy to spot them with my ATV's swiveling searchlight." His tea had cooled enough that he drank more easily, and he himself seemed to have warmed up enough that he talked more easily. "Of course we're also the regular butchers for the Niemis, so it doesn't hurt to drop by once in a while to size up their herd. But then tonight I see this, like sort of little construction site, and then I find you people camped out here with the heifers. Who the hell *are* you anyway?"

I felt like he had turned the tables on us, and I wasn't sure how. *He* was the one who had barged into our camp out of the night. But now he was looking at us skeptically as if we were the intruders.

"My parents own this property. They rent out the pasture to the Niemis."

Butch still seemed a little doubtful. "You bought the old Moreland place?" He set down his tea and crossed his arms, studying us. He had angular features and a few day's growth of beard. "What are you doing camped out here? You're building something."

"Well yes." Suddenly I felt hesitant telling this stranger about our project. "We're building a log cabin. Just a one-room cabin."

"But we're doing it the old-fashioned pioneer way," Janell put in. I wanted to stop her, but she went right on. "We're not using any power tools, you see? Just crosscut saws and axes and adzes and things."

I sighed. It all sounded a little silly, and embarrassing.

The butcher looked up into the dark trees for a while, as if he were contemplating our words or watching a squirrel. I was about to look up to see if there really was a squirrel when he unfolded his arms and took off a small backpack. "Mind if I smoke, Jeanie? It is Jeanie, isn't it?"

"Janell, actually." Her name was just uncommon enough that she was used to people mixing it up. "Go ahead and smoke if you like, Mr.—Boucher, isn't it?"

He smiled and took out a pack of cigarette papers. "Wallace Boucher, technically, but please, just call me Butch. Boucher means butcher in French. Did you know that? Hell, I guess I was born to the job." He opened a tobacco pouch, shook some shredded leaves onto the cigarette paper on his lap, and then pulled the pouch drawstring closed with his teeth. "I never did like the name Wallace. Kids in school called me Wally. Wally and the Beav. 'Hey, how's it goin', Beav?' Well, I ain't no beaver." He rolled the cigarette and licked the paper to seal it. Then he looked at us with narrowed eyes. "I'm Raven clan."

"Then you're a Native American?" Janell asked.

He shrugged. "A little. Enough." He waved the finished cigarette toward the shadows. "This is all old Sahalie Reservation land. The whole county was. The government took most of it away back in 1910 and gave it to white homesteaders. They took the rest away in 1954, gave the Indians some money, and told us we were Americanized. We weren't a tribe anymore. They said we were all just melted into the pot like everyone else. But I guess some traditions don't melt."

Butch flipped open a matchbook, bent back a single paper match, lit it one-handed, and cupped it against his cigarette. He took several long drags until the tip glowed a red hole into the dark. Then he held out the cigarette between his thumb and forefinger. "Share a peace pipe?"

Janell and I laughed uncomfortably. Neither of us smoked, and he seemed to be joking, but what if he wasn't? And was this really tobacco he was offering, or marijuana? The smoke didn't have the sweet, burning-weeds tickle of college dormitory joints, but it didn't slap you in the face like bus-station cigarettes either.

When he urged again, I took the cigarette. Holding my fingertips to form a small triangular mouthpiece, I sampled a mouthful of his smoke. It had a strange, earthy blend of scents—not unpleasant, but certainly not commercial.

Butch grinned, clapped me on the shoulder, and took the cigarette back. "There you see? Now we're friends."

I blew out the smoke. It left no marijuana hum in my head, at least not yet. "What is it?"

"Our own secret blend. Now that the tribe has been reinstated, some of us have been experimenting with the old traditions. Want some, Janell?"

She smiled and shook her head. "When did the tribe get reinstated?"

"Oh, it's been a couple years. The feds gave us a few scraps of old BLM land up in the woods—nothing to live on, but it's a token, a start. Have you seen our tribal smokehouse on the coast, in Taylorville?"

I wrinkled my brow. "I think I did see it, driving by. What is that, anyway?"

Butch tapped the ash from his cigarette into the fire. "It's my boss's idea. He sells smoked salmon and venison jerky to the tourists on Highway 101, along with a bunch of goofy Navaho blankets and fake silver crap from Hong Kong. He sees it as the tribe's revenge on the white man. It's just a first step, you see? Next we get back Skookum Rock, and finally we take over the whole county again." He grinned at me. "But that'll be a while. Friend."

"What's so important about Skookum Rock?" Janell asked. I wondered too. We had passed it on the Sahalie River Road. There was an "Oregon History" signboard not far from Bartola's Landing, but we hadn't stopped to read it. The rock itself, on the far shore of the river, was a hundred-foot lump of mossy basalt.

Butch flicked the last of his cigarette into the fire and shrugged. "That was the first land the Sahalie tribe had in these parts. Legend says the tribe was driven out from the North Coast in a war, but when they came down here they found this whole part of the coast controlled by three powerful evil spirits, the Skookum sisters. The sisters lived on this rock about six miles up the river and wouldn't let anyone pass."

He paused for a moment, frowning at the fire. At length Janell asked, "So what happened to them?"

"The Skookums?" He frowned again. "I don't know. No one really seems to remember that part of the legend. I think Coyote appeared and turned them all into a rat's ass or something. Whatever they look like now, I guess they're still lurking around in the woods. Anyway, the sign by the highway says if you leave gifts and stuff on the rock it'll bring good luck."

"That's not much of a legend," I said.

"Hey, I don't make 'em. That's all there is."

Janell swirled the cold tea in her mug contemplatively. "In any case, the legend says the land didn't really belong to the Sahalie tribe in the first place. If you want to give it back to the original owners you'd have to find these evil Skookum sisters."

Butch stood up and held out his hands, as if to ward off her suggestion. "Yeah, yeah. So just don't go looking for them. They're bad-ass powerful critters, lady. You'll wind up like old man Moreland."

"Clyde Moreland?" I asked. "You know what happened to the old homesteader here?"

"Yeah." Suddenly he laughed, and this time it *did* sound maniacal. "He was *butchered*."

"Bu—" The word stuck in my throat.

"Don't ask, friend." Butch slung on his backpack. "Look, folks, this has been fun, but I've got to saw beef in the morning. Thanks for the tea. I'll be back one of these days. Or nights."

Already he had slipped out of the campfire light.

Janell called after him, "Are the Niemis really going to kill the heifers? We've started giving them names like pets."

Butch's voice came back from the darkness. "They ain't all heifers, Janell."

"The bulls then, is that it? We've found two bulls, but we haven't named them yet."

There was a laugh from the dark pasture and the ATV's motor roared. Once again the spotlight blinded us on our rustic stage. This time the voice bellowed over the engine roar, like a director shouting to a pair of clumsy actors. "Count the BALLS, guys. One of those bulls is a steer. And you can name him MEAT."

The motor gunned and the light jerked us back into darkness. After a minute even the whine of the engine had vanished, leaving just the croak of frogs from the swamp. Janell sat back by the embers of the dying fire.

"Meat?" she asked.

I nodded. By now my head really was humming, and the night was spinning into a dream. Some mind-altering ingredient must have been in Butch's homemade cigarette after all. But I could clearly picture the pasture's black angus steer.

"The Niemis don't pay the rent in cash," I said. "Each spring we get 250 pounds of beef. Cut and wrapped. By the butcher."

5

The First Log

(July 1977)

There is an art to cutting down a tree. Unfortunately, it is an art none of us had.

—Don Berry, *To Build a Ship*, 1963

"Well, it *looks* easy enough," I said, creasing the book on log cabin construction open to the chapter entitled "TIMBER-R-R-R!"

Janell eyed me from across the rustic picnic table I had built for our camp. We were lingering over a breakfast of oatmeal mush, sweet cream, and cocoa with milk from the Niemi dairy. Now that the log cabin foundations were finally finished, I had spread out the drawings of our planned one-room summer house, along with the literature we had assembled on the subject: a how-to paperback sent by my sister Susan from San Francisco (inscribed "B+J: This *isn't* your Christmas present"), a copy of Thoreau's *Walden*, an extension service pamphlet on "Building a Log House" from the University of Alaska, and an October 1976 issue of *Sunset* magazine. This last had been saved for us by my mother. The magazine's headline read, "Log Cabin Renaissance Going on Now in the Northwest: It's Log Walls, Wood Stove, and Microwave."

"How many trees do you think we'll have to cut?" Janell asked.

"At least twenty-five. Maybe thirty."

Janell sighed and turned to the *Sunset* article. After a moment she read aloud, "Probably the biggest single boon to today's log cabin builders is the lightweight, 10- to 15-pound, direct-drive chainsaw."

In planning our back-to-the-earth adventure we had decided to go the pioneer route, using only a crosscut saw and an ax. But it was one thing to fantasize about Paul Bunyaning and another to stare it down over a bowl of oatmeal.

Silently we flipped through the glossy pages. A vaulted log palace soared up to picture windows at daring angles. Construction cranes dangled pre-milled, pre-cut logs like Tinker Toys. A vast living room stood carefully cluttered with fruit bowls, elephant-shaped vase stands, and curving, space-age tabletops. Of course we couldn't afford this kind of Lincoln Log mansion—we would be hard pressed to afford a chainsaw for that matter—but the photographs were alluring nonetheless.

I watched Janell from the side. She had tied her hair up with a blue bandanna, leaving a casual sweep of honey-blond hair across her ear. Her clear, warm skin glowed without makeup. The old-fashioned wire-rimmed glasses on her delicate nose gave her a studious air. We both wore blue work shirts, but she had embroidered a tiny wildflower on each of the collar points of hers.

"Would you rather go the *Sunset* route?" I asked.

She turned to the article's final page, a picture of the log cabin owners. A clean-shaven James Bond wannabe in a clashing plaid suit lounged in a sunken fireside conversation pit across from his wife, a pale woman with an enormous bouffant hairdo, long fingernails, and lip gloss.

"No," Janell said decidedly, as if awakening from a trance. She slapped the magazine shut. "No. I'll get the hard hats if you do the dishes."

I could tell she was still not entirely at ease as she gathered the hard hats, axes, and ropes from the supply tent. It took her several minutes to extricate the five-foot-long crosscut saw. The ungainly blade flopped around menacingly like a wounded shark, bristling razor-sharp, two-inch teeth.

I quickly rinsed the dishes and took the saw across my shoulder, carefully pointing the teeth out where they could bob without harm. "Ready?" I asked.

She nodded.

On our way up into the woods we stopped to inspect the six foundation piers one more time. We had brought only three bags of mortar mix, and our new bovine friend Tootsie had spilled half of one before we could shoo her out of the construction site. With what remained we had built the piers like trailside cairns, using tightly fitted flat rocks. Each pier started two feet below the ground on hardpan and stacked up pyramid-fashion to the marker strings we had staked eighteen inches above ground. In Norway, I had noticed that the farmers built their *stabbur* storage sheds high off the ground to protect them from rot and rats. In our rainforest, I figured air beneath the cabin floor would be even more important.

"Aren't the first logs supposed to be the heaviest?" Janell asked. She bit her lip.

"Let's cut the sill logs later. We should practice on some smaller trees first."

"Good," she said.

The trail I had built from the cabin site switchbacked steeply up a ridge into a dense hemlock forest. Sword ferns and salmonberry bushes rose from a thick bed of moss like green sea creatures in an underwater grotto, dimly lit by a distant sky. A hundred yards above the cabin site I stopped at what appeared to be a stand of telephone poles.

"A doghair thicket," I announced.

"A what?"

"That's what they call a place where the trees are as thick as the hair on a dog. They're fighting so hard for light they only have a few needles at the top, and hardly any branches below. Good straight wall logs."

"I hate to kill any of them," Janell said.

"A lot of them here will die soon anyway from lack of light. It won't hurt the forest to thin a few. How about this one?"

The tree I had pointed out was about ten inches in diameter and rose perhaps eighty feet in the air. Janell peered up at it. She sighed and nodded.

With the ax I scored a line around the trunk where the cut would go. Then I added an extra line for a V-shaped notch on the downhill side.

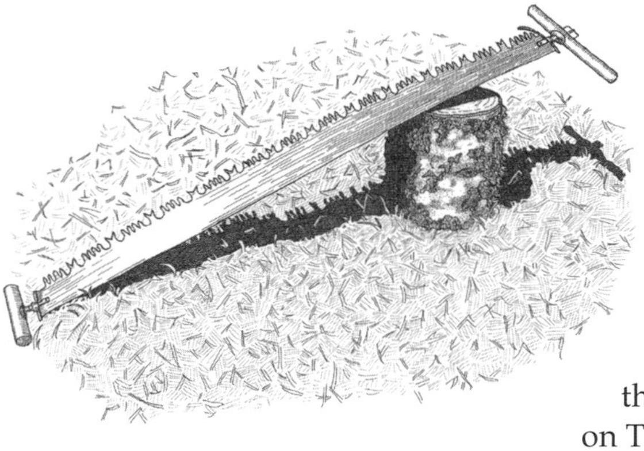

"Why mark two cuts?" she asked.

"If we just saw straight through, the tree will settle onto the blade. We'll cut a wedge out first the way we want the tree to fall. Then when we cut in from behind, the whole thing is supposed to pivot down on this hinge in the middle. I saw it on TV once. They had a logger who could aim the tree so well that he set up a stake a hundred feet away and made the tree drive it into the ground."

Janell is less talkative when she is nervous. The thought of felling this very heavy tree clearly worried her. In silence we set up the saw, each holding one of the handles at either end. After we had jerked the blade back and forth for a minute with little effect, she bit out the words, "Don't push. Pull."

Sure enough, when each of us took turns pulling, the blade sailed through the wood like a serrated knife through French bread. Bright curls of sawdust flew from the notch, accompanied by the sweet rich scent of fresh lumber. In another few minutes we had sawn out the wedge—a slice of cantaloupe bouncing merrily down the hill—and we were already well into the final cut in back.

Then a breeze swayed through the forest. Our tree tilted downhill, creaking ominously. We both jumped back, startled. After a breathless moment the breeze shifted directions. Slowly, incredibly, our tree swayed back until it was leaning at a frightening angle directly over our heads. I ducked behind another trunk. Janell looked up at the tree with wide eyes and began crab-walking frantically uphill through the moss.

But then the breeze passed and all of the trees straightened up, including ours. For a long time neither of us was willing to get near enough to finish the cut. By now our eighty-foot tree was attached only by an inch-thick hinge of wood in the middle. If it chose to defy our careful wedge-hint and drop on us, it could squash us like bugs, hard hats notwithstanding.

"Let's pick a different tree," Janell suggested.

"We can't leave this one here like this."

We approached the tree as warily as if it were a grizzly bear on a tether. I dug in my heels to prepare for a sudden eighty-foot dash. Every stroke of the saw now made the tortured tree groan, snap, and creak. The trunk swayed woozily, like a lamppost in front of a drunken man.

Finally the tree gave a small shudder. "Timber!" I cried, jerking the saw free. We raced for cover, our hearts pounding. The tree tilted slightly downhill, enough to show that it had been sawn entirely through. But then it merely nestled against the shoulder of a neighboring tree and stayed there, seemingly satisfied, as if it didn't care that it was no longer attached to the ground.

After a long silence, Janell said, "That's what we get for cutting trees on the back of a hairy dog."

I ventured forward, gave the severed tree a shove, shouted "Timber!" again, and ran for cover. The tree slowly bounced against its neighbor's branches, but did not fall. Before long I was back at the tree, yanking and kicking at the trunk. When this accomplished nothing, I looped a rope around the trunk as high as I could reach, walked downhill, and tried to pull the tree down.

"Bill!" Janell objected. "It could fall right on top of you."

As far as I could tell the tree didn't seem interested in falling anywhere.

"Wait, I've got an idea," I said. Using the blunt end of the ax as a maul, I pounded the trunk off of its stump. But as soon as the trunk slipped free, it rammed itself eighteen inches straight down into the forest duff, planting itself as firmly as if it were a pier pounded in by a pile driver. The tree looked as if it had been growing there all its life.

Janell gently lifted a patch of moss from the forest floor and placed it on the stump to hide the scar we had made. "Let's find another tree."

"No!" Now I was out for vengeance. "We're going to cut this one down again."

"Again?"

"Sure. The cabin will need some short logs on either side of the door. If we cut this one off waist high it'll come out just about right."

The second time we cut down the tree the job really was easier. Neither of us was alarmed when the severed trunk stuck into the ground as before, refusing to fall downhill. By the third time we cut it down, we felt like old hands at this kind of work. And so it took us by surprise when the tree really did tilt loose from its doghair neighbors, rip through the branches like a battleship launched into the woods, snap in half as it crashed across a gigantic old stump, and thump in two pieces onto the forest floor, splintering an elderberry tree.

We looked up at the little hole of daylight that had opened above our heads. Then we looked at the two halves of the broken tree.

"I guess I didn't aim it very well," I said. "That stump it hit must have been left from when this place was first logged seventy years ago."

"Look at the size of it," Janell marveled. The ancient rotten stump stood ten feet tall and swelled nearly ten feet wide at the base. Square notches remained where the early loggers had inserted springboards. Standing on those bouncy, narrow platforms they had been able to saw through the trunk above the root swell, where it was only six feet thick.

Suddenly our struggles with a mere ten-inch-diameter tree seemed puny. In fact, our entire forest shrank as we stared at the ancient stump. Once these hills must have been crowned with giants, the pillars of a great green hall in the Skookums' world of myth.

"Our beans are baking," Janell said.

I looked at her blankly. "Our what?"

"I have to go check on the campfire. Can you finish up with this tree by yourself?"

"Yeah, sure."

She cocked back her hard hat. "I'm cooking up a little surprise for you too." And then she was gone.

For the next hour I chopped off limbs and cut the logs to length. Launching the logs down the hill was easy enough, but then dragging them through the grass up to the cabin site proved nearly impossible. It took all the strength I could muster just to pull a single log alongside the foundation piers. What worried me was that this was among the smallest of the logs we would need. I returned to camp covered with fir needles, my clothes drenched with sweat. I splashed off in our wash basin, changed shirts, and collapsed into a folding chair. "At this rate we'll never finish the log cabin this summer."

Janell brought a bowl of nine-bean soup with crumbled crackers, and

I fell onto it hungrily. When I had recovered somewhat, I noticed one pot that seemed to be half-buried in the fire. I pointed. "What's that?"

"Your surprise. I've experimented with baking a chocolate cake in the Dutch oven."

"Wow!" Obviously, she was doing her best to make our camp in the woods livable.

She held up her hands to urge caution. "This is my first time, so I don't know if it will work. I had to put it on the coals and build a separate fire on top of the lid to cook it from both sides. And because cakes fall if you check on them too early, I haven't been able to look."

"Do you think it's done?"

She shrugged. "Here's hoping." With a shovel she scraped the burning wood off the lid and lifted the pot out of the fire pit. Then she blew the ash from around the rim and lifted the lid.

The unbelievable aroma of chocolate cake billowed up around us. But what I saw inside the cast iron pot was obviously not a cake. It looked more like a baked motorcycle tire.

Janell lowered herself to her knees and examined the thing, tight-lipped. With a knife she sawed through a thick black crust. When liquid cake batter spilled from the hollow inside, her hands went limp. She turned to me, downcast. "I don't know what I—"

"It smells wonderful." I gathered her in my arms. "Just don't think of it as a cake. It's more like a gigantic jelly-filled cinder doughnut."

At this she broke away from me angrily. "A cinder doughnut? I work hard to do something nice, and for you it's just a joke?" She threw down her oven mitt and walked off toward the cabin site.

There was nothing for it. After my insensitive jest, I knew I would have to eat my words. I put the motorcycle tire on a plate. Then I cut off the charred outer layer, crumbled the remnants into a bowl, and started in with a spoon. Actually, as a pudding, it wasn't half bad. I told Janell as much when she finally returned to camp.

She turned away.

"You know," I said, "I think we need a rest. Instead of cutting another tree this afternoon, why don't we go for a swim in the river?"

After a moment she said, "Only if I can wash my hair first."

"All right." I was used to her hair-washing therapy in times of stress.

"And you'll have to fill the wash tub so we can start cooking our dirty clothes while we're gone."

"Agreed," I said. After the troubles of the morning, I hoped the afternoon really would be a chance for a clean start.

6

An Ax Waiting to Happen

(July 1977)

> Anyone can build a log cabin. One of the cabins described in these pages was built by one man in three days for less than two dollars.
>
> —Bradford Angier, *How to Build Your Home in the Woods*, 1952

That afternoon we did not try to cut another log. Instead we took our swimsuits and hiked across the pasture on a cow path to the Sahalie River, followed by Lizzie, Tootsie, and the rest of the curious heifers. The path led to a park-like grove of maples and two gigantic spruce trees, seven feet in diameter. Having seen the stumps in the woods, I now knew that this was what the entire valley must have looked like before it was logged in the early 1900s. Presumably these trees had been left for fear they would fall into the river.

We changed into our swimsuits beside the giant spruces and made our way barefoot to the water. Mud squished up to our ankles on the steep shore. The water was chilly and such a murky green from its tidal meanderings that we could hardly see the bottom three feet below. I sloshed in, swam a few hard strokes to warm up, and then floated on my back. It felt good. I hoped we were washing away the morning's difficulties along with the dirt.

I got out first and dressed quickly, saying I wanted to check on the campfire where our laundry was cooking. In fact I used the chance to pick Janell a huge bouquet of wildflowers. I arranged them in a pitcher to brighten our wilderness campsite. Our first day of logging and Dutch oven cooking had not gone well, and I wanted to cheer her up.

When I presented the bouquet she said, "Oh, thanks. That was a nice thought."

"A nice thought?" I had hoped for a stronger reaction.

"Sure. You chose a colorful mix of flowers."

From her voice I could tell there was something wrong. "Don't you like it?"

"Oh, it's pretty enough," she admitted, "But most of these are aliens."

"Aliens? What do you mean?"

"That's what botanists call foreign plants that crowd out native species." She held up a bright cluster of dandelion-like blooms. "These yellow composites are tansy ragwort, introduced from Eurasia. It spreads along highways and overgrazed pastures."

"Why is that so bad?"

"It's poisonous. When cattle get tired of eating grass and try tansy, their livers turn to rock." She pointed to the greenery I had used to decorate the bouquet. "And this other is English ivy, probably planted by the old bachelor homesteader as a kind of primitive landscaping."

By now I was getting a little annoyed. I had gone to the effort to make her a bouquet, and she was dissecting it as if it were a fetal pig. "I suppose ivy is poisonous too."

She shrugged. "I don't know. But I do know that we should find every last leaf and pull it."

"Why?"

"In England ivy's a harmless ground cover. Here, where it doesn't freeze much in winter, ivy grows like mad year round, climbing up trees and choking them. Some of the hillsides around Portland have become wastelands of ivy-covered snags."

She set the pitcher on the picnic table and straightened the flowers. "Civilization can be pretty, but it comes at a price."

"You make it sound like human beings are aliens too," I said.

"You know, I wonder sometimes."

"You don't seriously believe the human race came from a different planet?"

She laughed. "No, but when people talk about joining the 'back-to-the-earth' movement it makes you wonder where they think they've been in the meantime. Civilization's gotten so out of touch, most people might as well be living on another planet. Then when they suddenly want to go back to Mother Nature, maybe it's no surprise if she doesn't welcome them with open arms."

This was starting to sound like a criticism of my entire log cabin scheme. I found myself getting miffed. "Maybe everything we've been doing is wrong. Maybe it doesn't matter if we cut our trees by hand, or use chainsaws, or blow them up with bombs. We'll still be fouling things up somehow. Maybe we're worse than English ivy, and this place can't wait to get rid of us."

I took the ax and walked off to the cabin site. What was the point of trying to please her? I needed some time alone.

The other day I had noticed some alder branches overhanging the cabin site, and now I started lopping them off to work out my frustration. Were we so different from the other animals that lived out here along the Sahalie River, I wondered? We were like a pair of migrating birds, building a summer nest. For us that meant clearing a site and collecting some big sticks. Didn't the Skookums' wilderness have room enough to let one more pair of animals in their back door?

Whack! I chopped off a tough alder limb the size of my arm. I swung the heavy ax to cut another branch. But for some reason the blade sliced through it as slick as butter. Before I could do anything, the ax had finished its downward arc and bounced off my boot.

With an eerie numbness I noticed that the laces on my right work boot had been neatly severed in four places. A two-inch slit had opened in the leather tongue. When blood began welling up through the gash, I managed to call, "Janell? Could you help me?"

By the time she hurried up I was sitting on the ground, taking off the bloody boot and sock, my hands smeared with red. "Oh!" she gasped. "I'll get the First Aid kit!" A moment later she was back, frantically pulling things out of the box: burn ointment, cotton swabs, an eye patch—nothing that seemed useful.

"Wait, give me the eye patch," I said. I clamped it to the top of my foot with my hand. Although the cotton quickly turned scarlet, it seemed to slow the worst of the bleeding.

"What happened?" she asked.

"I was cutting branches. I guess the ax was sharper than I thought. I don't know why it doesn't hurt more."

"That comes later. Lean back and keep your head down so you don't go into shock." She took a fresh gauze pad from the kit. When I lay back she peeled my hand from the foot, took a quick look at the cut, and grimaced. Then she pressed down the new bandage.

"How bad is it?" I asked.

"Pretty deep. You're lucky it runs lengthwise along your foot. I don't think you've cut any tendons or big arteries. But this isn't going to heal up by itself. It'll have to be stitched together by a doctor."

"Oh great. We don't have a telephone out here, or a radio. We don't even have a plan for sending smoke signals, for God's sake. The nearest hospital is eighty miles away. I've really screwed things up."

She clicked her tongue. "No you haven't. The Niemis have a phone and there's a clinic in Taylorville that should be open until five. We'll just rest here a while first. Then we'll see if we can't get you across the river."

My foot had begun to throb, but instead of pain I felt a strange lightheadedness. I closed my eyes. "I'm sorry I got mad about what you said."

She sighed. "That was my fault. I should never have started complaining when you went to the trouble to gather me a bouquet."

"But you were right. This shows you were right. We're not meant to be pioneers. No one is any more. Those days are gone."

Her voice was quiet. "I think you're a very good pioneer. I'm proud of what we're doing out here. It's always hard trying something new."

"Then you don't think we're from another planet?"

"No. It's about time we did something to show that we really belong on this one."

I winced. "It's been one hell of a rocky start." The pain had begun, shooting up my leg like an inserted knife.

Janell brought a basin and some cloths. I set about washing and bandaging my wounded foot. Whenever I stood, the bleeding would start again. Obviously the cut did need to be stitched shut, and the clinic in Taylorville would be closing soon. Grimly I put the bloody boot back onto my foot and tied the severed laces together loosely in front. Then, clutching Janell about the shoulder, I hobbled across the pasture to the boat landing. With each step my wounded foot lit on fire.

When we staggered up the far bank to the Niemis' field, I was faint from the pain. We found the farmer's eldest son, Joe, banging on his skunk-cabbage-whacker contraption with a wrench.

"Uh, hullo," Joe said, hardly looking up. "Did you see what I've gone and done?" He pointed to a pair of bicycle frames welded onto the vehicle's wing-like side blades. "I couldn't get up enough speed to make the blades cut through the weeds right, so instead I've added these choppers. They're connected to the fan belt with bicycle chains. What do you think?"

I shifted the weight off my bloody boot and groaned. "Uhnn, yeah. Might work."

Joe looked from me to Janell. "You didn't come for milk this time, did you?"

"No," Janell replied. "Bill cut open his foot with an ax. We're hoping to get to a doctor in Taylorville."

"Oh, well I can take you into town, sure, you bet."

"Thanks, Joe," I said.

"That would be great," Janell agreed. "We really appreciate you taking the time to help."

Joe slipped into the tractor seat of his modified Volkswagen and started the motor. "No problem. Hop in."

Janell looked at me uncertainly.

"Um—Is this thing street legal?" I asked.

"My skunk cabbage whacker? No, uh-uh, no way. Are you coming or what?"

I shrugged and climbed into the back. When Janell joined me, Joe let out the clutch. Wheels, chains, belts, and blades began whirring about us. The vehicle jolted forward.

"Aren't you afraid of getting stopped on the highway?" I shouted over the roar of the engine.

Joe laughed as if this was the funniest thing he had ever heard. "Yeah, the cops would shit a brick if they caught this rig in town. But they won't."

"Why?"

"We're just going up to the house to get Pa's pickup."

The lurching ride sent new jolts of pain up my leg. The world began to spin. The clattering din of the choppers surrounded us like a hellish spaceship's death weapon. "Skunk cabbages," I muttered.

"What?" Janell shouted.

"Skunk cabbages!" I spoke into her ear. "Are they aliens?"

She shook her head. "No, natives. They're harmless. They belong here."

The next hour or two were a blur. I vaguely remember being squeezed into the front seat of a pickup truck. Joe steered through Taylorville's back streets because, as he confided, he was "nervous about police," having lost his license once for unpaid traffic fines. I dimly recall the doctor telling his nurse, "Twenty cc's of Novacaine, and *schnell*, I have a board meeting at five." Another thing that stuck in my mind was the clinic's bill. Because we had no insurance the nurse demanded we pay at once. It drained nearly all the cash we had brought for the summer. Somehow Janell found an extra $10 bill for Joe, and he beamed.

The spinning didn't really stop until I climbed out of the pickup after the long drive back. I found a stick to use as a crutch. Standing at the gate by the Niemi farmhouse, I looked across the river. There, at the far side of our pasture, was a tiny brown clearing and the pin-sized log we had cut that morning.

I took a long, steadying breath, thinking how little we had accomplished, and how many obstacles we had met. "I should go thank George for letting us use his truck."

"I can do that while you wait here," Janell offered.

I shook my head. George would want to talk with me in his milking parlor, and Dolores would want to get her news from Janell in the kitchen. That seemed to be how the lines were drawn at the Niemis. "No, I can walk on my own with the stick. It's not far."

As it turned out, George wasn't in the milking parlor, so I limped on to the barn and found him there, feeding calves from a bucket.

"Well, if it isn't the traveler, back from town," he chuckled. "Looks like they patched you up all right."

"Five stitches. I wanted to thank you for letting Joe drive us in your pickup."

"The way that boy drives, we were both taking a risk. But that's what neighbors are for." He dumped a scoop of formula powder into the bucket, stirred it up with water, and held it out to the next calf. It wobbled up to him on spindly legs, stared with big, dewy eyes at the white soup, and jerked back, startled.

"This little guy's only three days old," George explained. "Come on, fella, you've got to learn to drink." He dipped the calf's muzzle into the bucket. The calf sputtered uncertainly, dripping white. Finally George dunked his hand into the bucket and wiggled his big, knobby index finger up from the liquid. The calf began eagerly sucking on the finger. After a minute George slowly pulled his hand away. The calf was left slurping formula, probably without quite understanding how.

"You really do have a way with animals," I said.

"Since Jack started taking over the milking, he's left me to feed the calves. Danged if their survival rate hasn't jumped twenty percent." He chuckled, and then said, "So I see you've got the first log for your place across the river. Is that how you chopped your foot?"

"No, I did that trimming tree branches." My voice sank. "The truth is, our logging operation hasn't gone very well so far. We had to cut our first tree three times to get it to fall downhill."

"Well sure, if you tried to fall it downhill," he laughed.

"What do you mean?"

"Well, if you aim a tree downhill in a thick second-growth grove like that, the stump'll stick in the ground like a stilt in a flower bed."

I looked at him, surprised. "Yes, that's exactly what happened. So we should have felled it uphill instead?"

"Of course." He shook his head. "And another thing—you left that log laying there in the sun all day with its bark on."

"So?"

"So by now its bark'll be glued on tighter than wallpaper. You'll have to whittle it off with a drawknife."

"Oh." I was learning more from George in two minutes than I had gleaned in two weeks from my books on log cabin construction. "I guess we should bark the logs right after they're cut."

"Peels off slick as a whistle. Leaves the logs kind of slippy, too, so they're easier to slide around. I couldn't believe you managed to drag that log through the grass with its bark on."

"Yes, that was hard." I sighed. "Obviously, we've still got a lot to learn about living out here."

By now George had finished feeding the calves and was washing out the buckets. My foot was throbbing again, and I knew I should let him get on with his other work, but there was one more thing I had been wanting to ask him. If anyone could clear up the rumors surrounding the history of our wilderness property, I figured it was George. It seemed as if the original homesteader on our property would have been a pioneer after our own hearts, but we had heard from both Joe and the "Butcher" that he had met a mysterious death.

"About Clyde Moreland, the old homesteader on our place. Do you remember what he was like?"

George dried his hands on a towel. "Old man Moreland? I reckon he started out here a lot like you kids. Came from the city, studied to be a lawyer. Then World War I came, and I don't know what all he did over there in Europe, but they say it changed him. Instead of lawyering, he buys this hardscrabble homestead across the river and starts building a house out of logs and cedar planks."

"What did he do out here for a living?"

George looked wistfully out the barn door to the hills across the valley. "Same as most folks in the valley back then. He hayed the fields and kept a few milk cows. There wasn't any road in those days. A boat came up the river to pick up milk cans every other day. People didn't buy so many things, so they didn't need so much money. When Moreland finally did have to go into town to shop every month, he always wore his old World War I uniform, even when he was seventy. I guess that was the only fancy outfit he had."

There it was, our back-to-the-earth idyll. In our own age, a self-sufficient homesteader like Clyde Moreland could have served as a poster child for the *Whole Earth Catalog*. But the picture George had painted of our predecessor made his life sound bleak and eccentric. It was a still life in lonely grays instead of vibrant greens. Moreland seemed to have chosen homesteading not so much to save the planet, but more as an escape, perhaps from the war, perhaps from the pressure of the legal profession, perhaps from the world in general. I couldn't imagine why anyone would want to kill a hermit of this ilk. Or was there more that George wasn't telling me?

"So did Moreland die when his house burned?"

George gave me a puzzled look. "The Moreland place never burned."

He started walking back across the farmyard slowly, so that I could limp along and keep up.

"What happened to it, then? There isn't any trace of the old house over there now."

"Moreland moved it. When the state finally built a road up the valley, he figured his house was on the wrong side of the river. So he hired a logger with a cat to drag it down to the river and barge it across on some big old spruce logs. It's still over here, on Lucas Hamilton's place. When Hamilton sold your father the land across the river, he kept a piece on this side with the old house for himself."

"Ah, so that's it. Then how did Moreland die?"

"Cancer. It was an accident. None of us were involved. It doesn't matter anymore." Suddenly George seemed to be slinging out words almost at random.

"What?" I turned to him guardedly.

He held up his hands. "Look, if you want to find out about things like that, you'll have to ask one of the old-timers."

"Like who?" I guessed George must be seventy himself.

"Like Mrs. Nelson. She's eighty-five. Lives by herself on the next farm, two miles downriver. She was mixed up in that whole Moreland business. But don't tell her I said so!"

Before I could ask anything else he clapped me on the shoulder. "Glad to see you're back on your feet. Watch out where you swing axes, now, and you'll do fine. Yes sir, you two are gonna do just fine over there."

He ambled on into the farmhouse just as Janell was coming out. She looked at me with some concern. "Let's get you back to camp. You look pale. Does your foot hurt a lot?"

"Yeah. I'm kind of dizzy." I leaned on her shoulder and began limping down the road to the riverbank.

"What was George talking to you about when I came out?" she asked.

"Oh, he was giving me a few tips on cutting trees. I also found out more about the old homesteader, but it's still mostly riddles. George seemed to think a neighbor named Mrs. Nelson might know more. How about your chat with Dolores? Any news?"

She held up an envelope. "We've got mail."

"Really? That's a first. Who's it from?"

"Your parents. They're coming to visit in about a week. To see if the cabin's done yet."

We stopped in the middle of the road, looked at each other, and laughed.

"Think we'll be ready?" she asked.

There were tears in my eyes, as much from the laughter as from my foot. "In a week? Oh sure, log cabins are easy."

7
The Bear Trees
(August 1977)

> Think, Laura—all those big, heavy logs in the barn walls. And the door is heavy and solid, made to keep bears out. No, the bear cannot get in and eat Sukey.
>
> —Laura Ingalls Wilder, Little House in the Big Woods, 1935

Although I limped for weeks, my wounded foot hardly interrupted our progress. Soon our days fell into a pleasantly wearying routine of work, food, and sleep. Cutting the trees really was easier now that we had learned to fell them uphill. Peeling the logs went faster once we fashioned a couple of maple barking spuds—flat-pointed sticks for prying off the logs' crusty hides. I even devised a set of wheels, using a pipe and a pair of old iron wheelbarrow wheels, that enabled us to drag all but the two heaviest logs up the grassy slope to the cabin site.

When night fell we would try to read by the flickering yellow glow of a candle, but soon our eyelids would droop and we would tumble into our zipped-together sleeping bags. There was a serene fullness to our exhaustion, earned from the day's labors.

Nowhere have I found such a perfect place for sleep as at the Sahalie—silent as the dark side of the moon. We wouldn't surface from that great, unconscious whirlpool of dreams until nine or even ten o'clock. When we finally emerged from the tent, stretching our satisfyingly sore muscles, we blinked filmy sleep from our eyes at the midday sky. Startled chipmunks would scold us, racing up the alder trunks, chattering, and flicking their tails in outrage.

Both of us had forgotten what day of the week it was on the morning our herd of heifers suddenly stampeded toward the far end of the pasture.

Janell fetched the binoculars from a supply can and adjusted the focus. "There's someone over there in red, waving a stick at the cows."

"That might be my mother," I said.

"It might?" Janell looked up at me, puzzled.

"Remember my parents' letter? They said they were coming to visit."

"Oh yes, I'd almost forgotten." She brightened, evidently glad for the company. She looked again through the binoculars. "Yes, there's your father, and Joe, and I think the dog too. Why don't you go help them while I put on some coffee."

I set off across the pasture. By the time I reached my mother, however, she was frantic.

"These cows ran up to attack us, and now they're chasing me!" She brandished her stick at one of the black-and-white Holsteins behind her on the path. "Shoo!"

The heifer bolted backwards and kicked its heels, but then trotted back to join the others. The entire herd was following my mother with intense fascination, as if she were a circus majorette leading a parade.

"They're just curious," I said, taking her backpack. "They don't get to meet a lot of new people."

"Then why don't they go meet your father?"

"Put down the stick and try holding out a handful of grass instead," I suggested. "Look, this one here is number sixty-seven. We call her Lizzie. She's tame."

Warily, my mother held out a long stalk of grass. Lizzie craned her neck forward, curled her giant, wet pink tongue around the stalk and yanked it in. My mother recoiled with an "Oh!"

By now my father had caught up, carrying an even larger backpack. "Say, son, you look like you've been going native." He grinned as he nodded at my uncut hair and beard. "We brought the things you asked for. And some fresh food."

"Thanks. Did you bring a newspaper?" We hadn't read any news for weeks. I had begun to wonder if the outside world was still spinning.

"Hot off the press. Say, I've taken a few days off work. Think your mother and I could pitch our backpacking tent over here and help out?"

"That'd be great. The log cabin's going up slower than we thought."

"We heard you cut your foot. Are you OK?" my mother asked.

"It's healing up fine. I'm—"

Suddenly several heifers bolted past us, and my mother clutched my arm. Joe had grabbed one of the larger heifers by its ears. He jolted about the field as it bucked and stomped. Finally he wrestled its head sideways, inspected its fear-widened eye carefully, and then let it go.

"Ha!" Joe said triumphantly, brushing off his hands. "Pa's been fighting pink-eye in the main herd. I told him this side of the river would be clean."

Mother marveled, "I don't see how you find the courage to do that."

"Do what?" Joe asked.

"Why, wrestle a cow. You could have been trampled to death."

Joe scratched his head. "By a heifer? No way, uh-uh. They're a little frisky, maybe, but they only weigh three or four hundred pounds. We've got a bull on our side that's over a thousand."

Mother shuddered.

My father added seriously, "I want you to know, Joe, that we're grateful for everything you've done to help us out here. I hear you were the one who drove Bill in to the doctor. And then today, you volunteered to ferry us across the river. Thanks. You're the best."

To my surprise, Joe actually blushed. He obviously wasn't used to this kind of gratitude. It occurred to me that his own family saw him mostly as a good-for-nothing who fooled around with skunk cabbage whackers. It was as if Joe had forgotten the power of praise. Now he seemed to swell a little as he savored the good words, like a desert plant after a rare rain.

"Aw, I wanted to see what Bill and Janell have been doing over here anyway," Joe replied.

"Come on up to camp for coffee, and we'll show you," I offered.

We walked together to the campsite and took off our packs. The Niemis' big yellow farm dog trotted up behind us, braced his paws, and

shook off the water from his swim across the river. We all held up our arms against the spray and laughed.

"Laddie!" Joe scolded. "You could have gone and done that back at the river."

While Janell poured coffee, my parents opened up their backpacks and began taking out a series of treats, like a pair of Santa Clauses unpacking Christmas presents. First came grapes and peaches, fresh from a fruit stand on the highway to the coast. Then came half a dozen pastries, a loaf of honey nut bread, and a pound of butter.

"Here's the yeast you wanted, Janell," my mother said.

"And here's your pack of typing paper," my father said, handing it to me. "Do you really think you'll get much typing done out here?"

"I've got my old portable typewriter in the tent," I said, a bit defensively. "But I'm not writing articles or anything. I'm just keeping a journal."

My father tightened his lips. I knew how much he wanted me to follow him into newspaper work. I had told him long ago that I wasn't interested in the stress and deadlines of a reporter's beat. Instead of journalism I had studied creative writing at the university. When it became obvious that short stories would not lead very quickly to a solid job, I switched majors, aiming to become a high school German teacher instead.

"This tool thing you asked for caused us no end of trouble," my father said, pulling a heavy handled blade out of the bottom of his pack.

"What is it?" Janell asked.

"It's called a froe," I said, turning it over in my hands. It consisted of a blunt, sixteen-inch metal bar attached sideways to a short wooden handle like a distorted golf putter. "The books say you need one of these to make shakes for the roof."

"Well, most of the tool stores I went to had never heard of it before. We finally found one at the back of an antique shop. Do you even know how to use it?"

"Actually, I don't," I admitted.

Joe set down his coffee. "I think I seen my grandpa use one before. You need a mallet to pound the blade into the end of a shake bolt." He stood a big piece of firewood on end, set the blade on top, and used a smaller piece of firewood to whack the blade into the wood. Then he pried the handle down, twisting the blade until it opened a lengthwise crack. But he couldn't quite split the firewood in two.

"Aw, it won't work on this alder firewood," he said, sitting back in his folding chair. "Besides, alder would just rot out after a couple years. You need cedar to make shakes. That's the only wood that splits right and lasts. "

"But there aren't any cedar trees around here now," Janell pointed out. "The original homesteader must have cut them all to make his house."

"And his barn. And his fenceposts. Probably did." Joe nodded. " Cedar trees grow back slow, or not at all."

"I see articles in the paper all the time about shingle mills in Oregon closing down," my father said. "I guess most cedar shakes are imported from Canada now."

"Where are we going to get enough cedar for our roof, then?" I asked.

"Oh, there's ways," Joe said mysteriously. "Besides, you ain't up to the roof yet, are you?"

"That's right, let's go see how much you've done on the cabin," my mother put in. "We can unpack and set up our tent later."

I opened the rickety gate I had built to keep heifers out of our camp, and we walked out to the cabin site.

"Oh! You don't have any logs up yet at all," my mother said. The yard was strewn with peeled, flattened logs and wood chips, but the six stone foundation piers still stood there, naked.

Janell and I looked at each other sheepishly. "Like I said, it's going slower than we thought," I said.

Janell added, "We haven't been able to move the two biggest logs at all. The sill logs are supposed to go on first, but they're still stuck back in the woods."

My father put his hands on his hips, sizing up our construction project. "Well, with all of us pitching in, we should be able to get those two logs out of the woods somehow. Then it looks like you've got the next fifteen or twenty logs cut to size, ready to go. What I'm thinking is that your mother and I are going to be staying here a few days. We'll need a different project to do, something extra that's smaller, where we won't get in your way." He frowned at a green puddle on one of the freshly cut logs. "Cow pies? Can't you keep the stock out of your work area?"

"I've kept them away from our tents, but I only had time to rig up a sort of alarm system for out here." I pointed to a flimsy barrier of poles and buckets. "When we hear the buckets tip over, we hurry out and chase the cattle away."

"You need a proper fence," my father announced. "That's what we can build for you. What do you say, Elsie?"

My mother bit her lip. "Bill, do you have a bathroom?"

"We, uh—" I hesitated. "We just use the woods, for now. You know, like on a backpacking trip?"

She shook her head. "I think we need to build you an outhouse."

"That really would be an improvement," Janell admitted.

My father considered this. "But as it is, the cows are getting into their water supply at the creek, too. That can't be good. A fence would keep cattle out of the whole area, so they wouldn't chase anyone. We don't have time to build both. Which would you rather have? A fence or an outhouse?"

I could tell Janell wanted the outhouse, and I wanted the fence, but we didn't say so. My mother, whose vote probably mattered more, was obviously torn. On the one hand, an outhouse would do away with the indignity of squatting in the woods. On the other hand, a fence would remove the threat of stampeding cows, something she seemed to take quite seriously. And of course there was the argument of the water supply.

Finally my mother sighed. "The fence first, then."

"Good," my father said. "We can start the fence this afternoon. But now let's help them get those two logs out of the woods. What do you say, Joe?"

Joe had been standing by, watching the outhouse-versus-fence debate with an amused look. But my father's invitation sent a dark flicker across his expression. "Aw, maybe I'll just wait here in camp with Laddie."

"Really?" I asked. "We could use another strong back. With all five of us, we might be able to do it."

Joe hedged. "I'm not so sure about going back in the woods."

"What, are you afraid of ghosts?" my father jested, obviously unaware how close he was to the mark.

Joe flinched. "Not now, uh-uh. No ghosts out here in daylight. In the daytime there's bears."

"Bears? I haven't seen any yet," I said. "Come on, we could sure use the help."

"Well, maybe," he said reluctantly. " But just for a minute."

I gathered up the ropes we would need and led the way on a trail through the forest to the sill logs. My mother lagged behind with Joe. I think she was interested that he could have shown such bravery against the stampeding heifers, and yet be afraid of bears. Mother had taught a year of high school biology once, long ago during World War II when there was shortage of men to serve as teachers. Ever since she had had an interest in wildlife.

My mother asked Joe, "Have you had a lot of trouble with bears bothering your dairy cows?"

"No, uh-uh, no way," he said. "But once I saw a big black bear the day after a cow had died of bloat. It was eating on the carcass."

My mother nodded. "Yes, black bears like carrion, if they can find it. They don't actually hunt anything bigger than a rabbit or a fish. Grizzlies will, but they've been extinct in Oregon for a hundred years."

"That's not what I heard about black bears," Joe countered. "They'll bust into your house and take all your food. Then they'll chase you down and eat you too. Have you seen their claws?" He held up his hand, the fingers curled menacingly.

My mother turned to my father. "Wes, wasn't there an article about bears in the paper this morning?"

"Bears? Well, there was that health department report. In the city section—ha!—it should have been on page 3A, in the regional roundup."

"What did it say?" I asked.

"Well, it was a sort of summary of deaths caused by animals in the past ten years. Only one person had died of a rattlesnake bite. Dozens had died from bee stings; allergies I guess. Other people had been killed by dogs, cows, even sheep—don't know how they managed that. But according to the report, not one person has been killed by a black bear in the entire history of Oregon."

Joe just shook his head.

When we reached the sill logs, I showed my parents the wheeled device I had built. "We've used this to haul most of the logs out. But the sill logs are too big. I can't lift them onto the wheels, and they'd just bend the axle anyway. So I've barked them and left some branch stubs to attach ropes. We'll have to try to drag them out."

My father examined the sixteen-inch-diameter logs. "These really are big. I thought you were supposed to be thinning the forest without taking big trees. Someday we could sell trees like these."

I pointed to the two stumps nearby. "These were going to die anyway. They'd been damaged somehow. See, all the bark has been scratched off at the bottom."

Joe's eye's widened. "Those are *bear trees!*"

"Bear trees?" Janell asked.

"Yeah, those scratches are claw marks! Man, that bear must've had paws the size of pitchforks!"

My mother knelt to examine the stump. "He's right. These are hemlock trees, so the inner bark is edible. When black bears come out of hibernation in the spring, they're so hungry they sometimes strip it off and eat it."

"No, man, they're not just hungry. They're marking their territory, *and we're in it!*" Joe looked about him at the dark woods as if every shadow might be a hungry bear. "Come on, let's get out of here."

Joe quickly looped the largest rope around a branch stub, slung the other end of the rope over his shoulder, and gave a tremendous yank. To my astonishment, the massive log jumped and skidded forward after him. The rest of us scrambled to help, tying on other ropes and pushing from behind. But that log rumbled up the trail to the cabin site almost entirely by Joe-power.

When he finally slackened his rope, Joe caught his breath, his chest heaving. For a moment he looked longingly across the pasture toward his own side of the river, where he might be safe from the bears, ghosts, and evil spirits that seemed to infest our property. But then, grimly, he took the rope and walked back into the dark woods for the second log. Only after it too had been dragged to the cabin foundations by the strength of his determination and fear, did he throw the rope aside. Then he whistled for his dog and marched off across the pasture toward the river without a word.

We watched him go in silence, awed by his sudden show of fearful strength. Laddie, the big yellow farm dog, slunk out of the supply tent and trotted across the field after him.

Struck perhaps by a suspicion, Janell went to check the tents. Soon we heard her give a cry of despair. By the time we arrived, her eyes were damp with angry tears. "Look what that stupid dog has done!" she cried. "He's pawed through everything, looking for food. All the pastries are gone, and the new loaf of bread, and the entire pound of butter!"

I blew out a long breath. "You're right, it's bad. But maybe it's worth it."

"Worth it?" Janell said. "How?"

I shook my head. "I don't think we could have gotten those sill logs out of the woods any other way."

That day we made more progress than we had for ages. With levers and pulleys, my parents and Janell helped raise the two sill logs into position. Each log spanned three of the six foundation piers. Then we hoisted the first two cross-logs into place. With a pencil I marked out saddle-shaped notches on the undersides of the cross-logs, matching the curving tops of the sill logs. Then I rolled the cross-logs over and

chopped out the notches with my ax. When I was done, I rolled the cross-logs back. They thunked into place, locking the outline of the cabin into a solid rectangle. After that, it was easy work to chisel out square notches every few feet along the sill logs for the smaller logs I had chosen to serve as floor joists. Then I tossed on some planks salvaged from the old barn to serve as a rough subfloor. Already it was possible to imagine the cabin as a house.

Meanwhile Janell had straightened the supply tent and was kneading bread dough to replace the loaf Laddie had eaten. This time she knew enough about Dutch oven baking that she built a large fire well in advance, so it would leave plenty of hot coals when it came time to bake the bread. To replace the lost butter, she skimmed cream from a gallon of Niemi milk cooling in the creek and shook it up in a jar until it turned to a watery soup with sweet yellow lumps.

My father discovered a source of fence posts near at hand for his own project. Clyde Moreland must once have had a shed in the pasture in front of our cabin site, because two rows of mossy pilings remained. These derelict foundation posts proved to be cedar. With some digging and some prying, my parents managed to pull several of them out of the ground. While my mother filled in the holes ("I'm always the one who seems to fall into them," she explained), my father used a wedge and a maul to split the pilings into posts of a suitable size for his fence. The split wood was as fresh, rosy, and pungent as the paneling for a brand-new cedar closet, even though it must have been in the ground more than forty years.

As we were washing up for dinner, Janell cautiously opened her Dutch oven. Inside, the single round loaf of bread had browned perfectly. She had decorated the top with an X-shaped slit, so the loaf resembled a giant hot-cross bun. She tapped the crust, and beamed when it gave a satisfactorily solid thump. The stew and fresh salad were almost ready too, she said. Then she added, "But we're out of drinking water. Could someone go fill the bucket from the creek, above where the cows have been?"

I took the bucket and started out. My mother said, "I'll go with you. That bucket's heavy when it's full."

The deeper shadows of evening were already creeping through the forest as my mother and I made our way up the trail along the creek. When we reached the stumps where the two bear-marked trees had been, I hesitated. "How far up the creek do you think the cattle have gone?"

My mother took the bucket silently and went on ahead. After making our way through ferns and salmonberry bushes for another minute we came to an alder opening where the creek meandered through a patch of giant-leaved skunk cabbage.

Suddenly my mother's hand caught my arm.

There, at the far end of the clearing, was a bear.

My heart sped. I could feel my mother's hand clench my arm more firmly. Neither of us dared to move, and hardly to breathe.

The bear was about the size of one of the heifers, but built much wider and lower, with massive shoulders. Its coarse black fur had become matted in places on its broad back. It sat back on its haunches in an odd position, as if trying to squat in a yoga pose. Its long pink tongue stretched out to eat the yellow spathes of the skunk cabbage blooms, one at a time, as if they were big yellow gumdrops.

My mother and I exchanged a glance of disbelief. I hadn't known anything liked to eat skunk cabbage.

Just then the bear raised a wet black nose in the air and blinked its beady eyes in our direction. It could obviously sense that something was hiding in the bushes, but the breeze was blowing toward us, so it couldn't smell what kind of animals we were. With an ursine sigh the bear rolled from its yoga squat and walked a few yards to a rotten log. There it paused, evidently struck by a new idea. It swung a massive paw at the log. Rotten wood exploded from the blow. The bear sniffed the crater it had so casually created, and licked up some wood grubs.

My mother, who had been watching with her mouth half open, now pulled aside a fern for a better view.

At once the bear turned toward us. It waved its snout a bit, apparently trying to get a better fix on us with its nearsighted eyes. Then with a huff it turned and gallumphed off into the woods.

When the crashing of the brush died away, I felt I could finally take a long breath. My mother looked less frightened than I had expected.

"Weren't you scared?" I asked.

"Yes," she admitted. "And yet no, not really. It was strange. Once the bear saw us, it ran away as fast as it could."

"But you were afraid of the heifers," I reminded her.

She nodded. "Cows are different. They're as crazy as giant puppies. They really might run up and trample you. People are killed by cows all the time. But that bear is a force of nature—a part of the forest. And it knows we aren't."

"Like the Skookums," I said.

"The what?"

I sighed. "Oh, a legend the locals have about the place. Joe believes there are ghosts over here."

"Yes," she said. "And he's right."

8

The Rains Come

(September 1977)

> At this place we have wintered and remained from the 7th of December, 1805, to this day, and have lived as well as we had any right to expect, notwithstanding the repeated fall of rain which has fallen almost constantly.
>
> —William Clark, The Journals of Lewis and Clark, 1806

The wind changed direction a few weeks after my parents left, late in August. Janell and I were rowing back across the Sahalie River, in *Earnest* of course, after a quick visit to the dairy farm. Every three or four days we made the trip over to the Niemis to check for mail and to refill our gallon jug with fresh milk for a dollar. This time, on an impulse, I stopped rowing, shipped the oars, and let *Earnest* drift with the evening tide. I sat there musing about the river and the clouds.

Janell stretched out across the boat's back seat and began reading through the newspapers Dolores had saved for us. "Your parents must have liked it here a lot," she commented.

"Why's that?"

"Your father usually writes his column about politics. That's what people expect of an editor. Here's what he printed this week." She read it aloud.

> I've spent part of my summer helping build a log cabin, rediscovering dormant muscles and some of the skills that vanished with the age of electricity and gasoline.
>
> My youngest son, Bill Sullivan, and his wife, Janell Sorensen, are using their summer respite from the University of Oregon to build a small cabin on our Sahalie River property

> near the coast. They are doing so without power tools—not even a chainsaw.
>
> Elsie and I spent a week earlier this month working with them. It was a rewarding experience, forcing us to adapt to a new kind of leisure. It surely wasn't the leisure of idleness. It was the leisure of doing something slowly, methodically, a small step at a time.
>
> The logs are almost up to window height now. My son and daughter-in-law may or may not get the roof on by the time they have to leave to go back to college, but it really doesn't make much difference. The race is in the running. Life is in the living. The log cabin is in the building.
>
> This summer I learned from them that the cabin itself isn't the important thing. It's the doing of it, the opportunity to spend a season along the Sahalie learning to live with the land.

Janell put down the paper. "What does he mean, we might not finish? We're working a lot faster now, and we still have several weeks left. What do you think?"

"I think the clouds have changed direction." I was still leaning over the edge, watching the upside-down sky in the river. Now I looked up at the real one. "All summer we've had little puffs drifting in from the north. Now there's a big dark layer of high clouds coming in from the south."

"What does that mean?"

I shook my head. The boat drifted around a riverbend. A breeze from the south rippled away the reflections, slowly spinning the boat. The giant maple trees along the river waved their boughs, as if stretching after a long afternoon nap. A few lazy leaves, already speckled yellow and brown, spiraled down to land in the water.

I was reaching for the oars when Janell held up her hand. She nodded upstream. A shiny dark head was swimming ahead of us near the bank, leaving a thin silver V. The animal's head seemed too small for a dog or a seal. I was trying to remember what I knew about muskrats and otters when the head turned back to face us, bristling whiskers. Suddenly it dived away with a shiny roll of sleek fur. For a split second I saw the raised tail—a defiant brown ping pong paddle. Then the beaver aimed an angry warning slap at us and was gone.

It was the first beaver either of us had ever seen, although we had lived most of our lives in Oregon, a place officially known as the Beaver State. We slowly drifted upriver with the tide, hoping to see the beaver resurface. But either it had retreated to a hidden lodge or it had swum underwater around a bend.

"That's strange," Janell said, and I was about to agree when I saw she wasn't looking for the beaver at all. Instead she had turned her head up toward the shadowy woods on the far side of the river. "There's a light up there in a window. It must be in that old shack by the road. I thought it was abandoned."

We rarely rowed upstream past this cabin, one of the few buildings within miles. A gust of wind bent back the alders, revealing a crooked tin roof, a dark gray wall of weathered cedar planks, and an ancient window with a dim yellow glow.

The evening wind was cold, and I shivered. "I suppose that's the house where Clyde Moreland died."

"The old homesteader? I thought his house was on our side of the river."

"It was. But George told me Moreland hired a logger to drag his house over here."

"How could he drag it across the river? And why?"

"He used some logs as a barge. After the highway was built on this side of the river, I guess he wanted to live by the road."

"Then maybe Joe should be looking for ghosts over here instead of at our place."

"Maybe so."

"There hasn't been a light over here all summer," Janell said. "I wonder who owns it now?"

"A lawyer, I think." The wind blew branches in front of the window, flickering the light. For an instant I thought I saw a face behind the pane, frightened eyes staring out into the twilight. When I looked again, the face was gone.

"Did you see that?" Janell asked. "Someone's in there. It might be a burglar."

"Or a ghost. Do you want to stop and find out?"

"No," she said quickly, and pulled her jacket tighter. "It's getting late. Let's go back to camp."

After a night of stormy winds I awoke to the hushed patter of rain. It had rained before at our tent camp that summer, but this sounded different. It was not merely another shower, nor the dripping of trees after a morning fog. There was a dull determination to the mournful gray sky that suggested these new southern clouds had the stamina to weep for days.

Already the tent was leaking where a puddle had formed in a sagging corner of the yellow canvas roof. The drip had drenched the relatively clean pants I had planned to wear that day. With a sigh, I pushed up the roof to drain the puddle, hung the wet pants on the candle tripod, and got dressed in my dirty jeans. Then I pulled on my tall rubber boots and went to start breakfast.

Outside, hemlock needles and alder leaves floated in puddles about our campsite. Drips from the trees had spattered mud on the legs of our folding chairs. I shook off the chairs and set them up under the supply tent's small rain fly. Then I gathered an armload of camp firewood, silently cursing myself for not covering the woodpile the night before. I noticed two salamanders crawling about the edge of the fire pit—orange-bellied, rough-skinned newts that seem to come out of hiding only after a rain. I carefully lifted them aside and began building a fire.

The paper matches were too soggy to strike, so I had to go find a box of wooden ones in the supply tent. Then I crumpled newspaper into the fire pit, crisscrossed kindling on top, and stacked up four pieces of firewood, log-cabin fashion. When I tried to light the fire, however, the paper merely blazed up and died, blackening the kindling. This time I cursed out loud. Only after my third attempt did the kindling reluctantly send up a few flames. My miniature firewood cabin sizzled and steamed fitfully.

It took an hour before our cocoa and mush were ready. By then the clouds had really opened up, pelting our camp with a roaring barrage of rain. We huddled under the tent fly beside the smoldering fire, cradling the bowls of mush to keep our fingers warm. Rivulets of rain streamed from the edges of the tent fly like silver chains, caging us within a world of water. When I wanted to rinse out my cocoa cup, I merely had to hold it at arm's length for a moment.

"This looks like a good day to finish my book," Janell announced.

"Don't you want to go put another wall log on the cabin?" I teased.

"No. Not right now." She took an Agatha Christie murder mystery from her raincoat pocket.

"All right, then. I'll catch up on my journal."

And so we cowered under the rain fly for the rest of the morning. We ventured out only to restoke the smoky fire or to divert puddles away from the tents. When Janell finally closed her book three hours later, I was fixing lunch.

"How was your murder mystery?" I asked, handing her a sandwich.

She blinked, as if getting her bearings. The rain had slowed to a drizzle and the sky seemed a little brighter. "Pretty intense, actually. This young couple bought a haunted house out in the English countryside. If they hadn't solved the mystery, they would have wound up as ghosts themselves. It turned out the murderers were still living next door."

I laughed. "So the story hit a little close to home for you?"

She chewed her sandwich thoughtfully. "Not really. We don't know if Clyde Moreland was murdered. Even if he was, it's not like

we'd be next in line. There haven't been any ghosts walking up to tell us their side of the story."

"Not yet, at least." I finished my sandwich and put away the lunch things. The long morning's inactivity had left me chilled and restless. I zipped up my coat and took the ax from the supply tent. "I think it's stopped raining for a while. I'll go work on the next log."

"Wait, I'll come with you."

We walked out together to the half-built log cabin. Inside, the walls were shoulder high. The back wall was solid, but the other three had carefully measured gaps—for a door on one end, a small window on the other, and a wide window on the long side facing the pasture. Wood chips from the corner notches lay strewn about the floor.

The next log, already hewn flat on both sides with my grandfather's adze, lay waiting in the yard. It was fifteen feet long, destined to span the top of the window frame. The log would have been too heavy for us to heft into place by brute force. But over the summer we had discovered a much easier way. We leaned two long poles against the cabin wall to form a ramp. Next we tied ropes to the top of the cabin wall and looped them underneath the log in the yard. Then we climbed up onto the wall and pulled both ropes at once. The heavy log rolled up the ramp like a pencil on a curled sheet of paper.

Once we had levered the new log into position, Janell sat atop a corner of the wall, swinging her legs and looking out across the misty field. After a moment she cleaned the moisture off her glasses and squinted.

"Bill, there's something out there."

"Where?"

"Out in the pasture. Look, it's coming our way."

A vague white shape was shimmering toward us across the field. "That's just one of the heifers," I said. But it didn't quite look like a heifer.

"No, it's tall and thin, almost like a person. But it's not coming from the boat landing, so it can't be one of the Niemis." Janell's voice climbed a note. "Bill, it looks like it's coming from that shack across the river, where we saw the light last night."

"Well it's not Clyde Moreland's ghost, if that's what you're thinking. It's probably just someone who was staying over there."

"Oh? Then how did it get across the river? And why is it coming toward us?"

"Who knows?" I looked closer. "Actually, there's two of them."

Janell and I jumped down from the wall, watching uneasily.

After a minute the two strange visitors reached the fence my parents had built, and let themselves through the gate. As they walked up to the cabin I could see they both wore long, light gray overcoats and had clear plastic galoshes over their shoes. The one in front was an elderly man with a white fedora covered in plastic, although the rain really had let up. He carried a black walking stick. Behind him was an even frailer looking woman with a clear plastic rain bonnet over wavy white hair.

The man paused briefly in front of the cabin, ignoring us entirely. He humphed at the stump we had set up as an impromptu step. Then, supporting himself with his cane, he climbed up into the unfinished cabin and walked past us to the front window's opening. He stood there examining the view, his feet braced slightly apart.

I was taken aback both by his brashness and by his age. His eyes and cheeks were little more than skeletal hollows. Flaps of loose skin hung from his chin like wattles. His bony fingers clenched and unclenched the brass duck-head mounted at the top of his cane. If Clyde Moreland had risen from his grave, I wondered, wouldn't he have worn his World War I uniform instead of a fedora?

Before Janell or I could speak we heard a tremulous "Oh my!" from the step. The white-haired woman was grasping the edge of the door opening, but she was having difficulty lifting herself up. "I'm sorry, could you give me a hand?"

I helped her up into the cabin. She straightened her overcoat and brushed aside her hair. I could tell she must once have been a beauty, but now she wore such heavy makeup that it cracked along wrinkle lines. The bright red of her lipstick gave the rest of her face a deathly pallor.

The man cleared his throat. "We'll be needing chairs."

"Chairs?" I hesitated, unsure how to ask these people who they were.

Janell put her hands on her hips. "Just who are you, anyway?"

The man turned and sized her up with raised eyebrows. "We're your neighbors, Miss Sorensen, and we've come to see what you're doing with my old farm."

"Your old farm?" Janell paled. The man not only looked like death, but he acted with the imperious arrogance one might expect of a messenger from the underworld. "Then you're—"

"Hamilton," I put in, finally figuring it out. "You must be Mr. Hamilton, the Portland lawyer who sold my parents this place."

The man touched his fedora and gave a slight bow. "The same. And this is Muriel."

The woman smiled, cracking more of her makeup. "Lucas gets these notions, and I can't do a thing. Why, yesterday he suddenly says, 'Let's go rowing on the Sahalie,' and the next thing we're shivering in that dilapidated old house. It's frightening the sounds you hear on a stormy night, splashes in the river and things. And then today we have to drag the boat down through the mud and tromp across the wet grass. Lucas just turned seventy-eight, but I still can't get him to act his age."

There was a pause while Muriel caught her breath. Lucas Hamilton leaned slightly toward me on his cane. "The chairs?" he asked. It sounded more like a command than a question.

Begrudgingly, I went to fetch our folding lawn chairs. When I returned, Janell and Muriel were talking about the change in the weather. I set up the chairs in a semicircle before the large window opening. We sat down as if for a business meeting.

Hamilton stood his cane in front of him with a thump, as if to call a court to order. "I do not subscribe to the *Oregon Statesman* myself," he intoned, "But my granddaughter in Salem reports that the Sahalie River has become a feature of your father's journalistic efforts. As I recall, the parcel he bought here has no road, no utilities, and no prospect of acquiring either. How does he intend to develop it?"

"We're just building a little log cabin," I explained. "We don't really need utilities for a primitive summer house."

"Peculiar," he said.

"And we think the isolation has its own charm," Janell added.

Hamilton clenched and unclenched his fingers on the cane's brass head. "Very peculiar. I have been paying taxes on that shack across the river for a dozen years, mostly as a memorial to my friend Clyde Moreland. Perhaps this fascination with rusticity will provide me with an opportunity to let it go."

"Oh I certainly hope so," Muriel exclaimed. Then she looked to Janell. "That place over there has *rats!* Seriously, we find rats' nests in the cupboards every time we come. And then thieves break in every year or so—there's nothing to steal, just a rattle-trap wood stove and some chipped dishes—but it's so close to the highway, and unwatched. This whole valley gives me the *heebie-jeebies.* Don't you feel it too?"

At this point I was ready to ask a few questions of my own. I looked squarely at Hamilton. "How is it that you wound up owning Clyde Moreland's house?"

Hamilton spread his bony hands. "The man had no family, and I was his best friend. His only friend, really, I suppose." He looked out the window opening. "We went to law school together, Clyde and I. When the war came, I finished my studies and passed the bar. Clyde didn't."

"Why? What happened to him?" Janell asked.

"Clyde enlisted to go to France instead. His troop was among those gassed in the trenches. He recovered in a French infirmary, but his lungs never were quite the same. Doctors said he needed fresh air. He ended up out here on the Sahalie, a scholar among the barbarians. I helped him whenever I could, even loaned him money now and then, like family. I think Clyde saw me as a lifeline to the world he'd been forced to leave behind."

The story corroborated much of what George Niemi had told me about Clyde Moreland, but I was struck by certain differences. George had portrayed the old homesteader as a shy man fleeing from the pressures of civilization, not an intellectual forced into the backwoods to recover from a war wound.

"We've heard different stories about how he died," I ventured.

"No doubt," Hamilton said, shaking his head. "I don't think anyone was entirely satisfied by the results of the official inquiry."

"What did it say?"

"That Clyde committed suicide. He was found outside his house on a rainy night, shot with his own military rifle."

Janell asked, "Why would he shoot himself?"

Hamilton sighed. "The man was in pain. His lungs had never been strong. Then he found out he had cancer."

"Maybe he just gave up," I suggested.

"Clyde was not a quitter," Hamilton said. "And even if he were going to end it all, why would he go outside on a dark, stormy night to do it? It was raining so hard that all the footprints were washed away. Any one of the ruffians in this valley could have killed him."

"Who do people suspect?" Janell asked.

Hamilton sighed. "It's amazing how many fools still blame me."

"You?" I looked at him cautiously.

"It's absurd, of course. I was the one who reported the crime. By then poor Clyde had already been dead for hours. The coroner established the time of death very clearly, and a witness proved I was elsewhere when it happened." He shook his head. "I just know it wasn't suicide.

Using a rifle was awkward and ugly—not like Clyde at all. I've always wanted to clear his name by finding the murderer."

"Who do *you* suspect?" Janell asked.

"It could easily have been the Niemis. They live the closest, and they'd been arguing with him about a fence for years."

I caught my breath. I remembered George insisting that his family had not been involved. Perhaps because I had grown to like the Niemis, I wanted to believe George. "I've heard a neighbor named Mrs. Nelson might know something about Clyde Moreland's death."

"Ah, the lovely Gretchen Nelson, erstwhile femme fatale. Remember her, Muriel?"

Muriel pulled her overcoat closer. "Lucas, it's starting to rain again. Finish whatever you came to do, and let's go home."

Hamilton turned to me intently. "Yes, by all means you should go talk with Mrs. Nelson. She was the only other one in the valley with a scrap of education—though only a scrap. She used to meet with Clyde to discuss higher things, and perhaps a few lower ones as well. In any case, her lout of a husband was a jealous fool. A prime suspect. He died of a heart attack shortly afterward. Still, I imagine Gretchen would remember if he had shot Clyde first. Yes, do visit her. I'm not in a position to investigate the case myself, but I would like to see it cleared up once and for all."

I glanced to Janell. "I'm afraid we won't have time to visit anyone this summer. We're still trying to finish up work on the cabin before school starts in September."

Hamilton gave a wheezing laugh. "Finish up? If you've only gotten this much done in two months you'll never get a roof on in two weeks." He used his cane to push himself to his feet." Come, Muriel, I'll take you home."

Janell confronted the old man. "We can keep working in the rain, you know."

He smiled at her as if at a child. "Miss Sorensen, the rains have not yet begun to fall. The Sahalie River Valley receives more than one hundred inches of precipitation each winter. Cattle drown in their stalls. This little log pile of yours will be a rotten ruin by spring, if it isn't swept away by a flood first."

"A flood? But we're almost a quarter mile from the river," I objected.

Now Hamilton turned his piteous gaze on me. "When the Sahalie floods, as it does every few years, it is fully a quarter mile wide. Clyde once built a large shed on this very site, just a few feet lower than your structure. It floated away in 1964."

Lucas Hamilton stepped down from our cabin, lent his arm to steady

Muriel on the step, and then led the way back across the pasture in the drizzle. At the gate Muriel turned to wave. "Good luck you two. Just watch out for rats!"

We did not finish the cabin that summer. In fact, the log over the window was the last one we raised before the rains wore us down. Day after day we would sit beneath the small tent fly, shivering at the streams of water that poured through the trees. We found a reject bottle of homemade wine that Janell's father had given us, a ghastly mixture of cherry juice and fermented zucchinis from his garden. Even emptying that dread jug did not slow the torrents.

Finally I threw a few boards across the top of the unfinished cabin walls, spanned a tarp over the whole thing, and nailed it in place. Janell packed our remaining dry food into one of the large waterproof cans. I greased our metal tools with shortening to ward off rust and packed them away in the other can. The Niemis kindly agreed to store our tents and our sleeping bags in their basement. I did not dare to ask George again about Clyde Moreland's death, remembering how abruptly our conversation about it had ended last time. Instead I asked about floods, and learned that Lucas Hamilton had not been exaggerating about the shed that washed away in 1964.

We dragged *Earnest* up beyond the highest flood level George could remember, startlingly close to the elevation of our sill logs. Then Janell and I packed our clothes and books in our backpacks, hefted them to our shoulders, and hiked up through the woods in the rain. After five miles on deer trails and logging roads we stumbled out onto Highway 101 at Taylor Beach, where the Greyhound bus from San Francisco to Portland makes a daily flag stop.

By the time night fell we were halfway home, watching the windshield wipers trying to shove aside the seemingly endless rains of the Coast Range. Janell had dozed off against my shoulder. I wondered if when she awoke—if when we both awoke from the long winter at the university—it would turn out that Lucas Hamilton was right, and we had only dreamed our cabin along the Sahalie.

9

The Dreadnaught

(June 1978)

A river smooth and seeming calm, hiding the cruel file-edge of its current beneath a smooth and calm-seeming surface.
—Ken Kesey, *Sometimes a Great Notion*, 1963

For most of that winter, living in a drafty 1940s apartment in Eugene, Janell and I were too busy with our university papers and practicums to spend much time thinking about our half-built log cabin in the Sahalie woods. We bicycled to class in the morning, walked along the paved Willamette River paths at lunch, and strolled through the city in the evenings. Because we had decided not to own a car—partly out of ecological conviction and partly out of economic necessity—the hundred miles that separated us from the Sahalie might as well have been a thousand.

A few times, however, news of the Sahalie did filter through to us. The first time was a weekend in November when my parents showed up at our doorstep in their Volkswagen squareback. Despite chilly weather, all the car's windows were open. My mother jumped out, wearing three coats on top of each other, and asked, "Quick, how much space do you have in your freezer?"

They had just been to Taylorville to pick up our annual rent for the pasture from the Niemis—250 pounds of beef, cut and wrapped. Now they were driving to visit everyone in the family, trying to unload the meat before it thawed.

Janell started clearing out the little freezer above our refrigerator while my father crawled into the back of the car, clunking the rock-like packages from box to box, picking out an assortment of round steaks, T-bones, and rump roasts. "Tongue? You like tongue?" he asked. "How about a nice ox-tail for soup?"

It was hard not to think of the black angus steer that had paraded about the pasture all summer behind Lizzie and Tootsie. We had named him Meat, and it had seemed like a good joke at the time. But now here were the cardboard boxes, printed with the logo of an Indian peace pipe and the words "Skookum Slaughterhouse." An unsteady hand had added in black marker, "Sullivan MEAT."

As Janell and I were loading our freezer my mother handed me a small extra package, marked with an X. "This is special for you from the butcher's apprentice. He says he knows you. A tall youngish man."

I recalled our strange evening visit from Butch, and answered with some hesitation. "Maybe. What is it?"

"Pastrami. It's his specialty. He says it tastes more like chicken than beef."

Janell and I looked at each other. I knew she was thinking the same thing: Raccoon. It would be harder to face than Meat.

"We'd better be going," my father said. "We still have to see Pete in McMinnville and Mark in Beaverton before all this thaws. Enjoy your steaks."

With that they were gone.

We didn't hear other news from the Sahalie for several months. Then, about the middle of January, a Christmas card showed up in our mailbox from Dolores Niemi. It depicted a madonna surrounded by candles—a card one might find on a dusty back shelf of a small drugstore. In careful cursive she had written:

> Dear Bill & Jeanelle—
>
> Thank you for your clever card I never do seem to get mine done until late! Maybe it's this stormy weather we've been having that makes my feet swell up so bad I can only wear slippers. I can see your little cabin from the living room window now since I had the boys trim an alder that was in the way. At the crest of the Thanksgiving flood George docked his boat by your step! The water was about eight feet below it. He was taking hay over for the cattle he forgot to swim back in time. Says he also caught you a roof in the flood. I don't like it when he's out on the river like that, but the boys wanted to. They brought your boat over here. It's not weathering the winter well, you may want to look for another. Hope you liked the meat.
>
> Have a Happy New Year, Dolores

We puzzled over this letter like CIA operatives trying to crack a code. What did it mean when she said George had "caught us a roof"? Could the river really have risen within eight feet of our cabin? And how could *Earnest* be weathering the winter so poorly that we needed a replacement?

I especially had trouble picturing George finding us an entire roof, apparently unattached to a house, sailing down the flooded river. Even if this were literally true, what chance was there that it would fit? And how would I go about moving it on top of our cabin walls?

Nonetheless, I let my family know that we were no longer on the lookout for roofing materials, but that we still needed used windows, a wood stove, and possibly another inexpensive boat.

The windows turned up a few months later in Salem. Janell's father had decided to remodel his kitchen, replacing his windows with insulated glass and aluminum frames. He said his old wood-frame windows from the 1920s were ours for the taking.

The new boat turned up in McMinnville. My brother Pete ran a computer consulting firm there. An unpredictable genius, Pete had surprised everyone by dropping out of the university's Honors College to spend a few years blistering his hands on a rough-and-tumble tree thinning crew for a forest management company. Then, just as suddenly, he had made a small fortune in his spare time by inventing a computer program that allows real estate agents to keep track of multiple listings. Now, while the royalties from his computer program rolled in, he dabbled in consulting work and rural real estate. Pete and I were enough alike in appearance that childhood acquaintances sometimes mistook one of us for the other at high school reunions. But we were dissimilar in style. While I rode a bicycle, Pete drove a twenty-foot Lincoln Continental. While I enjoyed working with words, he prefered numbers. From the first, Pete had ridiculed my log cabin concept as anachronistic nonsense. So I was a little uncertain when he called to say he had just bought me a boat.

"I hope it isn't some big ski boat," I told him on the telephone. "I don't have much of a budget for this."

"No, it's a rowboat. I got it at a garage sale down the block for $15. It's named the *Dreadnaught*."

"The *Dreadnaught*?"

From the sound of shuffling papers and an occasional clank I could tell that he was doing something else while he talked on the telephone—perhaps several other things at once. He often did this while talking, and as a result his conversation sometimes leapt about like a startled rabbit. "What? Oh, the *Dreadnaught*. My neighbor built it from plans in a magazine article. All it took was two sheets of ten-foot plywood."

"Why is he selling it so cheap?"

"The guy doesn't like boats. He just likes projects. Now he wants the space in his garage for something else. He never even put it in the water. Do you have any dynamite?"

"What?" I pressed the receiver closer to my ear, trying to sort out the noises coming from McMinnville. Someone sneezed and a distant alarm went off. "I'm sorry, Pete, I thought you asked if I had any dynamite."

"Dynamite?"

"Yes."

"Well, do you?"

"Uh, no."

He must have dropped the phone at this point, because it sounded as if I were inside a wooden box that was thumping down a flight of stairs.

"Bill? You OK?"

"Yes."

"Look, I gotta run. I've got some clients coming, but I want to try out this *Dreadnaught* thing. Does Janell's father still have a boat trailer we could borrow?"

"I think so."

"When are you heading over to the Sahalie?"

"The Monday after school's out, if we can get a ride."

"Good. You come to McMinnville and we'll all go in my pickup."

"That would be great. We've got some windows in Salem we'd like to—"

There was a crash on the other end, and excited voices, getting louder. "Sure thing. Bye, Bill," Pete said. Then the line went dead.

The Monday after school was out we were rattling down the Niemi driveway in Pete's pickup, with the *Dreadnaught* in tow. In some ways, I felt as if Janell and I were starting all over again. Just one year ago we had driven down this same driveway with the same boat trailer, dreaming that we would complete a log cabin that summer.

This time we were beginning with a different set of unknowns. I worried about setting out in Pete's *Dreadnaught* instead of in *Earnest*. Had our previous work on the cabin been lost to rot and floods, as Lucas Hamilton predicted? Had our supplies survived the winter in the waterproof cans at our camp? What kind of roof was it that George had caught for us? And would we ever find out who had killed our predecessor Clyde Moreland? Janell and I had agreed that the next step in that intermittent investigation would be to visit the mysterious Mrs. Nelson.

As we pulled up to the Niemi farmhouse, Laddie the farm dog made a show of barking at us. But then he lay down in the yard, put his head on his paws, and growled vaguely.

"There it is!" Janell exclaimed, pointing across the river to the tiny gray spot that was our unfinished cabin. By squinting I could just make out the dark square of the window opening. My heart beat a little faster to see the log walls still standing after the long winter.

"Sheesh," Pete said. "That's all the bigger it is? Looks like a roofless doghouse to me."

"I don't see any roof either," Janell said, "Unless—" There was a faint gray stripe in the grass below the cabin site. We all walked up to the farmyard gate for a better view of the distant field. From there we could also see a green John Deere tractor chugging up the Niemi's road from the boat landing.

"Who's that?" Pete asked.

"It's not George," Janell said. "Is it Joe?"

"No. It must be Jack. He's the younger son who's taking over the farm work." I waved and opened the gate.

Jack drove his big-wheeled tractor into the farmyard and set the brake, but he kept the motor running. He fidgeted in the seat and readjusted his baseball cap. "You bringing reinforcements this year?"

"This is my brother Pete from McMinnville," I explained. "He brought us here with his pickup, but he can only stay for the day. Are your parents around?"

"Naw, you just missed them. We finished up the morning milking by eleven, so they went on into town. Don't know where Joe's at."

There was an awkward pause. Unlike the rest of his family, this matter-of-fact young Niemi did not seem naturally talkative.

Janell ventured, "We were hoping we could launch our new boat down on your bank. And I think we left some tents in your basement."

"No problem. The basement door's unlocked. Just don't trip over the dog."

"Thanks," I said. Another awkward pause followed.

Finally Pete's patience gave way. "What about this roof thing? Bill tells me someone over here caught a roof in the flood. Do you know what that's all about?"

"Yup, I do." Jack made a chewing motion with his jaw, although I doubted he actually had any gum.

"How do you catch a roof?"

"Well, a roof's made of cedar, so what you do is catch yourself a cedar log."

Janell nodded. "I thought that looked like a log over there. Where did you find it? All the cedar trees were logged off long ago."

Jack straightened his baseball cap. "Yeah. But floods still wash a few old logs out of the canyons."

"Wood like that might get a good price at the mill," Pete suggested.

"Hell yes. A pickup load of cedar's worth a hundred bucks," Jack said. "My brother wanted the money for car parts. He wrecked his brush whacker in the demolition derby last fall. Me, I just wanted cedar for fence posts."

I asked, "So how did the log end up on our side of the river?"

Jack shrugged. "That one just did. When the water crested and there was all kinds of crap coming down the river, we took the boat up two miles and watched for logs going by. If they were cedar, we'd lasso them and start pulling for shore. It takes about two miles before we can get close enough to a riverbank to tie up to a tree. That one log didn't want to pull to our side for nothing, so we tied it up over there."

Janell commented, "That must be awfully dangerous, out in a little boat in a flood. Your mother mentioned in her Christmas card that she didn't like it."

"Aw, she thinks we should have learned to swim first."

Janell bit her lip and looked to me. I could tell she was thinking of the Niemis' boat, a fragile aluminum skiff with its deck covering slashed off by an ax. The Niemi men had been risking their lives every moment they were out on that flood.

"We need to pay you for that log," I said. "How much is it worth?"

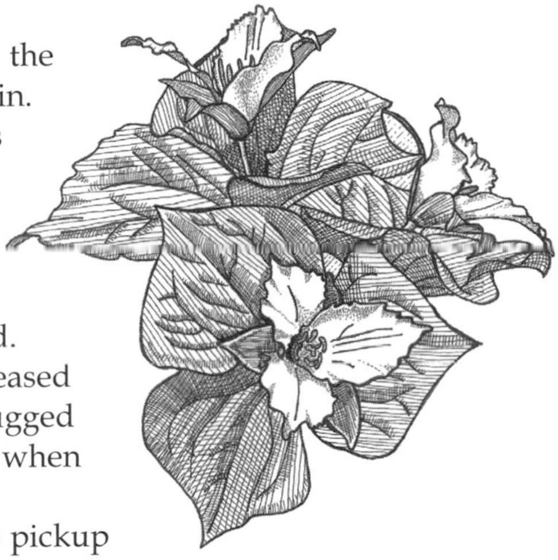

Jack squinted across the river at the gray stripe below our unfinished cabin. "Over there? Without road access, it's not worth much. How about if you just come help us buck hay bales the next few times we get a truck-load delivered?"

"That's a deal," I held out my hand.

Jack shook my hand. Then he released the tractor's brake lever and chugged across the yard to the barn. "See you when the hay truck comes."

The rest of us got back into Pete's pickup and drove down to the riverbank. Along the way we slowed as we passed *Earnest*. The Niemis had moved our old boat beside their road, perhaps to keep an eye on it during the flood, but then a tractor tire must have accidentally clipped the boat's stern in passing. The reason *Earnest* had "not weathered the winter well" was that its backboard had been ripped loose.

Pete snorted disparagingly at *Earnest*, swung the pickup past the riverbank with a flourish, and backed the *Dreadnaught* down to the boat landing's slope. We got out and Pete began untying the plywood boat from its trailer, obviously eager to see it launched.

"So the *Dreadnaught* has never actually been in water before?" Janell asked.

"Maiden voyage," Pete replied. "But the guy who sold it to me gave me a can of liquid fiberglass to use as seam sealer, in case we find any leaks."

He untied the last of the straps and stood by the winch at the front of the trailer, where the stern of the boat was still secured by a single piece of twine. Because Pete had loaded the boat onto the trailer backwards, who knows why, the boat's pointed prow now aimed straight down the steep slope at the deep, murky river. It looked like a gigantic ski poised at the top of an alpine run.

Pete unfolded the blade of his pocketknife. "Ready? Here she goes!"

With a single slash he severed the twine. At once the *Dreadnaught* rumbled off the trailer and slid down through the grass toward the river. When it reached the water, the prow sliced a neat V of white water on either side. But instead of bobbing up, the boat simply continued straight down into the murk. Without so much as a pause, the prow vanished underwater, followed by the seats, the oarlocks, and finally the stern. The backboard briefly shimmered white beneath the greenish water before disappearing completely. Not even a rope remained.

For most of a minute the three of us stood staring down at the river that had swallowed the *Dreadnaught* so thoroughly, half expecting that it would resurface, or at least that bubbles would rise to show us where it had gone.

Finally Pete said, "You'd think a boat made out of wood would *have* to float."

I weighed the possibility of taking off my clothes and diving into the river to look for the sunken *Dreadnaught*. Even if I found it, we would need to drag it up from the mud and seal its leaky seams before it could be of use. I decided Pete's boat had found its final resting place. "You know, I think I could nail the loose backboard on *Earnest* and seal it up with a few coats of that fiberglass you brought."

"I think you're right," Janell put in. "In the meantime we can start hauling stuff across the river in the Niemis' boat, so I can get camp set up."

Pete acknowledged this new plan with a distracted nod. He was staring at the murky Sahalie River with a strange, stunned expression that seemed to mix puzzlement, anger, and disbelief. Over the past year he had chuckled at the difficulties we had described from our first summer along the Sahalie. Perhaps he had imagined that he himself would be able to conquer our little wilderness in a single day if he set his mind to it.

At length Pete cleared his throat. "Dynamite," he said. "That's the ticket."

I looked at him with alarm. "How's that?"

"You don't want to waste your time crossing rivers in boats. You need a road to get you there."

"Well, there's the old gas line road, but it goes over hills so steep it's worthless."

"Right." Pete turned to me with renewed enthusiasm. "So you build around the hills instead."

"It's too steep. If you took a bulldozer on a slope like that it'd just fall into the river."

He rolled his eyes. "That's why you need dynamite. You set a whole string of charges along the cliff above the river. You wire them together and blow them all up at once. Kablooey! Instant road."

Janell and I looked at him for a moment in silence, thinking of all the ways this new scheme could backfire. She spoke first. "That's an interesting idea, Pete, but right now we just need to get our stuff across the river."

"OK, fine. Let's get this stuff across. We can do the road thing later. Besides, I've got a forest improvement project I want to work on."

"You do? What kind of forest project?" He had never shown much interest in the property here before. I worried about this new enthusiasm. Pete often went about things very differently than I did. Still, the property didn't belong to either of us, but rather to our parents, so I couldn't really object.

"After all that time I spent on a forest work crew, I learned a few things about upgrading a property like this. Since then I've been studying information from the Oregon Small Woodland Association and the Oregon State University Extension Service."

I wrinkled my brow. "I suppose they didn't like the idea of us cutting trees for a cabin?"

He shook his head. "No, that part of your plan is fine. That's what they call a precommercial thinning. But foresters have a lot of other intensive management strategies."

"Like what?" I wished he would drop the jargon and simply tell me what he was planning.

He waved his hand dismissively. "I can handle this by myself. Just leave it to me."

"Have you talked to our parents about this?"

"Sure. What do you think they bought this property for? Some kind of nature preserve? It's prime timberland."

After that Pete began carrying windows and floorboards down to the Niemi boat, but his mind seemed elsewhere. He hardly noticed when Janell exclaimed that the watertight cans had kept last year's camp supplies in surprisingly good condition. He said nothing when I proudly toured him through the log cabin. Straw on the floor showed that the Niemis had used the cabin to store hay during the winter. They had also nailed an extra tarp on my impromptu roof, and as a result the cabin logs were mostly dry, and entirely rot-free.

After lunch Pete fetched a chainsaw from his pickup and disappeared into the forest behind the cabin, farther back on the hill than we had ventured. For four hours we heard the angry whine of his saw, punctuated by the distant crash of trees.

When the shadows began to lengthen toward evening he reappeared at the cabin site with sawdust in his hair, his shirt pocket torn, looking tired and grim as he carried the chainsaw. "I'm going to have to come back and spend a few more days at this."

"What have you been doing?" I asked.

"Cutting weeds."

"Weeds?" Janell asked. "It sounded more like trees."

Pete shrugged. "Alder trees are weeds. Any forester will tell you that. Alders grow up fast and crowd out the conifers, but they're worthless at the mill. This whole place should have been sprayed with herbicide to knock out the deciduous trees after it was logged. It's just grown up wild. Now most of the alders are eight inches in diameter. It takes forever to weed them out."

I took him by the arm and turned him toward the little creekside alder grove where I had first been captivated by the spirit of the Sahalie, years ago when we had visited as boys. The evening light angled among the alders' white trunks, dappled by the alder leaves into a thousand glowing greens. "Pete, you've been a big help getting us moved in today. And I can't stop you from thinning the alders back on the hill if you want. But please don't cut the ones in this grove."

He nodded. "I understand."

"You do?"

"Sure. It's not like I'm planning to log your yard. A cabin like yours needs landscaping. I just want to put some responsible science into the rest of the forestry out here."

"Fair enough." I hoped we had reached a workable compromise.

Later that evening, after Pete had rowed back in the Niemis' boat and driven off toward McMinnville, Janell and I hiked to the back side of the hill to see Pete's work. I was shocked by what we found. It looked like a war zone. For a full acre, alders lay crisscrossed in a jumble of leaves and broken branches. The bittersweet smell of wilting leaves and sawdust filled the air. Here and there, conifers remained upright, lonely shadows of thin Douglas firs and Sitka spruces against the deepening sky. White stumps jutted from the debris chest-high, like ghosts. I could see that Pete had not even taken the standard precaution of sawing out undercuts. As a result, some of the larger trees had split and jackknifed dangerously as they fell. My brother could easily have been killed on this crusade.

"This is what the science of forestry looks like?" I wondered.

"Looks like a mess to me," Janell said.

"What should we do?" I asked.

She shrugged. "The forest will eventually recover, even from this. Nature is resilient."

"I suppose Nature is," I said, and sighed. "I just wonder if Pete is too."

10

The Spiral Bird

(July 1978)

> What is acceptable we call acceptable; what is unacceptable we call unacceptable. A road is made by people walking on it; things are so because they are called so.
>
> Chuang Tzu, On Making All Things Equal, circa 320 BC

A few mornings later I awakened before Janell. I lay there in our zipped-together sleeping bags, folded my hands behind my head, and gazed out the tent's mesh window at the speckled green of alder leaves. The vast silence—no car horns, no lawn mowers, no barking dogs, not even a refrigerator's hum—felt like the great peace of a sudden armistice after months of battling responsibilities in the city.

But there was a flavor to the silence, as even water from a mountain spring has a distinctive taste. I rolled that silence about in my mouth, savoring it, until Janell nuzzled against me, stretched, and blinked.

"Mmm—it's nice to sleep where it's so quiet," Janell mumbled.

"If you listen, there's a faint bird song," I said. Why hadn't I noticed it before, this background music of the Sahalie rainforest? "It sort of spirals upward like distant bells. Do you hear it?"

She closed her eyes, smiled, and nodded. "We never hear that one in town."

"Do you know what kind of bird it is?"

She lifted a shoulder. "I brought a bird book, but it's not very good at describing songs. They're all written out as 'chee-chee-chee' or 'tritt-tritt.'"

"All right, then, let's call it the spiral bird."

"There's a different bird song too. Do you hear that one?" With her eyes still closed, she lifted a finger each time the call came, a single rising tone.

"It sounds like a kid asking 'What? What?'"

"Must be the what-bird, then." She opened her eyes. "Want to go find them?"

"Sure."

We got dressed and began prowling up the creek. Although we heard many birds from a distance, they always fell silent when we approached. They seemed to melt miraculously into the salmonberry thickets. Frustrated, we finally we gave up and returned to cook breakfast.

"Those spiral birds sounded so close." Janell crumpled newspaper to build a campfire. "I can't believe we couldn't see them."

"Maybe they're invisible," I jested, fetching a pan for our oatmeal. "You know, evil spirits haunting the woods."

"You mean the Skookum sisters?" Janell struck a match and lit the paper. "The Sahalie is such a beautiful place, it's hard to believe the woods are as full of demons and murderers as people say."

We ate breakfast without more discussion. The magic of the morning had been replaced with an edge. When we were done we went out together to the construction site.

In our first few days of work that summer we had already accomplished a lot. We had added another complete round of logs, a fresh white layer above the dark, weathered logs of last year's work. Then we had chiseled out a dozen square notches in the top logs, spanned six smaller logs across the cabin as ceiling joists, and laid floorboards on top. Now when we walked through the cabin doorway it really felt like we were entering a room. Two large square holes remained in the room's ceiling, however—one at the far end for a future stovepipe, and one as a hatch to the future sleeping loft. Janell and I climbed the ladder I had mounted here. We surveyed our progress from atop the loft's deck-like floor. Soon we would have to start adding shorter logs, tapering the gables to a peak. The rest of the roof was still just an uncut cedar log lying in the pasture, where the Niemis had beached it in the winter's flood.

Suddenly a spiral bird sang out directly behind us like a lunatic with a glockenspiel. We turned and stared into the leaves. Nothing. The trickiness of these elusive birds was maddening. It reminded me of how much we still had to learn about the Sahalie. We hadn't even met many of the people who lived in the valley.

"You know," I said. "This might be a good day to go see Mrs. Nelson."

Janell looked at me. "The neighbor downriver? Yes, I would like to meet her. And not just because Lucas Hamilton thinks she's a murder suspect."

"Actually, he thought her jealous husband was the one who might have shot Clyde Moreland."

"Nonetheless." She frowned. "I wish there was some way we could call ahead to let her know we're coming."

"Unless you can yell two miles, I'm afraid we'll have to drop in."

"Maybe it'll help if I bring a jar of huckleberry jam."

"That's a great idea."

We climbed down from the cabin, loaded a backpack with supplies for a day trip, and set off across the pasture. At once the herd of dairy heifers rallied round to see us off. Leading the charge were two friends from last summer—Lizzie, the chummy black-and-white Holstein, and Tootsie, the headstrong black Jersey mix. Behind them followed a cluster of twenty frightened calves and a small, bewildered-looking bull.

"Oh, honey!" Janell cooed, petting Lizzie's white forehead. "Couldn't you get pregnant last year?"

"You think she was trying?" I asked.

Janell gave me a sad smile. "She's in the dairy business. All the other heifers from last summer must have had calves and moved on to the milking parlor. I guess last year's bull wasn't all that hot."

"Or else these two goof-offs had an attitude problem."

Janell coughed. "I beg your pardon?"

I backpedaled. "I just meant, maybe they were looking for more maturity before starting a family."

"Hmm. I'm not sure they'll go for this year's bull either." She sized it up critically.

"Yeah, he's even smaller than the new steer."

We fell silent, thinking of last year's steer, Meat. More than once we had stretched our meager food budget with a package of tough Swiss steak or gamy hamburger from the Sahalie butcher.

We continued to the boat landing. While Janell unlocked the boat's chain I fetched the oars we had hidden in a blackberry thicket. The river stood full and stagnant, bloated by the high tide. Without a current, the two-mile row downstream took nearly an hour. When the jungle of spruce trees finally gave way to the brushy bank of a farm, we chained *Earnest* to a log, hid the oars, and scrambled up the slope. We emerged onto a vast green pasture, tidy as a golf fairway. A few dozen thick-necked brown Herefords eyed us with alarm.

"Hello, girls," Janell called. Far away, on a bench above the field, stood a clapboard farmhouse and a picturesque red barn with a shiny new metal roof.

"Mrs. Nelson sure keeps her farm neat," I said. "No junk cars, no weeds. It's nothing like the Niemi place."

"I just wish she had a doorbell out here."

We hiked across the farm to a gravel road beside the barn. As we neared the barn an old gray dog trotted up toward us, sniffing and wagging silently. Only when its nose missed my outstretched hand did I realize the dog's clouded white eyes must be blind.

"Beulah?" An old woman leaned out a side door of the barn, holding a thirty-gallon milk can. "Well, what on earth—?"

"Mrs. Nelson?" Janell ventured.

"Who are you?" she asked, puzzled. "And where's your car?"

"We walked up from the river," I said. "We're your neighbors."

"Walked? Neighbors?" She set down the milk can and pulled a loose strand of white hair back from her weathered face. "It's been twenty years since a neighbor walked over to visit."

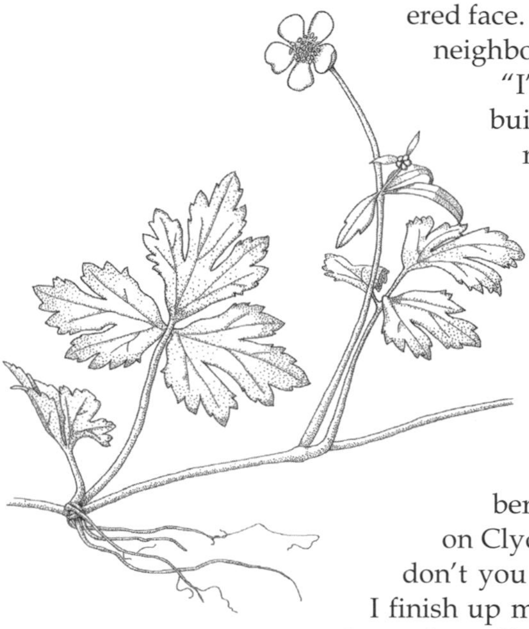

"I'm Bill and this is Janell. We're building a cabin two miles up the river."

Janell held out her jar. "I thought you might like some jam from the huckleberries I picked there last year."

"Now isn't that nice." Mrs. Nelson held the offering in her bony hands, admiring the blue of the berries. "You must be the ones on Clyde's old place. Well then. Why don't you come on into the barn while I finish up milking. We can go over to the house for coffee later, if you like."

We followed her inside. Again I was struck by the contrast to the Niemi's farm. While George's milking parlor was a gleaming command center of stainless steel pipes, Mrs. Nelson's old post-and-beam barn was pure Currier & Ives nostalgia, with dust motes in stray sunbeams, the smell of hay, and the coo of unseen pigeons.

"Now listen Maggie, we've got visitors, but it's all right." Mrs. Nelson pulled a stool beside a large brown Jersey cow and began squeezing foamy milk into a bucket, one fistful at a time.

"How long have you been living here?" I asked.

"Sixty-one years."

"Wow. That's a long time." I felt silly saying this, but I couldn't think of anything else.

She didn't seem to mind. "I grew up in Brookings. Taught school in

Myrtle Creek until 1917. Then my husband Ed and I homesteaded out here. Most of the county had been withdrawn from the Indian reservation about then because the Army wanted timber for the war effort."

She stood up and poured the milk through a strainer into an electric cooler. "More milk than I can drink from this old cow. Eight gallons a day."

"What do you do with it?" Janell asked.

"Mostly I just pour it on the garden. I used to give it away, but I ran out of bottles, and folks never bring 'em back. I've got sixty pounds of butter in the freezer here and more's a-coming. I give a whole fruit box of it to my son every time he comes up from Brookings. Here, take some." She opened a chest and handed me a block wrapped in waxed paper. It was shaped like a little loaf of bread with stripes on top.

"Thanks," I said.

"You coming up to the house, or are you in a hurry?"

"No hurry."

"Well that's good then." She led the way out past a garden.

"Do you really live out here all by yourself?" I asked.

She looked at me sharply. "And why shouldn't I?"

"Well, it's just—"

"That I'm eighty-three?"

"Well yes, and you've got such a large farm."

She aimed a finger at me, then turned it toward the barn. "You see that new roof? I crawled up there last summer, tore off the rotten wood shakes, and nailed on those metal sheets by myself. I drive my tractor out to mow and bale the fields, spray the thistles, and cut the weeds. I saw up and split my own firewood. The only thing I'm getting tired of is listening to people say I should go live in some retirement condo. How could I leave this farm?"

I held up my hands. "I didn't say you should!"

She studied me a moment. "No, I don't reckon you did, exactly."

"What a wonderful garden!" Janell said, changing the subject. "Do the vegetables grow this big because you water them with milk?"

Mrs. Nelson smiled sideways at Janell, acknowledging her tact. "Well maybe a little milk doesn't hurt. Only thing that won't grow is corn. I try every darned year, but it just never ripens in this climate. And then there's the rabbits. I've tried fences and poisons and traps, but nothing seems to work."

With that she led the way on into the farmhouse. It was a weathered gray building with small-paned windows. Cedar shakes covered the sides and roof. Half a dozen sheds in the same style nestled against it. We entered through a screen door to a pantry. Inside, age had tilted the walls and doors askew. She took us to a kitchen dominated by a gigantic, cast-iron wood stove. Rhododendrons bloomed pink in front of most of the windows, but the kitchen table looked squarely out across the pasture to the river. There were photographs on the walls, a quilt on a bench, and crocheted pillows.

Mrs. Nelson took off her apron, rolled down her sleeves, and untied her scarf. Then she sat down across from us, transformed from a rugged farmwife into a gentle great-grandmother. She wore spectacles, and had tied her white hair in a bun. She folded her bony hands delicately in her lap. "So tell me about this cabin you're building on Clyde's place."

While we told her about our project she listened intently, nodding occasionally. Finally she sat back. "Golly, that brings back memories. I guess some things weren't all that different when Ed and I first took up our homestead here."

"Really?" Janell asked. "We're new here so we're curious about the area's history. What was it like?"

Mrs. Nelson laid her hands on the table. "Well, Ed and I were among the first white settlers. In those days you could take the train as far as Illahee, and the wagon road went on to Murphy Landing, but then it was six miles by boat. That first winter Ed had some potatoes from a harvest job he'd had, so we ate those for a while. By spring I was down to grubbing roots and plants from the woods to give us a break from fish, fish, fish. Silverback salmon jumped everywhere in the river back then, so thick they'd land in the boat."

Suddenly she slapped the table and stood up. "Doggone it! I promised you coffee." She started building a fire in the wood stove.

"Did you have a house that first year?" Janell asked.

"We had a shack up here in the woods, but a skunk got in it and stunk it up, so we moved across the river to a cedar board hut. It wasn't much, and then the river flooded knee-deep inside one night and soaked the bed. After that we came back and smoked out the shack until we could stand the skunk smell. The regular house wasn't until two years later. Our first job was clearing the farm."

"Didn't the timber companies clear out the trees for you?" I asked.

She set a pot of coffee on the wood stove to percolate. "No, we were too far from the railroad to sell our trees. But that wasn't the worst of it. The whole pasture was one big beaver swamp. To drain it, Ed had to dig twenty-foot-deep ditches all around it, by hand with a shovel. I watched to make sure the bank didn't crumble down on him. Then we needed to cut down the trees, but we didn't have a saw blade big enough. We had to build fires at the bottoms of the spruces until they fell. Along each log, Ed bored holes every ten feet with a big hand auger and lit little fires in them. It was my job to blow on all the little fires to keep them smoldering. What was left of the burned logs we managed to cut up with the crosscut saw and stack for firewood. That was a sooty job."

She laughed. "I brought fancy French embroidery to work on during the long winter nights, but I didn't want to touch it when my hands were always so black." She pointed to a chest. "That embroidery project's still in there, unfinished, sixty-one years later."

"What about Clyde Moreland?" I suggested, hoping to steer the subject toward our investigation. "Do you remember much about him?"

"Oh my, yes." She poured us cups of coffee and set out a dish of homemade shortbread cookies, rich with butter. "Why, I remember the day Clyde moved in. He was just back from World War I, a handsome young man, smart in his uniform, and well educated. He'd studied to be a lawyer, you know."

I nodded.

"We got along so well in those early years," she went on. "He could talk knowledgeably about almost anything. And a heart of gold! He gave free lawyer advice to people up and down the valley. When the Depression came and people couldn't pay their taxes, Clyde would help them out, or even buy their farms if they wanted. Heaven knows where he found the money."

This was interesting news. Could Moreland have inherited wealth? According to Lucas Hamilton, he had no living relatives. But then Hamilton also said he had loaned Moreland money from time to time. "I suppose Clyde Moreland must have wound up owning quite a bit of land."

Mrs. Nelson eyed me across her coffee cup. "Yes, he did. As a matter of fact, that may have been his biggest problem. Jealousy's an awful thing."

We were getting dangerously close to the mystery of his murder. I took a risk. "With a beautiful farm like this, I'm sure you and your husband didn't have any reason to be jealous of Clyde."

She didn't blush. "Me and Ed? Of course not. No, the jealous ones were in the tribe."

"The tribe?" Janell asked. "You mean the Sahalie Indians?"

"That's right." Mrs. Nelson stood up to refill the cookie plate and our coffee cups. While she was pouring, she continued, "You see, Clyde met a Frenchman while he was recovering from a mustard gas attack in World War I. They were in the same hospital over there in France, and everyone was complaining about how there wasn't any work for veterans. Well, Clyde told him the U.S. government was giving away free farms to homesteaders in Oregon. So when they got out of the hospital, this Frenchman came along. But then it turned out you had to be a U.S. citizen to apply. The Frenchman married an Indian girl, but that didn't help, because Indians weren't citizens back then either. From that point on, they gave Clyde grief for owning so much land. I guess a lot of people in the tribe felt cheated. But especially the Bouchers."

"The Bouchers?" I asked, startled. "The Frenchman's name was Boucher?"

"Yes. Do you know them?"

"Well, there's a butcher in the valley with that name." I hesitated, remembering Butch's wild, threatening talk. He had wanted to reclaim Skookum Rock, and perhaps the entire county, for the tribe. Could his family's personal grudge against Moreland have led to murder?

"More cookies?" Mrs. Nelson asked, holding out a dainty china plate. With her wavering voice and her white hair bun, it suddenly seemed absurd that we could ever have suspected this gentle matron of any involvement in Clyde Moreland's demise.

"No, thank you," Janell said. "We really should be going soon anyway. But thank you so much for letting us visit. Your farm is as pretty as a park."

"Oh my, " Our elderly hostess turned aside at this praise, and gazed out the window at her farm's pasture.

Suddenly, incredibly, Mrs. Nelson's entire demeanor changed. Her hands clenched to fists. Her face stiffened into a horrific sneer. "God damn you varmints all to hell!"

Janell and I shrank back from the table. Had we done something awful to provoke her, or had she been gripped by this seizure on her own?

Mrs. Nelson grabbed a rifle I hadn't noticed behind a curtain ruffle. She flung open the window, aimed at the pasture, and fired. A deafening roar filled the kitchen, followed by a blue haze of acrid gunpowder smoke. "Bastards!" she cried, fumbling for shells from the lacy pocket of her dress. She reloaded and fired out the window again.

When she finally sat back in her chair, the rifle across her lap, Janell and I were cowering in the doorway behind the wood stove.

"Missed," Mrs. Nelson sighed. She took an apron from behind her chair and dabbed her eyes. "Ed never missed. Lord, that man was a shot! If anything got in his sights, it was dead."

"Wha—what were you shooting at?" Janell asked, emerging from behind the stove.

"What?" Mrs. Nelson looked up. "Oh my, did I startle you? It was just another one of those darned coyotes. I'm sorry. Would you two like some more coffee?"

I was still shaking from the rifle blasts. I made a show of looking at my pocket watch. "Look at that, Janell! The tide's going to turn unless we start rowing home soon." I thought we had learned more than enough about Mrs. Nelson for one day.

Janell didn't seem to take the hint. "Coyotes? I've never heard of coyotes attacking beef cattle."

Mrs. Nelson put the gun back behind the curtain. "Oh, coyotes don't mess with Herefords, that's true, but lambs—well, lambs are just candy to coyotes."

"Are there many sheep ranches in the valley?" Janell asked.

"No, nobody has sheep around here."

"Then why shoot the coyotes?"

Mrs. Nelson put her hands on her hips. "Well, of all the—! Coyotes are varmints. Don't you hear 'em at night, howling like crazies? When you've lived out here as long as I have, you'll know what's what." She took the waxed paper package of butter from the table and wrapped it in a plastic bag. "Now don't forget to take this with you when you go."

We said our good-byes at the door. "Now you all have to come visit again," Mrs. Nelson insisted. "I have so few neighbors. Promise?"

"All right," I agreed. She really could be winningly warm. Perhaps on a later visit we would find out if her violent temper—or her husband's marksmanship—had led to Clyde Moreland's undoing after all. "I hope you'll have more of those shortbread cookies when we come back."

"Well I will," she said. "Bye now."

Janell and I walked down the road toward the barn, with Beulah, the blind farm dog, trotting alongside as honor guard. The dog froze, however, when we passed the garden. Two rabbits had bolted from the cabbages and were sprinting to safety across a field. The blind dog jerked her head back and forth, whining helplessly.

"Nature needs varmints," Janell mused. "If this farm had a few more coyotes to chase the rabbits, I think Mrs. Nelson would have a more successful garden."

That afternoon, after we had rowed back to our own boat landing, a spiral bird began ringing its chaotic carillon at us from the salmonberry brush along the river.

"Welcome home to the land of invisible spirits," I told Janell.

"You don't think they're really birds?"

I shrugged. "Maybe."

She said, "Well, I don't think they're really invisible. It's like all the other demons. We just have to learn how to see them."

11

The Husicka

(August 1978)

I spent much of my summer vacation building an outhouse.
Well, someone had to build it.
—J. Wesley Sullivan, The Oregon Statesman, 1978

"Now there's a welcome sight," Janell said, adjusting the focus on the binoculars she had aimed across the pasture at the distant figures by the boat landing.

"What's that?"

"The editor of the *Oregon Statesman,* carrying a toilet seat."

I raised my eyebrows. "Boy, I guess he means business."

"Some things call for editorials, others call for action."

"Right. You straighten up the camp. I'll go see if my mother needs help defending herself against cow attacks."

I set out across the field. When I reached my parents they were indeed surrounded by heifers. "Ready to start your vacation?" I asked.

My father grinned and waved his toilet seat. "You bet!"

To my surprise, my mother was actually feeding Lizzie a stalk of grass. "You've got the tame cow over here again," she said. "The bouncy black one seems to have calmed down. And all the others look so small this year. Why's that?"

Joe Niemi was carrying a box of supplies up the riverbank from the boat. "It's 'cause they're first-year heifers," he said. He set his box down in the grass. "They're too small to breed yet. That big black Jersey's on her second summer. She ain't very bouncy 'cause she's pregnant as all get out."

"Tootsie's going to have a calf?" I asked.

"Any day now, from the looks of it." He turned back. "You want to help me get this stuff out of the boat?"

I looked down the bank. What remained in the boat was a stack of stovepipes and a small wood stove. I turned to my father. "You found us a stove!"

"It's both cast iron and cast off," he said. "Your cousin in Albany found it in a back-alley garage she was renting last winter. It wasn't up to code there, so she donated it to the cause."

"Looks like it'll do fine for us." The sides were rusty and plain, a single sheet of metal curved into an oval loop. The iron door, however, had been cast with decorative curlicues, and the stove's top consisted of a hefty piece of iron that would serve well as a cooking surface. "Did the stovepipe come with it?"

My father shook his head. "I had to buy special triple-walled, insulated pipe for the roofline. I know you're trying to use recycled materials wherever you can, but you don't want to risk burning the cabin down."

"It looks expensive."

"Sixty-four dollars."

"Ouch." I would have to pay him back.

"How much money have you put into this cabin so far?" he asked.

"Well, with the roofing nails and the foundation mortar, and now the stovepipe, it'll be almost a hundred dollars."

I thought it sounded like a lot, but my father just laughed.

Meanwhile Joe had finished unloading the stovepipe. Now he grabbed the stove about the middle, hefted it with a grunt, and began staggering forward, sloshing the boat from side to side with each step.

"Hey, let us give you a hand!" My father and I took the stove on either side and lifted it onto the grass.

Joe brushed the soot off his shirt. "Well, I gotta be heading back."

"Aren't you coming over to see the cabin?" I asked. "You can stay for lunch."

He looked up at the pasture, but then shook his head. "No, uh-uh. I'm grounded."

"Grounded? How?" I knew Joe was at least twenty-one—too old, in my mind, for this kind of control.

"Aw, I lost my driver's license again. Now everybody's giving me a hard way to go."

"I'm sorry."

"Aw, hell." He pushed the boat off and began paddling across the river with a hand-carved oar—evidently the only oar the Niemis still had. He called back, "Hope you get your husicka, anyway."

"Our what?"

"You know. Anyway, another hay truck's coming next week. My brother says he'll honk three times for you."

"I'll be there." I was still paying off my debt for the cedar log by bucking bales into the Niemi barn.

My father seemed to have gone into a kind of trance, taking deep breaths with his eyes closed. "I love the air over here!"

I looked at him uncertainly. The breeze along the river carried an earthy mixture of boat bilge, cow manure, and rotting leaves.

My father opened his eyes and rubbed his hands together. "Well! Are we ready to get to work?"

"Bill?" My mother called from the pasture, her voice a few notches higher. "The cows are starting to crowd closer!"

For the next week each of us took charge of a different project. My father focused on building the outhouse. My mother chinked the log cabin's cracks. Janell worked on the windows. I concentrated on the roof. All of us shared the camaraderie and optimism that comes when a major goal is in sight. After two years of work, the log cabin was nearly finished.

We all agreed that digging the outhouse hole should be our top priority. Last year my parents had narrowly decided to build a fence instead of an outhouse during their vacation. Since then Janell and I had often questioned the wisdom of that decision, especially in moments of need when we had had to search farther and farther into the forest to find bathroom sites that were still undisturbed.

So my father and I started to dig. We chipped through hardpan until the outhouse pit was seven feet deep. Then he took over, stacking up logs on his own.

The outhouse, my father announced, was going to be a miniature version of the log cabin itself. This was not merely a matter of architectural integrity, he pointed out, but also necessity, because we really didn't have any other building materials on hand. Occasionally he sawed the short logs he needed from my discarded treetops. Several times, however, he marched up into the woods, felled his own pole-sized trees, barked them, and cut them to length. The floor, door, and seat were built of lumber scavenged from the picked-over ruin of Clyde Moreland's barn. Day by day my father's closet-sized structure rose from the ground, crooked here and there, but fashioned with pride and rustic flair.

My mother found her calling as soon as she walked in our cabin's entryway. "Look at all the cracks in the walls!" she exclaimed. Now that the walls and ceiling of the main room were in place, it was hard to overlook the daylight streaming in through the gaps between the logs. Despite my efforts to flatten the top and bottom of each log with an adze, the cracks were often an inch wide.

"How will you ever be able to heat the cabin when it has holes like that?" my mother asked.

"The gaps are supposed to be chinked with clay or something," I admitted, "but we just haven't had time."

"Clay? In the Yukon, the gold miners used moss to plug the cracks in their cabins."

"And that worked?" I asked. "How do you know about log cabins in the Yukon?"

"My great-grandfather joined the Klondike gold rush in the 1890s. He kept a journal about it. Didn't you know?"

"No. What happened to him? Did he find any gold?"

"He caught pneumonia and died. Probably because he didn't have enough moss in his wall cracks." With that she grabbed a gunnysack and marched off across the pasture toward a riverside maple grove where the branches were draped with a thick layer of moss. Later that day she hauled back the bulging bag. Then she spent most of the rest of her vacation week carefully poking the moss into wall cracks with a stick.

Janell chose to deal with the windows. The first day I helped her hang our salvaged windows in the wall openings, screwing hinges onto the wooden frames. The next day she whittled curtain rods from maple branches. Then she set to making curtains, cutting the red gingham fabric my mother had brought, stitching seams by hand, and hemming the edges. She had to put her work aside countless times because it seemed I was always needing this tool or that bundle of shakes handed up to me on the roof.

My work on the roof went slowly. The whole process proved to be more complicated than I had thought. I had designed the roof to rest on a framework of twenty-seven purlins—long, straight poles that run lengthwise from gable to gable. These logs were awkward to wrestle up onto the slanting gable, and they had to be positioned precisely or the shakes would never lie flat. Each time I balanced another pair of purlins in place—one on either side—I quickly had to nail the next row of cedar shakes onto them to hold things together. But I was always running out of shakes, and that meant I had to climb down to split more from the cedar log in our front yard.

Fortunately, the cedar log had already been sawn into manageable lengths. A few weeks earlier my brother Pete had returned to whack away one more time at the alder trees on the far side of the hill. Although I did not care much for the slash-and-run forestry he had apparently learned from his tree thinning crew, I didn't object when he offered to use his chainsaw to slice up our cedar log.

I set out to learn how to split shakes. It is an art known as *riving*. Riving requires the use of a froe, the long-bladed antique tool my father had bought for me the year before. To rive properly, I discovered, you have to stand a bolt of cedar up like a chopping block. Then you position the froe's blade about half an inch from the edge and pound it into the block with a mallet. Next you pull back on the froe's handle. With any luck, this twists the blade enough to rip a crack down into the wood. After a bit more pounding and twisting, a fresh cedar board should pop off the block with a musical *poing!*

A well-riven cedar shake is a beautiful thing, richly pink and pungent. I stacked my most successful ones as if they were hard-earned gold bullion. I was almost sorry when they had to be bundled with a rope, hoisted to the roof, and nailed to the purlins.

Soon I discovered another difficulty in building a shake roof. Choosing the right shakes is as tricky as assembling a gigantic jigsaw puzzle. A shake that curves needs to be fitted against a matching curve. The next row of shakes has to be staggered slightly, to cover the gaps and nailholes of the shakes below. If the joints between shakes line up, rain will leak through. The stovepipe has to fit into the puzzle too, with its sheet metal flange woven into the rows of shakes the right way.

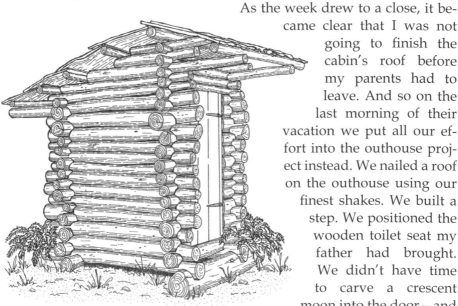

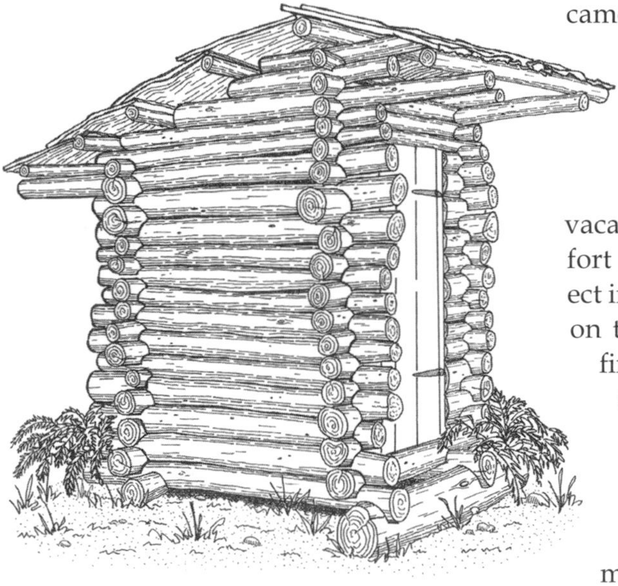

As the week drew to a close, it became clear that I was not going to finish the cabin's roof before my parents had to leave. And so on the last morning of their vacation we put all our effort into the outhouse project instead. We nailed a roof on the outhouse using our finest shakes. We built a step. We positioned the wooden toilet seat my father had brought. We didn't have time to carve a crescent moon into the door—and because the cracks between logs were unchinked, there was plenty of light and air inside without an extra vent anyway. My mother took pictures of my father standing proudly beside his creation, with his hardhat and ax. Janell hung a roll of toilet paper on a strategically located branch stub he had left on a wall log.

We even took turns trying it out while the others were in camp. Later we agreed that the building was pleasantest with the door open. Because the door faced across the pasture toward an unpeopled horizon, there was no lack of privacy. But sitting inside that log blind, I did feel exposed to a new outlook on the Sahalie world. An uninhibited hummingbird buzzed just outside the door to sip a foxglove bloom. Chipmunks chased each other with abandon up and down an alder trunk. Even the heifers grazing past didn't give me a second glance. I thought: If we ever finally spy a spiral bird, it will be from a blind like this.

When we were accompanying my parents to the boat landing to see them off I asked my father if he planned to write a column about his project. For the first time that week his face clouded, and he looked tired.

"People have liked my articles about the cabin so far, but I'm not sure they'd understand about the outhouse." He sighed. "Maybe I'll write it up anyway. In another week I'll be heading off to a conference in Victoria. By then someone else on the staff will have to answer the letters to the editor."

A week later, when we visited the Niemis to pick up milk, Dolores had clipped out my father's column for us.

> I spent much of my summer vacation building an outhouse.
>
> Well, someone had to build it.
>
> Let me make it clear at the outset that this is not just an ordinary privy. In keeping with the theme of the cabin it was constructed from materials at hand, as much as possible, and without the use of power tools. I made the seat box out of salvaged lumber. And the outhouse itself was made from logs, from the small trees we are thinning to make the larger trees grow faster.
>
> Bernard Eubanks of Salem has compiled a book on outhouses, called *Outhouse Lore*. Of the over 100 privies in the book, only one is in the style of a log cabin.
>
> I can understand why. It's a heck of a hard way to build anything.
>
> I had to fell and buck eleven trees and cut about eighty notches to put the thing together. With a seven-foot pit, it is designed to last a long time.
>
> My building has been christened the "husicka." When we talked with the Niemis about the project, they said, "Oh, you're building a husicka." It turns out this is the Finnish word for outhouse, and the Finnish tradition persists along the Sahalie, from the settlers of around the turn of the last century.
>
> The little building, like the bigger log cabin it serves, seems to fit into its surroundings.

A little wood stove is ready to be installed in the log cabin. The walls are chinked with moss. Finishing up the chinking was Elsie's project while I was completing the outhouse.

Now, Bill and Janell are busy finishing off windows and the door, all from reclaimed or native materials. Bill made a handsome nine-foot ladder to take them to their sleeping accommodations in the loft.

All those satisfactions that come with completing a project two summers in the making are now being enjoyed. These are of a different dimension from the satisfaction of building sentences at a typewriter or finally getting the thought to transfer itself to paper.

Getting two trees down, sawed, and out of the woods before breakfast produces a special satisfaction. It is akin to the feeling that comes when the tree, hung up in the branches of its neighbor, finally falls. And the sheer physical exhaustion at the end of the day, when the log walls are three rounds higher than at the start, can't be duplicated by punching the "execute" key on the video display terminal, to send this piece to the computer memory system.

Say what you will about the outhouse, it is real and functional, and it will be serving its purpose long after editorials written about supposedly monumental subjects are gone and forgotten.

The following week, while my father was in Canada, his substitute Don Scarborough ran the following column, entitled, "Quick, Honey, Dig the Outhouse."

Wes Sullivan usually fills this space. You know Wes Sullivan. He's the *Statesman's* editor and thinking man who takes us on rugged week-long camping and hiking trips, who tells us how he's building a cabin in the mountains using only his bare hands and his teeth. He's gone this week, preparing another episode of life in the beautiful Northwest.

How we envy him. Our life revolves around forty hours or more of pounding a video display terminal and trying to get three daughters through school. When I get a vacation I like to spend it relaxing with a cool glass of something.

But we do have some similarities beyond the years we spent together on the *Statesman* news desk. I, too, am building a cabin. Wes is helping a son do it the pioneer way. The first thing I did was rig up a power pole and line for all the wonderful labor-saving devices.

Wes told us recently his first job this year was to dig the outhouse. ("Well somebody has to," he said defensively.) I found an easier way. It was Mother's Day, so my wife dug it. The wedding ring created a blister so she quit after twelve inches. This was done deliberately to hasten the installation of indoor plumbing.

I started out married life a firm believer in letting each man do what he does best. The plumber would fix the washer, the electrician the water heater, and I would write obits.

So when the time came to build our long-planned A-frame on the Little North Fork, I quickly hired a carpenter and signed on as his first assistant. That was three or four years ago—time goes by so fast when you're having fun. Every day of vacation, every weekend I helped stack lumber, haul forms, saw two-by-fours, pound nails, and carry four-by-eight sheets of plywood up a tall ladder.

Even I don't believe it, but it all worked. The girls have their flush toilet, and the faucet eliminates the long trips with bucket to the river.

Pain and suffering are hard to remember after a while and this summer, with the carpenter's help, the place is so livable, and it all seemed so easy. Can Wes Sullivan say that?

"Maybe we should post these two newspaper columns in the husicka," I suggested to Janell. "You know, as a sort of housewarming."

"I'm not sure everyone would understand," she said.

"Why not?"

"Let's just say it's risky, putting newspaper in an outhouse." She smiled. "Some visitors out there mean business."

12

Raise High the Roof Beam

(September 1978)

> We pierce doors and windows to make a house, and it is on these spaces where there is nothing that the usefulness of the house depends. Therefore, just as we take advantage of what is, we should recognize the usefulness of what is not.
>
> —Lao Tzu, Tao Te Ching, circa 400 BC

It was a mistake, trying to play the music of the Sahalie first. The notes stumbled up into the dark trees above our campfire like startled bats.

"That's a strange warm up," Janell said, poking the fire.

I lowered the flute-like wooden recorder. "It was supposed to be the call of the spiral bird."

'Well, the real ones don't sound nearly that deranged. Besides, we never hear them at night."

"I wonder if we'll hear them when we're in the cabin?" The next day, if all went well, we would nail the last shakes on the cabin roof. I felt a thrill of anticipation at the thought of moving into our log home at long last, but also a touch of regret that this would be our last night under the stars, in the tent camp we had known for two summers.

I took up the recorder again and let a few melodies drift out on the night air across the dark valley. Greensleeves. The Gypsy Rover. Then I tried the call of the what bird, and hit it so close that Janell smiled.

The next morning we were awakened by a faint horn bleating in cadences of three.

"Is that an SOS?" Janell mumbled.

"Almost. It's another hay truck." Half a dozen times that summer I had been called to buck sixty-pound bales into the Niemi barn. It was what I had promised in exchange for the cedar log that provided our roof shakes. I couldn't stop payment now. "I guess I'll finish the cabin roof tomorrow." I kissed Janell good-bye.

"Maybe I'll work on the door," she said sleepily.

I put on my work clothes, grabbed a biscuit from the supply tent, and made my way toward the boat landing. Out of habit I counted the heifers grazing in a cluster. Everyone was there but Tootsie, so I thought no more about it. A first-year heifer might get in trouble by herself, but Tootsie was a big girl.

At the Niemi farm a big tractor-trailer rig had already backed its towering green load up to the barn door. Jack silently handed me a pair of hay hooks, steel question marks on wooden handles.

For the next three hours I was part of the Niemis' alfalfa chain gang. George would pull a bale off the truck and hand it to Joe, who would toss it up to me in the loft. Then I would thunk my hay hooks into the bale and carry it back to Jack, who would carefully fit it into a growing wall of giant green bricks.

All the time I could hear George's soft voice complaining to the truck driver that the bales were too tight, or too loose, or too damp. At intervals George would cut the twine on a bale, break it open, and sniff the hay. "This is definitely second cut," he grumbled. "I paid for first cut. Dairy stock need the protein of fresh shoots. And look at these thistles! What, do you want to blister their mouths?"

Joe and I were the weak links of the operation, it seemed, always a bale behind. We only had time to exchange a word or two with each bale. Our grunted conversation was as choppy as telegram text.

"Still grounded?" I asked.

"Left anyway," Joe replied.

"Where to?"

"Army office."

I thought about this for several bales. I knew Joe was not happy on the farm. His father treated him like a shiftless vagabond. But Joe wasn't a drifter by nature. And there weren't any freight trains he could hop to take him away from the Sahalie.

"Sign up?" I asked.

"Not yet."

"Why?"

Joe frowned, apparently struggling with an internal debate. After tossing up a few more bales he finally dumped one on end and stood there, looking me in the eyes. "You've been to Germany."

It sounded like an accusation, but I preferred it as a question. "Yes, for a year." Janell and I had bicycled across Europe and studied a few semesters at the university in Heidelberg.

"Is it better there?"

There was desperation in Joe's voice. Suddenly it hit me that this had been the Army's best offer: to send him to a military base on the far side of the planet. Janell and I had seen the gray garrisons of displaced Americans behind the autobahns at Wiesbaden and Fulda. Dazed recruits, many of them young black men, had stared out from behind the razor-wire fences as if the world beyond were a jungle of alien terrors. I couldn't see it as Joe's freedom train.

"I guess it's better there for the Germans."

"You mean—"

"Hey Joe," George interrupted. "We haven't got all day."

Joe winced, bent over, and threw me the next bale.

An hour later, when we had emptied the truck, Joe slouched off toward his collection of junk cars. A long, low moo resounded from behind the milking shed.

"Sounds like we got some unhappy customers out there," George told me. "We put off the morning milking until the hay was in. You want to pick up a free gallon on your way home?"

"Sure, thanks."

While George and I walked to the milking shed, his younger son Jack began herding impatient cows into the milking parlor.

"I guess you got a radio," George said as he flipped on the lights and started up the milk cooler. "I heard music over there last night."

"Oh, that was my recorder."

"A tape recorder? Must use up batteries fast."

I smiled. "Actually it's a little wooden flute. I learned to play it while Janell and I were in Germany."

"Oh." He set a glass jug under the milk tank's spigot. While he watched the white foam rise, he mused, "I used to play the fiddle once. My father brought one from the old country, you know. Taught me to play polkas and schottishes. But no one listens to those old tunes anymore."

"That's too bad."

The heartbeat-slow pump of the milking machine started up in the next room. Then the radio came on—scratchy reception of a twangy country station. Behind the door I could hear Jack's muffled voice yelling at the cows.

"You know," I said, "I wonder if the cows wouldn't be happier if they listened to polkas instead."

George chuckled. "I guess they did a regular experiment about that once. Some scientists tried playing all different kinds of music in a milking parlor. Mozart, rock and roll, harp music. They even tried—what the heck do you call it?—Gregorian chants. No matter what they played, production dropped. Finally they ran a tape of the farmer swearing. Right away the herd calmed down and the milk started flowing."

"I guess it's all in what you're used to," I said.

George nodded. He screwed on the jug's lid and wiped the drips with a paper towel. "By the way, how's that black Jersey on your side of the river doing?"

"You mean Tootsie? I didn't see her with the herd this morning."

His eyebrows rose. "I thought it might be time."

"Time for what?"

"They always wander off by themselves to have their calves."

"You think Tootsie—?"

"Yeah, I'll come get her tomorrow. Vacation's over for Tootsie. She'll be a working girl now."

His words struck a troubling chord within me. Somehow I didn't like the idea that one of our favorite heifers would be going to work, twice a day every day, in a noisy milking parlor. It seemed there was no such thing as a free day on this side of the Sahalie River.

I asked George, "Do you ever take time off for vacation?"

"Me?" He shook his head. "That's not part of dairying."

"Don't you get away at all?"

"Well, Dolores and I spent one night at Diamond Lake for our honeymoon, back in '49. Then we tried going to the State Fair in Salem once, but we couldn't find a parking space, so we drove back home."

He handed me the jug of milk. "Thanks for helping with the hay."

That afternoon I nailed up two more rows of shakes, but a big stripe of gray sky remained in the log cabin's roof, so we camped outside once again. There were no stars. Janell and I stared into the campfire. Far away, through the night air, we could hear the faint strains of a violin from across the river, playing a slow polka.

"Do you suppose that's a radio?" Janell asked.

"No, radios don't play those old tunes anymore."

"Then what is it?"

"It must be George," I said. "I guess tonight is his vacation."

Thick clouds were spitting a few warning raindrops when I started work on the roof the next morning. Within two hours I had nailed the last shake in place. For a moment I just stood there astride the rooftop with the hammer in my hand. Then the realization sank in that I was really done. The log cabin I had sketched on a notepad two years ago—the dream my father had doubted and my brother had ridiculed and Lucas Hamilton had said we would never finish—this log cabin in the Sahalie wilderness now stood beneath my feet.

I let out a crazy cheer and shook my hammer at the sky. "OK, clouds! Go ahead and rain!"

Janell came outside to the yard. "Are you all right?"

"I'm done! The roof's finished."

"Oh good. But what do you think is wrong with that cow?"

"What?"

"Haven't you heard it? One of the heifers is bellowing over by the boat landing. Something's wrong." She looked up at me. "Are you stuck up there?"

"No," I replied, a little irritated that she was not sharing in my celebration. Equally bothersome was that she was right about the cow. It had been mooing miserably for several minutes. I didn't want to think it might be Tootsie.

On top of all this, I really was stuck on the roof. By nailing up the last row of shingles I had sealed off my access route to the loft's ladder. Rather than admit I was trapped, however, I casually tossed my hammer down into the grass, put an arm around the stovepipe, slid down the shake roof on my stomach, and dropped ten feet to the yard. The fall knocked the wind from my chest.

"Careful!" Janell said, and then looked across the field again. "Do you think it could be Tootsie?"

I wheezed. "C-could be. We'd better go see."

We set out together across the pasture. The closer we came to the boat landing, the more obvious it became that something was indeed wrong. The heifers were stampeding back and forth amid a cacophony of moos, squeals, bleats, and shouts. Lizzie rushed up to us, grass hanging from her mouth, stared at us a moment with wide eyes, and then ran on.

At the riverbank we found George and Jack wrestling with a steer. On the far shore, Joe was holding a pathetically bawling black calf in his arms. Tootsie was stomping about in the shallows on our side of the river.

Janell hurried down to the shore. "Tootsie, you poor thing! Did they take away your calf?"

Meanwhile, George and Jack had managed to tie a rope into a make-shift halter around the steer's head. With Jack in control of the steer, George dusted off his shirt and turned to me. "That black Jersey must have had her calf two days ago. She'd hidden it down in the willow brush by the river. Just a bull calf, not worth much, but what with the tide we're lucky it didn't drown."

"Why did you take the calf across the river without Tootsie?" Janell demanded.

George glanced at Janell, but for some reason directed his answer to me. "Well, it's a motivator, you know? It's not easy convincing a cow like that to cross. Look at the trouble we're having with this steer. But put her calf bawling on the far shore, and she'll swim soon enough."

Janell spoke to the anguished Tootsie. "Honey, swim to your baby. You can do it." The calf on the far shore gave a forlorn bleat, but Tootsie still would not wade deep enough into the river to lose her footing. Janell turned to George. "You'll let them stay together, won't you?"

George chuckled awkwardly and spoke again to me. "When a cow comes fresh she starts out with lots of milk, you see, but if you leave the calf with her, production drops to match demand. So you feed the calf from a bucket and put the cow on a milker. It's the only way."

On the far shore a panel van drove into sight on the dirt road from the Niemi farmhouse.

"It's about time the butcher got here," Jack grumbled.

"The butcher?" I asked. "Why do you need a butcher?"

The truck downshifted for the hill, then swung in an arc across the Niemi pasture to the riverbank above Joe. It was a beat-up van emblazoned with the red peace-pipe logo of the Skookum Slaughterhouse.

"It's not for Tootsie, is it?" Janell asked, her voice rising.

"No, no." George laughed. He pointed to the steer. "As long as we were coming over, I thought we'd pay your rent."

"A steer a year, cut and wrapped by the butcher," I said mechanically.

"Right," Jack said. "So, as long you're here, you want to help? Your boat has stouter oars."

I sighed. Although I had mixed emotions about ushering this steer to its doom, it was in fact our rent. I could hardly refuse to help. "All right."

"Good," Jack said. "We'll tie the steer to the back of your boat and push him into the river while you row."

I fetched the oars from their hiding place in a blackberry bush and unchained *Earnest*. Soon I was rowing hard, trying to pull a stubbornly lock-kneed steer down the muddy bank. Jack and George shoved the animal off balance. It staggered downhill step by step until it stood knee-deep in the river. Jack and George couldn't wade any deeper in their rubber boots, and the steer wasn't interested in going any farther on its own, so I rowed in place for quite some time, tugging the rope this way and that, with as little effect as if the rope had been tied to a stump.

Janell ignored our efforts. "Swim, Tootsie!" she urged.

Joe held up the bleating calf on the far shore.

Suddenly Tootsie took a frantic step forward and sank under the river's murky surface with a splash. For a moment we all froze in place. We watched the river, holding our breath. An image flashed into my mind of the dreadful launching of Pete's *Dreadnaught*.

But then the black Jersey bobbed back up with a watery snort, pawing hard for the far bank.

"Atta girl, Tootsie! You can do it!" Janell called.

Meanwhile, our steer seemed to have been inspired by Tootsie's example. He plunged into the river on his own and began swimming after her. Before I could get my oars in action, the steer had swum past me. The rope pulled taut and spun the boat around. The next thing I knew, *Earnest* was being towed backwards across the river by a swimming steer.

"You're rowing the wrong way," Jack called.

"Hey, I'm just trying to keep up!"

"If it drowns, it's still your meat," George put in.

I managed to row a few awkward strokes backwards to give the steer some slack. He pawed onward, actually starting to catch up with Tootsie, paddling like a mad dog.

Our river rodeo had become a race. The spectators on the banks urged on Tootsie, or the steer, or both, while I fumbled with the oars in *Earnest*.

"Go, Tootsie! Swim!"

Behind us, the entire herd of heifers had stampeded to the shore to watch. They gaped at their two former comrades, swimming toward unfathomable fates.

Ahead of us, Joe began carrying the calf up toward the farm road, obviously confident now that Tootsie would make it across. At the same time, the butcher van's side door slid open and a youngish man in official-looking white overalls stepped out. Although I had met Butch only once, on a dark night the summer before, I immediately recognized his angular features and black ponytail.

After briefly surveying the scene, Butch flung open the van's back doors and swung out a crane arm with a large hook. It looked disturbingly like a portable gallows.

Tootise climbed up out of the river just ahead of the steer.

"I knew you could do it, girl!" Janell called.

Tootsie turned, dripping. The black Jersey cow stared back across the water at the lovely green pasture of her youth. Lining the bank was the herd of friends she was leaving behind. She opened her black, whiskered mouth wide and gave a long, loud, mournful moo.

Butch stood at the top of the bank with a rifle in his hand. He nodded to the wet cow and steer. "Which one's the meat, Bill? Or you want I should take them both?"

I shook my head. "No, just the steer. I'll untie it from the boat." I handed Butch the steer's rope without looking either of them in the eye.

"I see you finished the roof on your cabin," Butch said. "Looks good."

"Thanks." I didn't feel like talking. And this was certainly no time to ask the questions I had been saving for Butch. Ever since we had talked with Mrs. Nelson, I had wondered if Butch, or someone in his family, might have wanted to do in Clyde Moreland. His family apparently had an old grudge about what they saw as Sahalie Indian land.

"I keep meaning to drop by some night when there's a full moon," Butch said. "I've had to cut back on pastrami 'cause I'm fresh out of 'coon. Maybe next summer, huh?"

"Yeah, maybe." I nodded vaguely and pushed the boat off with an oar. Rowing back I passed the Niemis. They were paddling their boat in the other direction with a crudely shaped plank.

When I pulled *Earnest* up on our side of the river, Janell asked, "Do you think Tootsie will be all right?"

"Sure. Tootsie is lined up with a steady job. She'll be a good milk cow."

"What about Lizzie?"

I hadn't thought about the future of our other tame friend. It was a tougher question. This was Lizzie's second summer on our pasture. She was old enough to join the working world, but she hadn't had a calf. "I don't know."

"Maybe they'll let her stay over here for another summer," Janell suggested. "She's an awfully nice cow. I don't blame her for wanting to stay here."

"I don't blame her either." I locked up the boat and put away the oars. As we walked back across the pasture, followed by Lizzie and the rest of the heifers, a shot echoed from across the river. I kept walking, not wanting to think about the steer.

We moved into the cabin that afternoon in a steady rain. While Janell hurried back and forth carrying the sleeping bags, clothes, and kitchen supplies from our wet tents, I installed the cabin's 150-pound door.

The door was a project we had tinkered with for weeks. It creaked and groaned on massive, hand-carved maple hinges, but it swung true and latched firmly with a wooden bar. Instead of a lock, we left a latch-string hanging outside. The string was weighted with a nail. If we pulled the string in, only those in the know could open the door, because all that remained visible outside was a nail head like dozens of others on the front of the door.

We moved the picnic table inside, in front of the double windows overlooking the pasture. Janell tied back the windows' red-checked curtains with loops she had woven from macrame string. I hung up my grandfather's five-foot crosscut saw proudly, high on the back wall. I wished Grandpa could have seen the log house we had built with the saw from his attic.

We hung up coats, the adze, and a few other tools on branch stubs that we had left on some of the wall logs to serve as pegs. Most other supplies we simply stacked on the floor until we could build more appropriate furniture.

Because we had no plumbing, I nailed a plank on the wall outside the door to serve as a washstand. There, protected from the rain by the cabin's broad eaves, Janell set up a dish rack, a small washbasin, and a huge enamel coffeepot filled with water.

I lit a fire in our little woodstove. It smoked at first, filling the cabin with the nostalgic smell of wintry hearths. Then the stovepipe warmed and the draft took hold. Soon a roaring fire was simmering a pot of noodles. As the little cabin warmed, condensation on the windowpanes fogged the rainy twilight into an early night.

We ate dinner by kerosene lamplight. A gap beside the stove door cast dancing yellow ghosts across the wall logs.

"Let's leave the dishes for tomorrow," I suggested.

"We don't have to go to bed just because it's dark outside," Janell said. "We're not camping anymore."

"I know." I winked. "I'm just looking for an excuse to get you to bed."

She blushed at my suggestive tone, but let me reel her into my arms.

I carried the lamp up the creaking wooden ladder through the trap door to the loft. The purlin logs that ribbed the underside of the roof were high enough that Janell could stand up straight in the middle, but I had to crouch to undress. We crawled into our double sleeping bag, blew out the lamp, and snuggled together in the sudden darkness.

A gust of wind hurled a rattling shower of raindrops against the cedar shakes inches above our heads. The noise of dripping water seemed to be all around us. Was the roof leaking?

I sat up, fumbled for a flashlight, and flicked the beam along the underside of the roof. I was a little surprised to see the shakes really were still dry. Earlier that day I had noticed winks of daylight angling through the gaps between the shakes. Although I had laid them out according to the advice in a book, carefully staggering the gaps, a part of me had still doubted it would work.

Before I turned out the flashlight, I noticed Janell had folded her hands behind her head. "You're not worrying about leaks?" I asked.

"No, I was thinking about Tootsie."

"Oh." I turned out the flashlight. "It's tough, her leaving like that."

"I don't want to leave either. Now we've finally moved into the cabin, and next week we have to go back to the university."

"That's not so bad," I said. "In a few months we'll have to start applying for jobs."

There was a pause before she spoke again. "Do you really want to be a high school teacher?" Her voice wavered in the dark.

I didn't have an answer, so I asked a question of my own. "Do you really want to teach grade school?"

"I think so. I like working with kids. And as teachers we'll have the summers free. Then we'll always be able to come here each June. Will you still want to, now that the cabin's done?"

"Oh, the work here is far from done," I said. "For starters, there's lots of furniture left to build. Chairs, a table, a woodbox, a tool closet maybe."

"And a kitchen cabinet."

"Right, a kitchen cabinet. And eventually we'll want to add on."

"Add on?"

"You know, we'll want to build an addition with another room or two."

"Really?" she asked.

"Sure. We'll need more space when we have a family."

Neither of us spoke for a while, thinking about the repercussions of this tantalizing yet frightening prospect. We lay there listening together to the rain on the roof. The storm had slowed. Syncopated drips from the trees pinged musically on the cedar shakes above our heads. Because the shakes were slightly different lengths, the notes varied in pitch. *Pong, pang, bing!* We were sleeping beneath a giant marimba, struck to a ragtime beat by the rain. Now and then a maple leaf slid down the scale, a slow riff.

It wasn't the spiral bird, but it was a song of the Sahalie nonetheless, a wilderness lullaby played by the winds on our new roof.

13

The Volcano Blows

(May 1980)

> To the sick the doctors wisely recommend a change of air and scenery. If you are chosen town clerk, forsooth, you cannot go to Tierra del Fuego this summer; but you may go to the land of infernal fire nevertheless.
>
> —Henry David Thoreau, Walden, 1854

Nine months after we finished the roof of our one-room log cabin, Janell and I graduated from the university and landed full-time teaching jobs. For the next year we spent all our energy in Sherwood, Oregon, a small, conservative town that was being swallowed whole by the strip malls and condos of Portland's suburbs. Janell seemed to like her fourth-grade class. She glowed when we decided in the middle of the school year that we should start a family.

I had a tougher time in Sherwood High School. I had signed on to teach German, an elective course with motivated students. But just before school started, the previous German teacher suffered a miscarriage, canceled her maternity leave, and demanded her job back. Suddenly reassigned to sophomore English, I found myself facing class after class of surly adolescents, bitter that they had been forced to sit through another required course.

By May of 1980 I was wrung out. We eagerly accepted my parents' offer to whirl us away to the log cabin for a weekend to see how the place had weathered the winter.

The four of us hiked in along a new trail I had cleared through the riverside forest the year before. Three-petaled trilliums bloomed as big and white as Easter lilies along the path. As always on the first visit of the season, I worried about what we would find when we reached the cabin. I couldn't help envisioning our little log house crushed by falling trees, gutted by fire, or washed away by floods. My heart sped up. Perhaps my strongest fear—and I don't know why it hit me this year in particular—was that the place might have been ransacked by intruders. I imagined we would go upstairs, like the three bears, and find an evil Goldilocks still sleeping in our bed.

"Look, someone's been hiking on your trail," my father called back. He stopped at the crest of my new path, where it switchbacked down toward the pasture. He knelt beside something on the ground.

When my mother caught up with him she exclaimed, "Say! Someone *has* been hiking on your trail."

"Do you think it's broken?" Janell said when she joined them.

Struggling under a heavy backpack, I was the last to catch up. I found them gathered around a bit of greenish glass protruding from the fresh dirt of the trail. "Oh. It looks like a bottle."

"Yes, but who would bury a bottle out here? And why?" my father asked.

"Maybe there's a message inside." My mother had brought a shovel, planning to weed some of the poisonous tansy plants from the pasture that weekend. She began using the blade to work around the glass.

"I think bottles in the ground send a different kind of message than bottles in the ocean." I looked up the slope. "This is where Clyde Moreland had his house, before he moved it across the river."

"The old homesteader?" My father looked uphill, and then squinted out through the alders at the pasture. "That makes sense. Before these trees grew up he probably had a view of the river and the whole farm from here."

"So what you're saying is, this was Clyde's garbage dump," Janell said. "A bachelor like him probably just threw his trash out the window."

"Right. And when I built the trail last year I scraped off the top layer of duff. Now the rains have started washing things out."

My mother turned over a shovelful of dirt speckled with white chips. "Hey, I dug so deep I hit china."

"An old dinner plate, anyway," Janell said.

The bottle itself came loose in the next shovelful. My father carefully scraped the dirt off the glass. It was a large blue-green canning jar, completely intact, inscribed "Mason's Pat. Nov. 3, 1858."

"Wow! That's old," my mother said.

"That might just be the date of the patent," I put in. "Moreland didn't start his farm here until after World War I."

My father held up the jar proudly. "Add this to your shelf as a relic of the homesteaders' patron saint. I guess that's the message: Clyde Moreland wants to keep in touch. Did you ever find out what happened to him? Was he really murdered?"

Janell shrugged. "Everyone we talk to over here seems to think so, but they all blame someone else. The old lawyer thinks the neighbors shot him. The neighbors think the butcher did it. The butcher thinks evil spirits got him."

"Maybe a clue will turn up right here in your trail," my father suggested. "Archeologists say the best way to understand people is by the garbage they leave behind."

"Maybe. Right now I want to go see if the log cabin's OK." I led the way down the hill and struck off across the pasture. I couldn't shake the ominous feeling that we would find the place in ruins.

The grass in the pasture was already hip-high, dotted here and there with the yellow blooms of tansy ragwort. As we parted our way through the waving green sea, a dozen black-and-white backs angled to head us off, a convoy of submarines on an intercept course.

"Gosh, the farmer puts smaller cows over here every year," my mother said. "These are no bigger than calves. Except for that giant white one."

"Lizzie!" Janell exclaimed. She pulled a handful of grass and held it out to the full-grown Holstein. "Oh, honey! You're limping!"

The big white cow still had a dirty yellow tag in her ear identifying her as "67", but she seemed wary and worn. It took Janell a minute before she could get close enough to pet the fur on her nose. "Look, Bill, you can see her ribs. I think they just left her here all winter by herself."

"She's lucky it didn't flood."

Lizzie lowered her head so Janell could scritch her ears as well. "I know you don't want to leave this side of the river, honey, but you've got to have a calf someday. You just have to."

"We need to get rid of these tansy plants before the cows start eating them," my mother said. She dug her shovel blade under a stalk and slowly pried up the roots. "Oof. It's harder than you think."

"We can do that tomorrow," my father said. "Let's go check the cabin first."

My heart was still beating too fast as we neared the end of the field and the cabin came into view. The windows were not broken. No shakes seemed to be missing from the roof. The stovepipe stuck out at its usual jaunty angle. The woodshed was full, and the picnic table still stood in the yard. Why was I so afraid something was wrong?

I climbed the step and carefully pried loose the secret nail that hid the door's latchstring. Then I lifted the latch and swung the heavy, creaking wooden door inward.

At once a horribly sour, musty smell billowed out the doorway. The ghastly odor nearly knocked me backwards off the step.

"Good Lord, did something die in there?" my father asked.

I ventured inside, with Janell close behind. The table and woodstove were still where we had left them, but smaller objects lay on the floor, as if strewn by clumsy vandals. Sticks of kindling. A spoon. A mangled potholder. Huge clumps of moss.

"What the hell's been in here?" I whispered. "A wolverine?"

Janell pointed to a dark brown liquid slowly dripping from the ceiling to splash in a corner of the floor. "Whatever it is, I think it's still upstairs."

"Open the windows. Let's get some air in here," Grimly, I grabbed the pointed maple stick we had used to debark the cabin logs. "I'm going up to meet Goldilocks."

I pushed open the loft's trap door with the stick. There was a rustling noise upstairs in response. Janell and I exchanged a worried look. She squeezed my arm silently.

Rung by rung, I climbed the ladder. With my stick at the ready, I raised my head slowly through the trap door.

The stench of the loft was dizzying. But even in the dim light I could see a giant green blob lurking in the far corner behind the stovepipe.

"What is it?" Janell asked from below.

"I'm not sure. Maybe some kind of nest."

"Mice?" my mother asked from outside.

"I don't think so."

"Just throw it out the window," my father said.

I swallowed. "That's not as easy as it sounds." I propped open the little upstairs window beside the ladder and crawled out onto the loft's floor on my knees. Slowly, I began advancing toward the nest. Brown, pellet-like droppings littered the floor around a pile of moss, shredded newspaper, and cloth. A ghastly puddle of brown urine explained the drips we had seen downstairs. Finally I was close enough that I nudged the nest with the end of my stick.

Nothing happened.

I poked harder, and the front of the nest fell open. To my surprise, it was empty.

Then I saw the bulging black eyes. All this time a rat the size of a boot had been clinging to the underside of the roof, crouched on a purlin log just inches from my face. "Augh!" I cried, swinging my stick against the roof with a whack. The rat leapt across my legs and cowered in a corner behind our sleeping bag.

"Bill?" a voice came from below. "What is it?"

"A rat!" I swung the stick frantically, over and over, but the rat scurried about the loft so nimbly I couldn't seem to connect. Finally I landed a glancing blow and it shot toward the open window. "Look out! He's coming your way!"

"Look at the size of that thing!" my father exclaimed. "Quick, Elsie, hit it with your shovel!"

I heard a clang against the wall logs, and then a scream. I scrambled down the ladder and out the door.

Mother was shuddering in my father's arms. "It—it—it jumped right on me!"

"That's all right," my father consoled her. "I think you scared it away."

Janell stood in the doorway, gripping a broom as a weapon. "Are you sure it's gone?"

I nodded. "For now."

We spent the rest of the day cleaning the rat's mess out of the cabin. We swept and scrubbed the stained floors. I lit a fire in the stove with the door open to smoke out the worst of the smell.

As we sat around the table for a dinner of canned spaghetti, I flipped through a guidebook from our shelf. "Here it is: Pack rat, alias wood rat. You can tell because the tail's hairy."

"I'm glad its nest was empty." Janell said. She looked at me awkwardly. "I guess the rat was planning to start a family. Maybe it will find a better place out in the woods."

My father shrugged. "It probably thinks this is its home. And it can get in here anytime it wants. I remember the 'mouseproof' Norwegian design you talked about when you were building the cabin, with foundation piers eighteen inches high. Well, I saw that rat jump four feet."

My mother sighed. "It's my fault, really."

"What's your fault?" I asked.

"I'm the one who said you should insulate the cracks with moss. Maybe moss works in the Yukon, but here the rats just use it to make nests. We need to pull it all out and chink the cabin with cement instead."

"Or you could just get a cat," my father suggested.

Daylight had begun to fade. A first bat dipped through the gray sky outside the cabin window. I piled the dinner dishes together and lit the kerosene lamp. "All right, this coming summer we'll chink with cement. Maybe we'll even get a cat. But what about tonight? What if the rat comes back?"

"I'm sleeping out in the yard," my mother said quickly. "Wes brought a tent we can use."

"If you kids have trouble here in the cabin just give a shout," my father said. "Still, it might be a good idea to keep a couple of flashlights and a machete handy."

Janell bit her lip. "I think I'll sleep outside in the hammock."

"Fine, sleep outside." My voice betrayed just a hint of irritation. "But I'm not about to give up this cabin to a rat."

We went to set up our separate sleeping arrangements. My parents staked their tent in the yard. Janell carried her half of our zip-together sleeping bag out to the hammock. I undressed in the loft and crawled into my half of the sleeping bag. Before I blew out the lamp I scrutinized the logs in every corner of the loft, just to make sure none of the rafter logs had a pair of beady black eyes.

Without the lamp the darkness was so profound I couldn't see the window, much less my own hand. A cold wind whistled through the cracks between the logs where the moss was missing. Tree branches above the cabin rustled and creaked in the wind. I listened tensely, dreading that I would hear the scurrying of tiny feet.

I don't know how much of that long night had passed when the door downstairs slowly creaked open. I quickly twisted out of my bed, grabbed the flashlight, and aimed it at the ladder.

Janell smiled at me weakly, her hair tousled. "It's awfully cold in the hammock. Are you—are you still alone up here?"

I nodded. "I can't sleep either. Come on in." We zipped the sleeping bags together and huddled for warmth, glad to be together again.

When we woke up the sun was trying to break through a mist over the pasture. I rolled over for a better look out the window, and groaned.

"What is it?" Janell asked.

"My parents. They're already out there, digging up tansy plants."

She sighed. "They must have skipped breakfast so we could sleep. We should go cook pancakes for them."

"Yeah, we should," I said. But neither of us began getting out of the warm sleeping bag.

"They've been really nice, bringing us here for the weekend," Janell said. "We should tell them."

"Tell them what?"

"You know, that they'll be grandparents in September."

I nodded. They would be excited by our news, but their lives would not be revolutionized. This would be their third grandchild, after my oldest brother Mark's two kids. For me, however, the impact of a child loomed as large as a comet on a collision course.

Janell went on. "Someday we should talk about the changes we'll need to make here at the cabin."

"You mean, like adding an extra room?"

"That too. But I was thinking more about babyproofing."

"Babyproofing?"

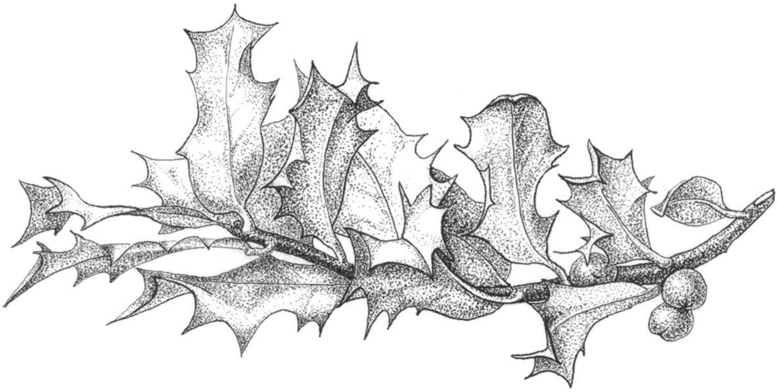

"You know. If there's a kid crawling on the floor, rough-sawn planks aren't exactly the best choice."

"I suppose not."

"And all those sharp tools piled downstairs? We'll need to put them in cupboards that latch. Can you build something like that?"

I nodded absent-mindedly. "Sure. I'll buy some finished lumber this summer."

"And a woodstove with an oven?"

"Maybe. I don't know."

She looked at me from the side. "You're worried about something else, aren't you?"

"Oh, it's this whole thing about money. I know we've saved some this year with both of us working, but next year you'll be staying home with the baby. That means I—" I stopped in mid-sentence, afraid to go on.

"That means you can't quit at the high school, no matter how miserable you are?"

I rolled my head away from her. "It kills me the way those kids groan when they see a book. Shakespeare's a snake pit to them, and it's required."

"Maybe you could get a job at a newspaper, like your Dad."

"No. I'd have to have a degree in journalism. With my background, all I can do is freelance. It'd be fun to try writing articles about the outdoors—travel, hiking, that sort of thing. But there's no paycheck there for years. Maybe ever."

She held my head to her chest and stroked my hair. For a long time neither of us spoke. Finally she said, "Let's go make breakfast."

I got dressed and went downstairs, afraid that I was arcing closer to some terrible collision. The cabin looked cluttered, unbabyproofed, and it still smelled like rats. I decided to build a fire in the yard and cook our pancakes over the old iron sheet we had used when we were camping.

Janell set up our lawn chairs around the picnic table. By the time my parents returned from their weeding work in the pasture, breakfast was ready.

We ate in the yard, watching the last of the morning fog melt from the hills in the sun. My parents talked cheerily about how they had learned to uproot a tansy plant *and* shake off the dirt, all in one step. When they paused for a fresh batch of pancakes, Janell said, "Bill and I have some news for you."

Everyone looked to me expectantly. I felt my face go red with a sudden confusion. Did I really want to announce this news?

Before I could speak a series of deep booms echoed across the field, like the concussions of an artillery barrage.

"Good Lord, what's that?" my father exclaimed.

We all looked out across the pasture. I couldn't see anything out of the ordinary.

"It sounded like dynamite. Is somebody blasting?" my mother asked.

I thought of my brother Pete's threat to build a road into our property with dynamite. "Not that I know of."

"Maybe the Niemis' fuel shed blew up," Janell suggested.

"Could it be sonic booms?" My father looked at the sky.

"In that case you think we'd see—"

Suddenly my words were cut short by the earth-shaking roar of a gigantic explosion. The shock wave swept through the valley, rattling glass in the windows and scaring great flocks of birds from the trees. The heifers bolted across the pasture, bawling.

We gaped at each other. Nothing in my imagination could shake the Sahalie idyll so violently.

My father spoke first, his voice steeled with seriousness. "I need to go call the newspaper."

"What on earth happened?" my mother asked. "Was it a nuclear attack?"

"I don't know, but this is one time I wish we had a telephone out here." He turned to me. "Where's that boat of yours? Let's go see the Niemis."

My father and I dragged *Earnest* through the pasture, rowed across the river, and hiked up to the Niemi farmhouse. We found their family huddled inside around a television, watching impossible news reports of flooding rivers, flattened forests, collapsing bridges, and blackened skies. The entire upper half of Mt. St. Helens, a volcano in Washington state, had blown up in a cataclysmic eruption. Dozens, perhaps hundreds, of people were dead or missing. The sound of the blast had reached us here, 150 miles away.

"This is the news story of the century," my father said impatiently. "I've got to get back to the newspaper office in Salem."

"What about my apartment in Sherwood?" I asked. "It's only fifty miles from Mt. St. Helens."

"Naw, that's upwind," Joe said. "They're saying the mountain blew north. No problem."

"Let's get going," my father said.

We hurried back to the log cabin, packed up as quickly as we could, and hiked out to my parents' car. Because they had to take us home first, my father took the road toward Portland—toward ground zero. The closer we came, the darker the sky ahead grew. Billowing ash clouds boiled up from the horizon. As we drove into Sherwood a deathly snow of gray ash began to fall, covering the grass, dimming the town to shades of black and white.

We quickly thanked my parents outside our apartment. Before we could finish our goodbyes their car was already driving off in a swirl of dusty ash. We were left on the sidewalk of what seemed a ghost town after Armageddon. In the distance, where the clean, Fuji-like cone of Mt. St. Helens had once stood, I could just make out the eerily broken silhouette of the smoking volcano.

It occurred to me that even this catastrophe would not delay my return to work in the morning. For a terrible moment I wished the eruption had destroyed Sherwood, high school and all.

Glumly I unlocked our apartment door, walked across the front room—leaving the gray footprints of a zombie—and saw there on the kitchen table the papers I still had to correct before facing my sophomore classes in the morning. One hundred and thirteen three-part essays stabbing at *A Midsummer Night's Dream.* I would be up half the night grading them.

I sat at the table and buried my face in my hands. Never had I felt so low. Was it possible that I had awakened that same morning to sunshine at the Sahalie log cabin? Ahead stretched endless Monday mornings in a town struck dead by nuclear winter. Is this where I had wanted to be?

Then a light hand touched my shoulder. "You don't have to do this."

I wiped my eyes with my hand and looked away from her. "Yeah, I do." We knew each other well enough that we both knew what we meant.

"No, I'm serious. I've been thinking." She walked to the sink and ran hot water to fill a teakettle. "How much money have we put away this year?"

"What?"

She put the kettle on the range on high. "My salary this past year was almost $11,000, and yours was $13,000. How much of that have we saved?"

"Most of it. We've probably only spent $3000 all year. Of course we've been living like chipmunks, eating oatmeal and rice, paying cheap rent in a small town."

"That's what I thought." She thunked two mugs onto the counter. "Bill, we have $21,000 in the bank. If we keep on living like chipmunks, we have enough to last seven years."

"But, with the baby—"

"Babies don't want their fathers wasting away on nothing but summer dreams. You've got to live the rest of the year too. As soon as school's out next month, I want you to tell the principal you aren't coming back. Give freelance writing a try instead."

"That's crazy. Freelance writing is a shot in the dark. Nine out of ten novel manuscripts wind up in drawers, unpublished. Even articles for the *Oregonian* only pay fifty bucks, if they get in at all."

She filled a tea ball with dried peppermint, dropped it into a mug, and poured in steaming water. "Once I met a crazy man who talked me into bicycling across Europe. That same daredevil convinced me we could build a log cabin in the woods when we were broke." She pushed the mug of hot tea across the table to me. "Now I think he needs a push from a crazy woman."

"Janell—" My voice cracked. Could she really be willing to risk this much for me? "Freelancing could drag us into some awfully hard times."

"Not more than seven years' worth," she admonished, her finger in the air. "If you can't make a living as a freelance writer by then, well—"

"Then I'll get a job clerking at K Mart, I swear."

She smiled and let me pull her onto my lap. For the longest time I simply held her there, unable to speak.

14

Baby On Board

(July 1981)

> The Sage returns to the state of the Uncarved Block. Truly, the greatest carver does the least cutting.
>
> —Lao Tzu, Tao Te Ching, circa 400 BC

"Are you sure this is a road?" Janell asked. We were in an ancient green pickup truck borrowed from my brother, bouncing through a jungle of head-high grass past gigantic stumps. Between us our ten-month old daughter Karen clapped her hands in her car seat and goggled at the green world. The frantic little meows that had been coming from the pet carrier at our feet suddenly paused, and instead our new striped Siamese cat, Kitsa, let out a weird, wailing howl of despair.

"Hang on, everyone, we're almost there," I said. This summer we had decided to drive as close as we could to our log cabin, rather than ferry across the river in our increasingly leaky wooden boat, *Earnest*. Besides, we had a ton of stuff to haul in. I had heaped Pete's pickup bed with lumber for the cabin addition's floor, a 1930s woodstove with an oven, a half dozen boxes of food, a toy scooter for the baby, and a large two-wheeled cart. Every foot closer we could drive shortened the distance I would have to cart our gear by hand.

"It's sure looks different since they logged the trees along the river," Janell said. "Are you positive this is the old gas line road?"

"I can feel it."

"You can feel it?"

I was concentrating on my driving. The truck's hood mowed a swath through the grass, like a Land Rover on a Serengeti safari. Grass pollen and slugs covered the windshield so thoroughly I had to use the wipers, and still could hardly see. But I knew there was gravel in the old road's ruts. When the tires hit the right track the steering wheel had a special, almost imperceptible jiggle.

Suddenly the grass curtain parted before us, revealing a puddle where a creek crossed the road two feet deep. Unable to stop, I gunned the engine instead, hoping for the best. Janell braced her hands against the dashboard. The cat wailed. Little Karen squealed.

The truck plowed into the creek, arcing muddy water over the hood. For a frightening moment the tires spun in the mud. Then they found the road's gravel and took hold. We clambered victoriously up the far bank, drove a few more yards through the grass—and stopped short at a seven-foot wall of wood.

I caught my breath. "I guess this is as far as the truck goes."

Janell peered out at the obstacle ahead. Lying across the road was a huge spruce log wider than our pickup truck was tall. "This must be the tree your father wrote about, the one that caused all the trouble."

I nodded, remembering the story. The only old-growth trees in the Sahalie Valley were along the riverbank. Early loggers had left them rather than try to fell them into the river. Last winter one of the biggest spruces had blown down on property owned by the Willamette Pacific timber company land. The trunk had spanned both the gas line road and the Sahalie River itself, entirely blocking river traffic.

Everyone agreed something had to be done. The timber company said the gas company should remove the tree because it was on their right-of-way. The gas company argued that it was the state's responsibility to clear navigable waterways. The state insisted the federal government should take care of it. Finally, after weeks of wrangling, one of the Taylor County commissioners got so tired of bureaucratic inaction that he boated up to the tree and chainsawed through it himself, clearing the channel.

My father's weekly column described the results of that bold move. Voters removed the county commissioner from office in the next election. And the Willamette Pacific timber company decided to cut the rest of its old-growth trees along the river before they could cause more trouble.

Janell and I got out of the truck to survey the situation. To the left the spruce log jutted to the riverbank. I leaned out to count the rings, but gave up when I reached two hundred. We walked back past the truck, exploring the log in the other direction. There the trunk flared up into a thirty-foot fan of upended roots. Beyond was a water-filled pit resembling a bomb crater.

"You're right about the truck not going any farther this year. How close do you think we are to the cabin?" Janell asked.

"It must be a mile. But our property line's pretty close, and from there the river trail's in good shape. As long as we're not in any rush, I'll be able to haul everything in with the cart, one load at a time."

"Even the stove?"

"I suppose, if I take it apart."

"For today, let's just hike in with the perishables."

"In other words, the cat and the baby."

"Right."

Karen was already howling in the car seat in the truck. The cat had shifted to an ominous low moan. Janell outfitted the baby with a lace bonnet against the sun and transferred her to a backpack carrier. I loaded my own backpack with groceries, locked the remaining food boxes in the truck cab, and set off with the pet carrier.

This year I wasn't too worried about finding rats in our log cabin—we had chinked the cracks with cement the previous summer—but I was disturbed by the increasingly loud sound of a chainsaw.

"Sounds like your brother's attacking our alders again," Janell commented.

"No, Pete's in McMinnville. Besides, the sound's coming from the Niemi farm."

She looked back at me. "I hope the Niemis aren't cutting down their trees too. They've got a dozen big spruces on the bank, and one of them really does lean out over the river. They're an important part of the view from our cabin. Seeing the stumps here is bad enough."

"Let's row over tomorrow for a look. Then we can pick up a gallon of milk."

"And Dolores can meet the baby, and George will tell us whatever news he's got," Janell added.

At the high point of the river trail, where the Clyde Moreland house once stood, we discovered two new bottles exposed by winter rains. One was an ornate pint flask for Old Mr. Boston's Whisky, with a stern post-Prohibition federal warning on the bottom prohibiting re-use or re-sale of the bottle. The other was a square purple vial for Tox-All Fly Killer.

"Your father said we might find clues about the old homesteader in his garbage dump," Janell said. "What do you think of these?"

"I think Clyde didn't buy many luxuries when he went into town. But when he did, he thought about his loved ones."

"His flies?"

"No. His cows. I can picture him massaging their backs with this salve so they won't have to swish their tails so hard on hot summer days. Afterward, he'd invite Old Mr. Boston home to ease the painful memories of World War I."

"Sometimes I don't think you're taking this murder investigation seriously." She smiled all the way down to the pasture. But when the band of heifers galloped across the field to meet us, Janell's expression sobered.

"What is it?" I asked.

"Lizzie. She's not here this year."

The big black-and-white Holstein was indeed missing. "Perhaps she'll show up later. She limped last year, so she might be slow. How old would she be now, anyway?"

"Four and a half."

"That's getting pretty long in the tooth for an old maid at a dairy farm."

"I know. I'm afraid they might have left her here for the winter again, and she didn't make it."

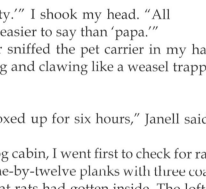

One of the heifers coughed, catching its breath after the run. Another looked back into the woods and mooed.

"Moo, that's right," Janell said. "What happened to Lizzie, your number one moo?"

"Moo!" Karen said, standing up in her backpack. She waved excitedly at the cattle.

"Did you hear that?" Janell exclaimed. "Karen said 'moo!' That's her third word."

"After 'mama' and 'kitty.'" I shook my head. "All this proves is that 'moo' is easier to say than 'papa.'"

A spotted brown heifer sniffed the pet carrier in my hand. The cat inside went berserk, hissing and clawing like a weasel trapped in a beehive.

"Kitty!" Karen crowed.

"The poor cat's been boxed up for six hours," Janell said. "Let's get her to the cabin."

When we reached the log cabin, I went first to check for rats. The new floor—a layer of smooth one-by-twelve planks with three coats of glossy sealer—showed no sign that rats had gotten inside. The loft held no rat nests.

But when we let Kitsa out of her carrier, she did not seem to share my confidence that the house was rodent-free. This was a young cat that had spent her entire life locked inside a Eugene apartment, a place where the most athletic prey she could stalk was a beetle. Now she began methodically sniffing about the perimeter of the room, hot on the trail of some mysterious, grander quarry, her true purpose fulfilled at last. She inspected the new cupboard, the woodbox, and the tool closet with its babyproof latch. She hardly paused at the dishes of cat food and water we put out for her. Instead she twisted her head toward the trap door in the ceiling, and, with an agility I would not otherwise have believed possible, sprang from the table to the ladder and up into the loft. A minute later, having exhausted her search of the upstairs, she leapt back down through the trap door like a cougar and hunched behind the woodbox on full alert.

I was busy changing Karen's diaper, and Janell was still unpacking, when Kitsa pounced. A moment later the cat trotted proudly into the middle of the floor.

"She's got a mouse!" Janell exclaimed. "Get it away from her, Bill!"

"Why? Isn't the cat supposed to catch mice?"

"Oh, just don't let her hurt it. Throw it outside, please?"

I shrugged and left Karen diaperless, wiggling on a blanket on the floor. I put a pair of potholders on my hands and took the mouse out of Kitsa's mouth. "It's sure a tiny thing. See, it's not hurt at all, just a little stunned. What kind of mouse do you suppose it is?"

"A deer mouse. Look at that cute mouse tail. And those little mouse eyes." Janell reached out a finger as if to stroke its head.

Suddenly the mouse leapt out of my hands and raced across Janell's loosely buttoned shirt, evidently looking for a place to hide.

Little Karen waved her hands gleefully. "Mouse!"

"Get it off me! Where is it?" Janell danced about the cabin, jumping and swatting at her shirt. "For God's sake, where'd it go?"

"Mouse!" Karen squealed.

"Will you two hold it down? You're distracting the expert." I pointed to the cat. Kitsa was crouching beside the tool closet, watching the shadows behind a bag. The cat was obviously certain that its mouse had somehow escaped from Janell's shirt. When Kitsa pounced again, I didn't try to take the mouse away from her. Instead I plucked up the cat with my potholders and threw both of them outside.

Janell sank back into a chair. "I don't know how she learned, but that cat sure can mouse."

"Mouse!" Karen was still wiggling on the floor, naked and loving it.

I looked to Janell. "I know, I know. Don't say it."

"Say what?"

"'Our daughter's fourth word is 'mouse,' and not 'papa.' That still doesn't prove anything."

Although the next morning was Saturday, wailing chainsaws from the Niemis' side of the river woke us up shortly after dawn. At breakfast we took out the binoculars and determined that the falling trees were not the dozen graceful spruce giants along the river—at least not yet.

Relieved that our view was intact, I spent the morning carting in loads of food and supplies from the pickup truck. Then I unloaded the lumber and the new woodstove onto the grass and drove the truck back a mile to the county road, where Pete had arranged to come get it in a few days.

That afternoon we went to visit the Niemis. I carried an empty milk jug in one hand and had Karen in a carrier on my back. The growl of chainsaws grew louder as we rowed across the river and walked up the road to the farmhouse.

The doorbell didn't work, as usual, but Laddie's barking and then Karen's crying soon brought George to the door. "Well, looky who's here," the old farmer said, grinning. "This must be that new little Sullivan we read about in the newspaper. Come on in. Dolores and I are just in the kitchen doing the bills."

In the kitchen I set the backpack carrier on the floor and took Karen out.

"Oh, let me hold her," Dolores said. She set Karen on her knee. "Aren't you adorable. I bet you're going to start talking soon."

"She already says four words," Janell said, and smiled wryly at me. "New since yesterday are 'moo' and 'mouse.'"

"A real farm girl," Dolores laughed.

George pulled up extra chairs for us and cleared half of the kitchen table, sweeping back a pile of bills with his big, worn hand. "So you two have just come down from Portland?"

"Actually we moved back to Eugene last year," Janell said. "I'm taking some time off for the baby and Bill's been writing."

George looked to me. "Working for the newspaper like your Dad?"

I sighed. "No. I'm just doing a few freelance articles." I had written dozens of stories in my first year as a freelancer, but only a couple had sold. The clock was ticking away on my seven-year deadline to earn a steady living.

"Anything to help pay the bills," George said. "That's why we signed on the loggers. You probably heard them up behind the barn, cutting hemlocks. It's a heck of a deal. We get paid, and they let daylight in to dry up the mud on our cow trails."

Janell leaned forward. "Are they going to cut the big spruce trees along the river?"

"They'd better," George said. "That's what they were supposed to log first."

Janell flushed. "Those trees have been there for hundreds of years. Don't tell me you're worried about them falling into the river?"

Dolores was clapping Karen's hands pattycake. "If enough fall in the right place, maybe we could plank them and have a bridge."

George shook his head. "The government would just send someone to saw through it." Then, although Janell was the one who had asked him a question, he turned to me. "Maybe you should cut the trees on your side too."

"I don't think so," I said. "Their roots are holding the bank. If the trees along the river are gone, there won't be anything to stop the next big flood from carving into the pasture."

"And the fish need shade," Janell added. "Every summer the river gets warmer. The fish runs are dying out because the water's too warm to hold oxygen."

"Do you reckon?" George pushed back his cap and scratched his white hair. "Seems to me those spruces just shade my pasture, keep the grass from growing. And this Mortensen fella we signed up, he says spruce timber's selling high."

I could see this was not going well. I held up my empty glass jug. "So, George, do you think you could go up to the milk shed with me to sell me a gallon?"

"If you want."

I maneuvered him outside, leaving Janell and Dolores to find less controversial topics.

To my surprise, George didn't want to let the subject go. As we walked across the yard, accompanied by the whine of saws and the occasional thump of a falling hemlock, he admitted, "I worry about this Mortensen."

"Your logger? Did he come recommended?"

"He just came. Drove up to the farm one day and made an offer out of the blue." George led the way into the milk shed. He put my jug under the tank's spout and opened the spigot. "I find out later he's actually a carpet layer in Taylorville. He moonlights as the boss of a gyppo crew on evenings and weekends."

"What's a gyppo crew?" I asked.

"A bunch of half-assed independent loggers that don't know—"

Suddenly the chainsaws outside stopped, and George paused. Three seconds of silence passed. Then I heard the unusually loud crash of a very close falling tree, and the lights went out.

"Damn," George muttered. He closed the milk spigot and set my jug aside.

"What happened?" I asked.

In reply he opened the door. A large fir tree beyond the barn had fallen through a set of wires. "That line powers half the Sahalie Valley." He strode up the road, his expression grim.

Ahead of us, George's business-like younger son Jack had already sprinted out of the barn. He gesticulated at a logger by the stump. "Idiots! This morning you drag a tree through a fence and lose half our herd in the back forty. Now you cut our power. Without our coolers, we could lose a thousand dollars of milk a day!"

"Huh?" The logger looked up blankly. He was a skinny, red-haired man with grease-stained overalls and a dented silver hardhat. He tapped his left temple. "Deaf on that side. My reg'lar job's welding in the junk-yard shop. Got a spark in that ear. Try this other."

Jack stalked to the man's other side and shouted, "You weren't supposed to cut trees so close to the powerline!"

The logger shrugged. "Mortensen said to cut all this up here."

"Where is this boss of yours, anyway? After all, he's getting fifty percent of the profits at the mill."

"Is he now?" The logger raised his eyebrows. "Don't that beat all. He just gives us four bucks an hour, shows up at quitting time each day. Should have been here by now."

As if in reply, a white Impala turned down the Niemis' drive. Jack threw up his hands. "You yell at 'em a while, Pop. I'm calling the electric co-op." Jack stormed off toward the farmhouse.

The Impala slowed as it passed the fallen tree. Sparking wires jerked about the field like beheaded snakes. When the car reached us the door opened and a large, dough-faced man in a plaid suit eased out of the seat. "George, my pal! Cheer up. The power company will get a repair crew to fix your wires. You and I are going to make some nice money out of this fir."

George ran his hand over his jaw. "You're supposed to be logging down by the river."

"OK, OK," Mortensen said. "Next weekend we'll pull out the cedar logs I saw down there on the bank. The mill's giving top dollar for cedar this year."

"No, the cedar logs are ours." George shook his head. "Your contract said you'd cut the spruce trees along the river, not steal our cedar."

"How am I supposed cut spruces six feet across? My guys don't have saws that long."

The red-haired logger jerked a thumb toward George. "I saw a really big chainsaw in the farmer's woodshed. Maybe we could borrow it?"

George gave an exasperated groan. "All right, you can borrow my saw. Just finish the job."

"That's my pal," Mortensen grinned, but George was already walking angrily back to the dark milk shed.

15

The Niemi Spruces

(August 1981)

A man is rich in proportion to the number of things which he can afford to let alone.
—Henry David Thoreau, *Walden*, 1854

In the days that followed Janell and I would occasionally glance across our pasture to check that the big trees were still there. The twelve ancient spruces stood at attention along the Niemis' bank like a riverside honor guard. It hurt, knowing they had been condemned in a hasty court-martial to face Mortensen's bungling executioners. Or might there be a last-minute reprieve?

Most of our time was spent juggling the demands of an overexcited cat and baby, both of whom radically changed our log cabin lifestyle that summer.

Ten-month-old Karen insisted that she be involved in everything we did, whether we were fetching water or going to the outhouse. It seemed she would only fall asleep while being lugged about in a backpack. She howled if we dared to put her in a bed. As I hiked around with her, waiting for her to nod off, I would whisper in sing-song, "Papa. I'm your Papa. Come on, Karen, say 'Papa.'" If she replied at all to this prompting, she usually said, "Moo."

Our striped Siamese cat, Kitsa, discovered that the field outside was hopping with rodents and promptly put into effect a frustrating new workplace policy: She would catch mice only *outside* the cabin. Then she would bring them inside to eat. We soon learned not to open the door if she begged to come in with a muffled meow. That meant she had a mouse. If Kitsa did slip inside with her prey, she liked to let it loose on the floor to toy with it for a while.

Each morning when we swept out the cabin we discovered a few no-longer-cute tails, a head or two, and perhaps a blue, slug-shaped intestine or a bright green, pea-sized gall bladder. Despite this carnage, I suspected that several of Kitsa's toys had escaped, and as a result, the mouse population inside the cabin might actually be increasing.

The biggest technological advance of the summer proved to be our new wood-fired range. I made four laborious trips to cart in the stove's many parts. Then I polished them up, assembled them, and made a few repairs. Finally the antique stove gleamed like new. Only a few cracks in the enamel revealed its age. We felt as if we had upgraded from a fiddle to a Stradivarius. Instead of a mere woodburning drum, we now had a refined baking and cooking instrument, with a thermometer on the oven door, an adjustable damper on the side, two circular cook plates over the firebox, and a warming rack above. As soon as the stovepipe was attached, Janell set to work on a culinary concert, successfully baking bread, cookies, and cornbread all in the first day.

Using a wood-fired range, we learned, can be a complex performance art. Mastery requires a knowledge of wood, its varying degrees of dryness, and which kinds burn best. When the oven is in use, the firebox must be filled with smaller sticks. The stovepipe damper must be left open farther. When the goal is to heat water and to provide warmth for the cabin, the sticks are larger. Slightly wet wood is permissible. The damper is turned down.

My trips to the woodshed became more and more complicated. Not only did I have to haul Karen on my back, but Janell might instruct me to bring "popcorn wood" or "laundry logs," depending on the cooking task at hand.

Diapers turned laundry day into a formidable chore. After the usual rinses, the cloths had to be cooked for an hour in an enamel tub on the stove. Then we would haul the steaming pot into the yard, where Janell would scrub the diapers on a washboard with soap, rinse them again, and run them through a hand-cranked wringer to squeeze out the water. Karen insisted that she be allowed to help at every stage of this process, slowing things down even more. By the end of laundry day Janell's hands were raw and her back was sore. My arms ached from wringing out the many pairs of blue jeans that would not fit through the cranked rollers. The sense of accomplishment, however, was profound when we looked out the window to see a long line of drying diapers fluttering in the yard—a proud white arc of signal flags flying from our log ship's deck.

We had been at the log cabin almost a month, and had begun to hope that the Niemis had changed their minds about the spruce trees, when the whine of chainsaws returned. Janell and I tried not to watch on that long Saturday. Every hour or so the saws would pause, and a screech or a crack made us look up. Another of the giants would be tilting away. In an eerie silence, a cloud of dust would rise above the Niemi pasture. Only several seconds later would the thunderous boom arrive.

By the end of that day, nine of the twelve trees were gone. We were heartbroken.

But three trees remained. Several days later they were still standing. I couldn't figure out why they had been spared. When I saw the loggers' cars reconvening on the pasture the next Saturday, my curiosity got the better of me. Taking along an empty milk jug as an excuse, I rowed across the river to see what was up.

It turned out that Mortensen's crew had started by cutting the easiest trees first. Six of the twelve spruces had leaned over the pasture. These had fallen the right direction without trouble. The next three trees had stood as straight as flagpoles. By cutting large notches on one side of the trunks, the loggers had convinced these spruces to fall conveniently into the pasture as well.

The final three trees, however, leaned decidedly toward the river. Of course these were the trees that had alarmed George in the first place. But how could they be felled without spanning the river?

When I tied up *Earnest* and climbed the bank I found Mortensen's part-time loggers discussing the problem with Joe. Something about the Niemis' elder son seemed to draw him toward frivolous or dangerous challenges, especially if they allowed him to avoid routine farm work.

"We could do her like a spar pole," a young-looking member of the Mortensen crew suggested. "You climb the tree, lopping off branches on the way up. Then you climb back down, cutting the trunk into forty-foot lengths as you go. When you get to the bottom there you are, standing beside a pile of logs. I saw it in a movie once."

There was a moment of silence as we all looked up at the tree, imagining this feat of derring-do. The spruce was four feet in diameter and stood nearly 200 feet tall. Whoever climbed it would be sixteen stories off the ground when the logs started dropping past him.

Mortensen's lean, red-haired logger shook his head. "I'm no movie star. There's gotta be an easier way."

"Sure there is," Joe said. "You simply pull the tree down with a cable. What do you think, Bill?"

I held up my hands and backed away. "Don't ask me. I'm just on my way to get some milk."

"What kind of cable?" the red-haired logger asked.

Joe pointed to a shiny pickup truck behind him. "I just put a winch on the front bumper of Pa's new truck. It's got two hundred feet of airline cable."

"But the tree's two hundred feet tall," the first man objected.

Joe rolled his eyes. "If we tie the cable a hundred feet up the tree, I'll have a hundred feet of cable to spare when it falls. No problem."

Heads nodded in agreement.

While the loggers went to work on Joe's plan, I walked up to the farmhouse to get my milk. Laddie barked like mad, but no one else was home—who knows why. The milking shed was unlocked. I had seen George open the cooling tank spigot often enough that I knew how to fill the jug, but I felt funny about doing it by myself. Finally, afraid of unwittingly violating some health department regulation, I decided to head home with my jug empty.

By the time I returned to the riverbank, the loggers had already sawed out a large, wedge-shaped undercut on the pasture side of the trunk. Joe backed up his truck until the cable was taut. I noticed that the loggers had tied the line only thirty feet up the tree, and not a hundred. Perhaps it had proven difficult to climb higher while carrying the cable. Nonetheless, Joe waved to me and gunned his motor, obviously confident that this thirty-foot margin of safety sufficed.

Suddenly the tree gave a resounding *craaack!*

The loggers dropped their tools and ran.

Joe calmly engaged his winch. The little spool began cranking in the cable.

But the giant spruce showed no interest in being cranked. With ponderous grace, it swayed away from Joe and toward the river, dragging the truck along like a pull toy.

My heart leapt to my throat. If the tree insisted on falling the wrong way, it might yank Joe over the bank with it.

I could see Joe frantically pulling on the truck's emergency brake. The tires locked up, leaving a pair of grooves in the pasture.

And then the tree gave an enormous creak. Miraculously, it paused in mid-air. Had some unfelt breeze—some unseen hand—touched the tree's crown? The leaning tree swayed to a stop and let the cable go slack.

"Get out of the truck, Joe!" I yelled.

"What?" He cupped his hand against the noise of his engine.

"Jump!" Now I could feel the wind, a solid gust from upriver. The tree wagged its long branches and began tilting back toward the pasture.

Joe started to shout "What?" again, but then he must have noticed the tree's shadow racing across the field. Above him, a gigantic spruce was careening through the sky. Open-mouthed, Joe slammed the truck into reverse gear and hit the gas. For a moment the truck went nowhere, jerking about like a bucking bronco on a leash. Then Joe remembered to release the emergency brake. Instantly the pickup screamed backwards across the field.

From where I stood I heard two sounds almost simultaneously. The first was the monumental *BOOM!* of a two-hundred-foot tree smacking a foot-deep groove lengthwise into the pasture. The second noise was small and tinny by comparison. It was the sound of the Niemi truck ripping off its front bumper at the end of the cable while backing up at forty miles an hour.

After this adventure the Mortensen loggers disappeared from the Niemi farm, never to be seen in the area again. Joe was grounded for a month for destroying the bumper of his father's new truck.

Janell hoped the whole matter was now closed, but I could tell the two remaining trees rankled George. The giant spruces poked out over the river like a pair of intercontinental missiles poised for a strike.

I was reminded of the previous summer, when George had told me about mowing the thistles in his pasture. After driving his tractor back to the farmhouse, George had noticed a single thistle plant still standing between swaths in the middle of the far field. For weeks he watched resentfully as that thistle grew. He tried not to notice when it bloomed. But when it finally started going to seed, he couldn't bear it any longer. He hiked out there and cut the damn thing with his pocketknife.

I think those two last spruce trees got to George the same way.

It was August when the Niemis finally took action. I was finishing the foundation piers for our log cabin addition, but I stopped work when I noticed George's pickup truck driving down to their pasture. With binoculars we could see George standing there, apparently offering encouragement, while Jack climbed the larger of the two trees with a chainsaw. Jack lopped off the tree's limbs as he climbed. He did not, however, attempt the death-defying strategy of sawing the trunk into logs on the way down. Instead he and George got back in the truck and drove away. The one spruce stood there like a gigantic telephone pole with a Christmas tree on top. The other spruce—the one that leaned the most—was untouched.

Janell and I mused about this for days. The oddly crippled spruce and its intact neighbor were in the center of our view from the cabin window.

Then one evening at twilight we heard a chainsaw start up again at the riverbank. Why would the Niemis work at night? And what else could they cut but the spruce's trunk? I hiked across the field to see.

Sure enough, Jack was cutting down the limbed tree. And just as surely, it would span the river when it fell. The trick was that a forty-foot tugboat had steamed up our little river and was waiting nearby. This explained why the operation was being undertaken at dusk. The government has rules against hauling logs by river because tree bark contains acid that kills fish.

I retreated discreetly to watch. The tree groaned, tilted loose, and whistled through the starry sky. The colossal splash arced two sheets of water up from the river on either side. When the waves settled, the tugboat approached and a man jumped out onto the log. He chainsawed off its top and ditched it in the willows on our bank. Then he tied a cable to the log, climbed back aboard the tugboat, and gave the motor full throttle.

The small end of the log swung downstream in the frothy white wake of the tug. The large end of the tree rumbled down the bank from its stump, slapped into the sandy mud on the Niemis' side of the river, and—

—And nothing. The log's butt end simply stuck there in the mud. The tugboat churned furiously, wagging the log this way and that. But the log did not pull loose.

I could overhear bits of an argument on board—something about the tide going down, and the dangers of night sailing on a narrow river. Finally they tied the log to the remaining spruce tree with a rope and chugged off without it.

A few days later, as the end of summer approached, Karen and I went to get milk from the Niemis one last time. I was expecting George to be bitter about the tugboat's failure. To my surprise, he sounded almost cheerful. "Oh, a flood will take out that log one of these days."

"What about the last leaning spruce tree, the one that's still standing?" I asked.

"Nice-looking tree, isn't it?" He handed me the full milk jug and wiped his hands on his jeans. "Picturesque."

"But it's the one that made you hire the loggers in the first place, to keep it from falling across the river!"

He shrugged. "If it's been there two hundred years, it'll last a few more. Besides, it's probably the only thing keeping my bank from washing away. Might even be good for the fish."

George's mysterious change of attitude left me speechless. He led the way out of the milk shed and stood there, waiting to close the door behind me. I knew I should say something. After all, it was time to say goodbye until next year.

"Bye-bye," Karen said, standing up in her backpack carrier.

"Well, I didn't know she could say 'bye-bye,.'" George chuckled. "Did your papa teach you a new word?"

"Moo!"Karen said happily. In fact, 'bye-bye' was her seventh new word of the summer, after 'moo,' 'mouse,' 'no,' 'juice,' 'moon,' and even 'bug'—everything, it seemed, except 'Papa,' despite my efforts to train her.

Karen's words reminded me of something else, a question I had been meaning to ask all summer.

"George, do you remember the tame Holstein that used to be on our side of the river? The one we called Lizzie?"

"Number sixty-seven?" The old farmer shook his head sadly. "That was an awfully old heifer. I know you and Janell liked her."

My heart sank. This was hard, especially after the debacle with the spruce trees. Still, I felt I had to know just how heartless George had become. "Then Lizzie—?"

"I'm sorry. I'm afraid you won't be seeing her on your side of the river again." George sighed, but his eyes betrayed mischief. "Lizzie finally had her calf last spring, so we brought her over here."

"What! I thought—"

"You thought what?" George chuckled. "Lizzie's one of our best milkers. See you next summer, Bill." He headed toward his farmhouse, smiling.

I was left there in the road, speechless once again. Finally I walked down to the river with Karen, bailed *Earnest*, and pushed off. We drifted downstream beneath the single large spruce that remained on the Niemi bank.

"I don't know, Karen," I mused. "Maybe they're not such bad neighbors after all. Tell Papa what you think."

Karen bounced in the carrier on my back and said, simply, "Papa."

16

Great, Grand Parenting

(July 1984)

> The universe is wider than our views of it. Be a Columbus to whole new continents and worlds within you, opening new channels, not of trade, but of thought.
>
> —Henry David Thoreau, Walden, 1854

During the next two summers I built an extension onto the log cabin to make room for the additions to our family. Karen now had a baby brother, Ian.

One morning I was in the front yard building furniture for the new upstairs bedroom when a six-year-old boy suddenly appeared, unpacked a shiny new hatchet, and began chopping at my newly installed porch post.

"Hey!" I cried. We don't get a lot of visitors at our log cabin and I didn't recognize this boy, but I was damned if I was going to let him attack our cabin. "Hey, stop it!"

The boy kept whacking our porch post. Our cat Kitsa ran under the house to hide. I had to walk across the yard and grab the boy's arm before he stopped swinging. He looked at me blankly, as if a tree branch and not a person had caught his arm.

"Joshua?" I asked. At this close range I recognized him as one of my brother Mark's two children. I still had no idea how or why Joshua was here. Mark, my oldest brother, was an electronics engineer for a computer company in Beaverton, near Portland. Mark rarely took his family to the Sahalie. In fact, Mark's family rarely left the city at all.

"What?" Joshua asked.

"Don't chop the porch post."

"But Grandpa Wes said I could."

"He did?" I paused to puzzle this out. My parents often babysat Mark's children, sometimes for days at a time. They must have decided to hike into the log cabin as a diversion.

"Grandpa said I could use my new hatchet when I got here."

"Well you can't chop on the house."

Joshua shrugged, walked to the closest alder tree, and began whacking into the bark.

"Please don't chop live trees either." I redirected the boy toward a log by the woodshed. Almost without breaking his rhythm he switched to attacking the log.

"Kids, kids, kids!" Karen squealed, dashing out of the house. She was nearly four years old now, with rosy cheeks and excited green eyes. Barrettes held back her shoulder-length brown hair. She wore a blue gingham dress styled after the illustrations in *Little House on the Prairie*—her favorite bedtime book this year. "Papa! Brianne's coming!"

Playmates were hugely important to Karen. After several weeks with only her two-year-old brother Ian for company, she was desperate. Behind her Ian toddled into the doorway, lugging a good-sized rock. My young son's eyes—blue, like Janell's—surveyed the world with an expression that was surprisingly business-like for his age. His blond hair was far lighter than either of ours. He did not yet speak, perhaps because his sister surrounded him with more than ample verbiage. Lately he had become a fan of the concepts of "big" and "heavy." He liked to carry a large rock with him and preferred storybooks about trucks and dinosaurs.

Karen rushed down to the fence and climbed onto the gate in her excitement. "See, Papa? It's Brianne."

Sure enough, Mark's five-year-old daughter Brianne was bobbing across the pasture. She seemed to be sailing above the tall grass like a low-flying owl. Only when she was closer could I see that she was being carried on the shoulders of my father, a man now better known as Grandpa Wes. Behind him, Grandma Elsie waved to us cheerily.

"Am I a good hiker, Grandpa? Am I?" Brianne demanded, clinging to my father's neck. "Am I as good a hiker as Josh?"

"Of course you are," my father sighed. He greeted me with a sheepish smile. "Hi. Mind if we drop in for the weekend?"

"Glad to have you."

My father stooped stiffly to let Brianne crawl down. The two girls ran up toward the cabin, talking excitedly. My father rubbed his neck. "I've got to find a better hiking motivater for that girl. I'm still kind of new to this grandparenting business."

"You obviously made a hit by buying Josh a hatchet."

"I hope he doesn't get in trouble with it." My father looked up toward the sound of chopping in the yard. "I'd better go see."

I took my mother's backpack. "I'll make room for you upstairs in the new bedroom."

"Oh, don't do that," my mother objected. "Wes and I don't want to be underfoot. We already set up our tent on the other side of the pasture, where the old homesteader had his house. Actually, Wes and Pete have been talking about building a platform or something there. Maybe even a guest cabin."

"Really?" The idea of yet another cabin on our remote Sahalie property worried me. Did we need another building out here? And what would it look like? Pete's involvement was particularly unexpected. He had occasionally thinned alder trees from the forest, and he had talked about dynamiting various things, but he had not shown much interest in our construction projects.

"So far they've just been sketching on napkins," my mother assured me. She waved to Janell in the cabin window.

"Come on in," Janell called. "I'm just starting to fix lunch."

When my mother and I walked into the cabin's new front room we found Karen and Brianne already playing on the room's oval rug. Karen marched out a rag doll with button eyes, a red-checked apron, and a matching bonnet. "OK, Brianne. Your doll can go to the barn with Laura to help milk the cows."

Brianne laughed. "I don't think so!" She opened the pink plastic satchel she had been carrying and took out a long-legged, high-heeled plastic doll in a sequined swimsuit. "Barbie wants to drive to the beach instead. Come on!"

Karen watched with bewilderment as Brianne took out a pink convertible sports car, jammed the dolls in side by side, and raced them across the plank floor. They hit the log wall like a mismatched pair of crash test dummies.

"Time for a Band-Aid!" Brianne exclaimed.

Karen looked up uncertainly. Janell had come to the kitchen doorway. She suggested, "I wonder if you girls would like to help make cookies for lunch."

"Yeah!" both girls cried at once.

"I'll come in a minute," my mother called in after them. Then she added to me, "First I want to see what you've done with the cabin addition."

I gave her the tour. The addition was the same shape as the original cabin, but it was three feet taller, so the new upstairs bedroom had plenty of headroom, and it was several inches wider, so the new wall logs could notch into the ends of the original cabin's front logs. The downstairs of the original cabin now served as a kitchen, with new cabinets and a sink, but still no running water. For an impromptu refrigerator I had nailed a cooler box outside the back window. Foods that needed to be kept properly chilled still had to be stored a hundred yards away in the creek.

The new downstairs room was a combination parlor and dining area, with built-in benches and bookshelves around the walls. In one corner I had carefully fitted planks into a vertical log to make a spiral staircase, with a rope as a handrail. We used a board to block Ian from clambering on the steep staircase when we weren't watching. Upstairs a double bed with a foam mattress took up most of the new master bedroom. I had fashioned the headboard from wide planks, with two heart-shaped holes chiseled out for decoration. A kid-sized, three-foot-tall door led to the cabin's old loft, which now served as a bedroom for Karen and Ian.

From the upstairs window I could see my father in the yard, showing my hand saw to Joshua while Ian toddled nearby. "I should go help Dad keep an eye on the boys."

"You and Janell deserve some time off from parenting," my mother said. "I know how stressful that can be. After lunch why don't you just leave the kids with us?"

I sighed. "That does sound attractive."

"Go ahead. Take the afternoon off."

"All right. Actually, there's a neighbor down the valley Janell and I have been meaning to visit for ages. Maybe we'll go see Mrs. Nelson again." I looked to my mother. "What will you do all afternoon with the kids?"

"I'm thinking I'll convince them to help me pull tansy weeds in the pasture."

Unlikely as this sounded, I did not scoff, knowing from experience how persuasive my mother could be.

While she went back downstairs to help Janell and the girls with lunch, I went out to the yard to see how my father was doing with the boys. I found them huddled around the picnic table with my tools, examining them one at a time. Joshua's fascination made it clear that he had never seen a hand saw up close, and had never actually banged a nail with a hammer. Ian hefted the bit-and-brace with a grunt. This crank-shaped device obviously fit Ian's definition of "big" and "heavy."

"What's that for, Grandpa?" Joshua asked.

"It's an old-fashioned drill." Grandpa Wes set the tool's point on a piece of scrap lumber and showed Joshua how to crank the handle.

When the hole was finished Josh said, "Weird. Now can I use my hatchet for something again?"

My father nodded. "I think you *might* be old enough that Uncle Bill would let you split some kindling. What do you think, Bill?"

I thought this would be far better than attacking porch posts or trees.

I brought out a stack of old cedar shakes I had set aside for kindling. My father got a glove to put on Joshua's left hand. Then, like a golf pro giving a lesson, he helped Joshua stand one of the shakes on a chopping block. Joshua was about to whack at the shake with his hatchet, but my father caught his arm and lowered it gently until the blade rested on the shake. Then he had Joshua lift both the hatchet and the shake together. When Joshua tapped the shake against the chopping block, the hatchet split off a perfect pink piece of kindling with a musical *poing!*

Joshua beamed. Before long he was splitting kindling on his own, surrounded by a growing jumble of pungent cedar. He teased Ian, "You're not old enough to use a hatchet yet."

Ian banged a stick on the picnic bench, pretending he was cutting wood too.

My father and I retired to oversee the operation from folding chairs. "This is sure better than yesterday," my father said.

"Did you have Joshua and Brianne then too?"

He nodded. "I tried to entertain Josh by taking him to my office at the newspaper. All he saw was shelves of dusty reference books and cabinets full of old files. Grandpa's work might be important to some people, but not to him."

"Six-year-olds live in a different world."

"But they shouldn't," my father said. "And out here at the Sahalie, they don't. Here a grandfather is a person of importance. I was the one who found the trail along the river. I knew how to set up the tent. I was there when Josh discovered a salamander. I was Brianne's assurance that the cows wouldn't bother her in the pasture."

We were interrupted by the bang of the cabin's front door. The two girls dashed outside. Brianne stopped before us, breathless, with an empty jar in her hands. "We're going to get milk for lunch!"

"It's in the creek," I said, pointing toward the alder grove.

"Grandpa showed *me* how to cut kindling!" Joshua taunted the girls in a sing-song voice. Ignoring him, they ran on to the creek.

My father looked out across the pasture and mused, "I don't remember many things about my own Grandpa Sullivan, but the memories I do have are not about his work as justice of the peace. What sticks in my mind are the things we did together outdoors. Riding on his horse Halley. Crossing the Marcola River in a little cable car suspended between trees. And cutting kindling."

"You learned to cut kindling from your grandfather too?" I asked.

He lowered his voice. "No, my father made me cut kindling as a chore. I hated it. My most vivid image of William Henry Sullivan is of the grandpa who cut so much kindling when he visited us in Portland that I was off the hook for two weeks. I never would have believed it would become one of my favorite pastimes."

"That's not such a bad memory to have of a grandfather."

He nodded. "I don't know what these kids will remember about me when they're grown. But I'll be content if they think of me as I do of my grandfather, as a man who really knew how to split kindling."

"Eeee!" Brianne and Karen rushed screaming out of the alder grove, their hair flying and their milk jar forgotten.

I jumped to my feet. "What's wrong?"

"Grandpa! Uncle Bill!" Brianne gasped, her eyes wild. "There's something awful down at the creek!"

"What?"

"It was this big and this high," Brianne said, stretching her arms to describe something the size of a garbage can. "It went *Whoosh!* past us," she added, zooming her hand through the air like a jet fighter. "And it made a loud noise, *Stomp! Stomp! Stomp!"* She stomped ominously toward us with the heavy gait of a Frankenstein.

"What do you think it was?" my father asked.

"I don't know!" Brianne shrugged helplessly. "We didn't see it."

I frowned and looked to Karen. "And what do *you* think it was?"

Karen was quiet a moment before answering. "I'm not sure either. But I *think* it was a woodpecker."

17

A Bird of a Different Feather

(July 1984)

> I found myself suddenly neighbor to the birds; not by having imprisoned one, but having caged myself near them.
> —Henry David Thoreau, *Walden*, 1854

And so Janell and I had the afternoon off from parenting. She agreed that it would be interesting to go visit Mrs. Nelson again. We both had a few more questions we wanted to ask her about Clyde Moreland. Janell suggested, "Let's walk through the Niemi's farm on the way. Maybe they can tell us about that strange voice."

For the last few evenings, just after sunset, we had heard a peculiar wail from the Niemis' side of the river. It sounded like a very drunken man loudly attempting to imitate the howl of a cat in heat. I couldn't picture either Jack, Joe, or George performing this weird nocturnal aria.

After we rowed across the river and hiked up the Niemis' road, I heard a smaller, higher version of the wail coming from their farmhouse. "Is that the same voice we heard last night?"

"I hope not," Janell replied, pushing the doorbell. "Because this one's a baby."

George opened the door with his usual half-embarrassed grin. "Well if it isn't our pioneer neighbors. Come on in and take a look at what we just got."

In the living room Dolores was bouncing a small child in a red-and-white-checked dress on her knee. When we walked in the toddler suddenly stopped crying and looked at us with large dark eyes. One of her eyes aimed slightly to one side, as if it had its own ideas. The girl's hair was jet black, and her skin seemed slightly tanned. The overall effect was stunning—an intriguing and exotically beautiful child, perhaps two years old.

"Come in!" Dolores exclaimed, beaming. "What do you think of our future granddaughter?"

I was struck by how this pretty child revealed Mrs. Niemi as very young and very old at the same time. Nobody talked to us about the mysterious disease that had obviously struck Dolores in recent years. Her legs had swollen to purple-streaked stumps and her white hair was almost entirely gone. More ominous yet, the forces of dirt battling the farmhouse appeared to be gaining the upper hand. Even the magazines on the coffee table were piled five inches deep, askew. But this baby on her knee had fired a bright, child-like glow in Dolores' sunken eyes.

"She's adorable," Janell said, bending down beside her to coo.

"But, uh—how does that work with the future granddaughter business?" I asked. "Are you thinking of ordering one like this?"

George chuckled. "No, Cherie here came ready-made. Jack's gone and gotten himself engaged, you see?"

I didn't see, and must have showed it, because Dolores added, "You know how Jack is always working here on the farm while Joe's in town larking around? We were afraid Jack would never meet a girl. So one day Joe brings home MaryLou on a date, and guess what? Sparks start flying between her and Jack instead."

I nodded. Once again Joe had lost out. Joe was always losing out. Of course, Joe's hard-working younger brother probably looked like a better investment to MaryLou. I wondered if she realized what kind of life she was committing herself to as a Niemi farmwife. Dolores was likely to recruit her as an assistant—or a successor—in her farmhouse struggle against dirt.

"Turns out MaryLou was a two-for-one deal," George said proudly. "Now we're watching Cherie while Jack and MaryLou are out shopping for wedding things."

"She has beautiful black hair," Janell said.

"We think the father must have been part Sahalie," Dolores said. "MaryLou doesn't talk about it much."

Cherie clapped her hands, and suddenly both future grandparents focused on the business of pattycake, tossing and turning imaginary cakes marked with a B.

"We didn't mean to barge in," I said, still standing.

"Can't you stay for coffee?" Dolores asked.

"Not really," I said. "My parents are watching our kids for the afternoon, so we're just out on a hike, heading down the valley toward Mrs. Nelson's."

George went with us to the door. "So how are things going with your magazine articles?"

"All right," I lied. Although I had sold dozens of articles as a freelance writer, they had paid next to nothing. I had started work on a historical novel set in frontier Oregon, but I knew nothing about how or where to sell book manuscripts. The truth was that I had used up four of the seven years Janell had granted me to make a career of my freelancing. Our bank balance was still dropping.

Janell said, "I'm planning to take a part-time preschool teaching job in the fall to help make ends meet." She glanced to me, as if to remind me she would not be extending my seven-year deadline.

I looked back to George and changed the subject. "You should come over sometime and see the addition I'm finishing on our cabin."

"I'll do that," he said. "And speaking of cabins, don't be surprised if you see one go up in flames before long."

"What! Whose cabin would that be?"

"Clyde Moreland's. The new owners next door said they plan to burn his old place."

Janell and I looked at each other. She asked George, "So Lucas Hamilton finally sold the original homestead house? Who bought it?"

"I asked him the same question," George said. "He told me, 'There's one born every minute.' He was asking the moon for that shack—over $200,000, they say. Turns out the sucker was Hank Wilson, the rich son of the county commissioner who dug all the gravel pits. He and his wife want to build a fancy retirement house with a river view. For them, the old Moreland cabin was just in the way."

I recalled Lucas Hamilton's visit to our log cabin years ago, when he told us he was keeping Moreland's homestead in memory of his long-time friend. But Hamilton had struck me as a greedy old man who might have other motives. He had even suggested the Niemis were suspects in Clyde Moreland's murder. I decided to test that theory gently.

"Maybe you'll get along better with these new neighbors. From what I hear, you and Clyde had quite a fight over a fenceline once."

George chuckled, a bit nervously, I thought. "Well, Clyde did wave his old World War I musket at me once. I never paid much attention to our fence, and I reckon our cows wound up in his yard a bit too often. But that sort of thing goes on all the time. Take Bartola's peacocks, for example."

George and I had made our way out to the front porch while Janell waved goodbye to Dolores and the future granddaughter. But Janell turned in time to catch this last sentence.

"Peacocks?" she asked. "What about peacocks?"

"Don't you have one yet?"

"No."

"Well, you must have heard ours. Sounds like a crazy cat with a loudspeaker."

"So that's the voice," Janell said. "Where did this peacock of yours come from?"

"It wandered here from Bartola Landing, the marina five miles down the road. Barry Bartola raises ducks, pheasants, and these peacocks on the side, you see. He pens up the hens because they're valuable, but he lets the males strut around free. Each year the old cocks drive off the young males, and they hit the road. They're not good fliers, but they're great walkers. Why, nearly every farm in the valley has a peacock or two, and the Wilsons' gravel pit on Root Creek has five. Some folks say Barry shouldn't go infesting the valley with big useless birds, but nobody's quite mad enough to shoot him yet."

"Yet?" I remembered Barry Bartola from the time we had bought our old wooden boat at his marina years ago. He seemed like a stingy but otherwise harmless old man who traveled everywhere on a riding lawnmower.

"Barry's made more than his share of enemies, even before he got the peacocks. It wouldn't surprise me if he was the one who shot Clyde."

"The marina owner might have shot Clyde Moreland?" Janell asked. "Why?"

George gave an awkward shrug. "Go ask Mrs. Nelson. I've got a future granddaughter to deal with today."

Janell and I decided to walk the cow path under the powerline, and not take the county road, for the two miles to Mrs. Nelson's farm.

"George isn't the type to shoot somebody over a broken fence, do you think?" I asked.

"He'd never plan to, no," Janell replied, looking straight ahead. "But if he got to arguing over a rifle on a rainy night—"

"I'd like to find out more about this Barry Bartola."

"I'd like to find one of his peacocks."

We kept a lookout for peacocks, but saw hummingbirds instead. One at a time the thumb-sized birds would zoom up to us, each with a ruby spot on its throat like a shining scarlet jewel. The rest of their feathers were an iridescent blue-green: peacocks in frantic miniature.

"Why are they buzzing me?" I asked.

"They're checking out your red backpack. The color birds see best is red. Flowers pollinated by hummingbirds are always red: foxgloves, columbine, fuchsias. Your backpack makes you look like a giant flower."

A hummingbird hovered before me, its wings beating like a big bee's. The blurry rhythm was so efficient that when the wings jerked the bird away at a right angle, the little body wagged behind an instant before it zipped after the wings into the blue.

When we reached Mrs. Nelson's gray shake farmhouse and knocked on the wavy glass of the door, I was alarmed to see the eighty-nine-year-old woman hobbling up to meet us on crutches.

"Well isn't that nice," she exclaimed. "It's those Sullivans, come visiting again like they promised. Took you a few years, though, didn't it?"

"What happened to your foot? Are you all right?" Janell asked.

"Aw," she waved a hand at the cast on her leg disparagingly. "Stepped in a mole hill and twisted my gall-danged ankle. I'll be jiggered if it's slowed me any though. Now come on in, and don't mind if I've already got company."

We followed her inside to the kitchen, where a gangly, sleepy-eyed teenage boy was finishing supper. He poked the last of a sandwich into his mouth and washed it down by drinking most of a quart canning jar of milk.

"This is Kevin, my great-grandnephew from San Diego," Mrs. Nelson said. "Kevin, swallow that before you say hello to the Sullivans."

Kevin swallowed. "Hi." Then he picked up a medium-sized mixing bowl and began eating potato salad with a casserole serving spoon.

"Kevin asked for a larger bowl because he eats that much," Mrs. Nelson explained. "He's sixteen."

Kevin swallowed again. "Do you guys know anything about fishing?"

"Not very much," I admitted.

"Well I stayed up late last night reworking all my gear, and this morning I caught two from the bank. They were so little I gave them to the cat, but I saw a couple really big ones out in the river. Grandma makes me fish from the bank."

"You can fish however you like, but I told you I don't have a boat," Mrs. Nelson snapped. "Now go make your bed. You didn't do it properly this morning." I could see his bed, a fold-out couch in the living room, covered with an unruly quilt.

The lanky boy finished the rest of the milk from his canning jar, gathered up a bag of fishing gear, and slouched out the back door, conspicuously rumpling his bed back into a couch on the way.

When the door closed behind him Mrs. Nelson let out a long breath. "I've probably had a dozen of these kids over the years." She shook her head and cleared away the supper dishes. "Well, sit down now, won't you, and I'll get us some coffee."

"You've had a dozen teenagers come here from San Diego?" I asked, sitting down.

"I get them from all over to heck and gone. It seems everyone in the family has a cantankerous sixteen-year-old boy they don't know how to handle. So they ship them off to the farm for a week or two to see if Grandma can't straighten them out."

"Does it work?" Janell asked. Now that she was planning to go back to teaching, Janell seemed particularly interested in how different people handled behavior problems.

Mrs. Nelson thunked the coffeepot onto the wood stove. "When they live under this roof, darn it all, they live by my rules. For goodness sake, you'd think they never had to get up on time at 7:30, make their beds, wash their faces, and comb their hair! Well, it's not much for rules, but by golly they do it here or there's no breakfast."

She slammed a couple of spoons onto the table so hard the coffee cups rattled. "They can have all the oatmeal they want, and whole fresh milk, but I'm not going to town to buy these sugar cereals. They'll live on farm food here."

At this point Mrs. Nelson strutted back a step, ignoring the cast on her foot, and threw back her shoulders to mimic the haughty stance of a teenager. "One of them came swaggering in, saying he was going to be a football star. Well I saw a round lump in the back pocket of his pants, and I asked, 'What's that?' 'A yo-yo,' he says, kind of sheepishly. 'Well, let's see it, huh?' "It's broken,' he says. 'Well, maybe we can fix it. It's been a long time since I've seen a yo-yo. Bring it on out.' So he brings out the snuff can. "Snuse?' I say. 'You eat this stuff?' And I just drop it in the stove fire. I tell him that's why he's so awful pale and thin. If he wants to be a football player, I tell him, he needs to be eating oatmeal and whole milk instead of that garbage. Well! By the time that one left he'd come around enough that he made his mother stop on the drive home to buy oatmeal."

Janell and I laughed. "Are you making progress with Kevin?" I asked.

She gave a weary sigh and poured the coffee. "It's only his second day. As soon as he came he plopped down and asked, 'Grandma, where's the pop?' I said I didn't have any, so he said he'd just go buy some. When I tell him it's fifteen miles each way to town, he says he'll just take my car. Well, I tell him he can't fool me. No license, no drive. So now he's out fishing, and meanwhile there's three cords of wood by the front door that sure could use a teenager splitting it up for winter."

She squinted over the coffee cup as she sipped. "Oh, I'll bring this one around too. But I'm getting tired of reforming all the dingbat city teenagers in the family. Money's no bribe for this one, either. His parents are both bigshot California executives. They're too busy to talk to him. Instead they throw twenties at him all the time."

Mrs. Nelson set down her cup. "Here I've been yakking! Tell me what you're up to. I hear you've got kids now too."

"Yes, Karen's three and a half, and Ian's almost two," Janell said.

"Oh? Where are they?"

"Back at our log cabin," I said. "My parents came to visit and offered to baby-sit for the afternoon so we could go for a hike. I'm afraid our kids are probably being spoiled, even as we speak."

"You should bring them to see me sometime."

I smiled, imagining Karen and Ian confronting Mrs. Nelson's fierce will. "Or you could come visit us at the log cabin."

"Well, now that's hard without a boat." She looked out the window. "I haven't been to Clyde's place since he moved his house across the river in 1950. Did you hear Lucas Hamilton finally unloaded that property of his on the Wilsons?"

"Yes, and George Niemi says they plan to burn down Moreland's old cabin to make room for a big new house."

"Really?" She shook her head. "I remember when Clyde built that cabin, back in, what was it? In 1922, I suppose. We called it the 'house on the stump' because he'd built it on top of a big ten-foot-wide stump as a foundation. Clyde threw a big housewarming party for all the homesteaders up and down the valley. I remember people were having such a good time they tossed empty whiskey bottles out his front window down the hill."

Janell looked at me in amazement. "We found one of those bottles a couple of years ago. The rain washed it out of the trail below the old cabin site. It was a flask for Old Mr. Boston whiskey."

Mrs. Nelson nodded. "Clyde took a nip now and then. But Barry Bartola got himself so drunk at that party he started a fight and dang near drowned on the way home."

"Were he and Clyde enemies?" I asked. At last it sounded like we might be able to make some progress in our murder mystery investigation.

She looked at me sharply. "No, but there was something going on between them. After Clyde died, Barry wound up owning several big pieces of Clyde's old land downriver. I never did figure out how that worked. Suddenly Barry opened Bartola Landing and started selling five-acre lots all along Wilson Road. Just last year Barry wanted to build an RV park at Skookum Rock. But I think he tripped himself up this time."

"Oh? How's that?"

"Well, when he sold the last lot at the end of Wilson Road to Valerie Boucher, he forgot to leave himself a road right-of-way across fifteen feet of her land. Now the only way he can develop Skookum Rock is to bully her into letting him drive through. Except she isn't the bullying sort."

"Skookum Rock is sacred to the Sahalie," Janell said. "If this Valerie is related to the Boucher we know, I bet she doesn't want to see Skookum Rock developed at all."

Mrs. Nelson smiled. "I bet you're right."

"Grandma!" a voice outside bellowed. "I've got a real fish! Now what do I do?"

"Duty calls," she said somberly.

"For us too," I said. "We need to get back before dark."

Evening had pinkened the hills when Janell and I returned to the log cabin. We approached guiltily, knowing we had overstayed our outing and missed dinner. But Grandma Elsie and the four kids were playing a game of Go Fish in the kitchen, and Grandpa Wes was smiling from a rocking chair on the porch.

"See?" I've already finished next week's column. What do you think?" He handed me a notepad covered with his looping longhand scrawl. While Janell went in to join the card game, I read the column through.

> Long ago I learned we can't dominate our environment along the Sahalie River. But with persistence and by concentrating on specific and limited objectives, we can carve out a small enclave.
>
> Our family log cabin stands as testimony to the determination of Bill and Janell, the builders. But stretching across the twenty-acre pasture are huge blotches of thistle and a profusion of the darker green spots of tansy ragwort, offensive to our vision as we sit in the front yard of the cabin surveying our domain.
>
> As I look out at these irritants I think back to Clyde Moreland, the original homesteader of this property who, in the 1920s, cleared the trees from the pasture with a horse, a winch, and a cable. I still can see the rusting cable above the grass in the center of the pasture.
>
> What that one man lacked in size, tools, and muscle, he made up for in motivation. Fueled by inner fires of determination, he wrought the miracle we enjoy.
>
> Multiply that by the millions and we have America today. But where is the font of such inspiration? How can we will ourselves to do the impossible? What does it take to break the shackles of our own, self-imposed limitations?
>
> I gained a hint of that earlier this week as I brought two of our granddaughters back to the cabin from the other side of the pasture.

It was nearly dinnertime. We easily could have gone round by way of the pasture, but I suggested going over the hill through the forest. The girls, Brianne, 5, and Karen, 3, were agreeable, so off we went.

I had forgotten how overgrown this section had become. This little-used trail is covered by a low tangle of salmonberry and wild blackberry runners. While I'm used to slogging through in my high-topped boots and jeans, each stickery vine seemed to present an insurmountable obstacle to the little girls, especially to Karen, the youngest.

Foot by foot we slowly progressed until we reached the base of the hill. We had exhausted Karen's patience to the point of tears as we started up the backside of the hill. Going back meant reencountering all the stickers we had just conquered.

Desperate, I drew on my years of parenting, reminding the girls of a story they both know well. We must have worn out three books of *The Little Engine That Could,* the story of the tiny engine that pulls the train of toys over the mountain to the good little girls and boys on the other side by puffing, "I think I can, I think I can."

The idea of dinner waiting on the other side of the mountain captured their imaginations, and to the chanting of two tiny voices repeating, "I think I can. I think I can," we started up the hill.

The stickery vines no longer presented an obstacle, but a challenge to a newfound determination. The two little engines stormed the trail with a fierce zeal. And when Karen whimpered and faltered as a vine became tangled in her hair, another shot of "I think I can" set her going again.

The hill was much higher and longer than I remembered, but at last the top was in sight and the beat quickened.

All the way down to the cabin we marched to the ringing, triumphant call of "I thought I could. I thought I could. I thought I could."

At one point the trail down is so steep, huge steps have been carved. Karen stopped and as she tried to manage those steps, I heard her mutter under her breath, "Well, it's back to 'I think I can' again."

And then home to the cabin and dinner and stories about having conquered the mountain.

I came away from the experience chastened by the importance of the stories we tell our children. What inspiring pictures are

> we planting in the minds of today's youngsters that will give them the courage and the determination to conquer tomorrow's mountains, to put their vast reservoirs of untapped, purposeful power to use for the betterment of their world?
>
> As for me, I find humbling the awesome power of the Sahalie to produce growth. But as those thistles produce a purple haze of flowers, I know that letting them go to seed will just make matters worse next year.
>
> I don't know if I will be able to cut them all this summer, but I think I can.

While I read my father's column, Brianne skipped past to take a jar of milk to cool in the creek. Now she suddenly rushed back to the porch, her eyes wide.

"Grandpa Wes! There's something down at the creek!" she gasped.

"What is it?" he asked, but from his smile I could tell he had doubts.

"This time it's *not* a woodpecker," Brianne insisted.

"Was it this big?" Grandpa Wes teased, holding his arms outstretched.

"Well, yes, about that big."

Grandpa Wes looked to me. "I don't want to ask if it went *whoosh* like an airplane."

"It *did!*"

This was serious.

"All right, Brianne, let's take a look," Grandpa Wes said, and then whispered to me, "I think somebody here needs to learn a little lesson about stretching the truth."

We followed her back down the twilit path to the creek.

"See?" she said, pointing.

Beside the stream a full-grown peacock faced us in full ornamental array. Its iridescent tail feathers were fanned and a halo of feathery doodads waved above its head. The bird looked at us and loosed the weird cry of a thousand-pound drunken cat.

"Good Lord," Grandpa Wes breathed. "She was *right!*"

I smiled. After my talk with the Niemis that afternoon, I knew where the spectacular bird had come from. But I decided to let my father puzzle over this little mystery a while. "Score one for granddaughters, Brianne," I said.

18

The Assessor

(August 1984)

'Modern improvements' are wont to be pretty toys, which distract our attention from serious things.
—Henry David Thoreau, Walden, 1854

Toward the end of summer I awoke early one morning to a buzzing whine. It sounded as if a confused bumblebee was trying to get in the window. When I put on my clothes and dragged myself downstairs I saw my father out in a corner of the pasture, waving a little gas-powered garden weed cutter at the seemingly endless stands of five-foot-tall Canadian thistles. My mother was out there too, digging the few remaining tansy ragwort plants with a shovel.

"What's that noise?" Janell asked sleepily from upstairs.

"My parents. They've come back. They're trying to weed the entire pasture by hand."

"Oh God. I guess we should make breakfast for them."

I started a fire in the woodstove. An hour later, when my parents finally trooped up to the cabin to say hello, I was already feeding pancakes to Karen and Ian.

"Mmm. Smells good," My mother said.

"Come on in," I said. "You must be hungry after starting so early."

"It's a huge job," my father admitted. "But we have to start somewhere. I don't want those thistles going to seed."

They sat down and filled their plates.

My mother pointed out the window to a black spot on the far side of the river. "What happened to the old shack across the river?"

"Wasn't that Clyde Moreland's original house?" my father asked between bites.

"The new owners burned it down," I said. "Yesterday morning it was still there. Then we went for a hike. When we came back in the afternoon there were just a few blackened posts."

My father shook his head. "A lot of history went up in smoke with that place."

For the rest of that day, my parents whacked away at the weeds in the pasture.

Ian, his hair blond from the sun, took off all his clothes and stomped naked about the yard with a watering can, dousing logs and shoes. I hammered together drawers for a dresser I was building.

Just before lunch Karen insisted I needed to go with her to the husicka. Although she was toilet trained, she wanted company when she was near that black hole, a vortex so dark it seemed to swallow time. I followed her to the outhouse and waited outside for ten minutes. Finally I checked and found her dropping pinecones down the hole.

"We don't put anything but potty and poopy down the hole," I said.

"Why?"

"Because when this hole fills up I'll have to dig another."

"When *will* the hole be full?"

"Not for ages, I hope. Not till you're grown, Karen."

She considered this. We walked back to the cabin. While she was washing her hands she told Janell, "Mama? Do you know when Papa says I'll be grown up?"

"When's that, sweetie?"

"When the outhouse is full."

Janell laughed and I shook my head.

At dinner we picnicked in the yard with my parents. The last of the yellow tansy blooms were gone, but a haze of thistles still covered the field like a purple mist. My father's weed cutter had hardly nicked the corner of the twenty acres.

"Dad, it's hopeless," I told him. "You can't cut all the thistles. None of us can. Only a miracle could stop them from going to seed."

Exhausted from his day's labors, my father looked out across the thistle blooms. I could tell he was wishing with all his heart for that miracle.

The next morning when I stepped out of the cabin into the bright sunshine, I was astonished to see a giant green John Deere farm tractor with a scoop bucket and a mower bar in the middle of our field. The tractor purred like a magic dragon as it devoured row after row of thistles.

Grandpa Wes was in the front yard, sitting in a chair in the sun. "You see?" he said. "If I hadn't struggled out there with a brush cutter all day,

Joe Niemi wouldn't have taken pity on me and come over to finish the job. At this rate he'll be done in a couple of hours. It just shows you the power of 'I think I can.'"

The tractor clattered past, mowing another ten-foot swath.

"It's a good thing we pulled the tansy first," my mother said. "If he cut them, they'd just come back and bloom anyway."

"Pulling, cutting—actually, I don't think it will matter much in the long run." We turned to Janell. She had just emerged from the cabin with a plant book in her hand.

"Why's that?" Mom asked.

"Because fresh seeds come in the silt every time the pasture floods. Besides, tansy is a new alien here. It will keep on spreading until a natural enemy shows up."

Dad gave a half-smile. "Maybe Elsie *is* its natural enemy."

Janell tilted her head. "They've found a caterpillar that eats tansy in Asia. It's the larval form of a cinnabar moth."

"Why don't they bring it over here?" I asked.

She shrugged. "They don't know yet what else it might eat. If it likes corn or wheat, it would be a disaster. But in the end, the quickest way to stop an alien is always to bring in another alien."

"I suppose Canadian thistle is an alien too?"

Janell considered this. "I don't know if it's really from Canada. But according to my book, mowing won't help much. The roots are a matted layer a foot deep. They send up new shoots each year. To get rid of the thistles we'd have to take off the cattle."

"Take off the heifers?" my father asked, concerned. "That's our rent."

"As long as they keep eating the soft plants and leaving the spiny ones, the thistles are going to spread."

"Enough!" my father said, holding up his hands. "I'm just glad the thistles won't be going to seed this year." He leaned back and took a deep breath of Sahalie air. "This place is priceless. I mean it. Everything we've got here—the cabin, the view, the ambiance. I wouldn't sell it for a million dollars."

"Mama!" Karen called from the cabin window. "There's a poo-poo at the gate."

My parents looked puzzled. Janell and I, however, understood. Karen used the word "poo-poo" to mean "people."

I walked across the yard and saw there really was an unfamiliar man by the gate, wearing a white business shirt and a necktie, of all things.

"Don't shoot!" The man waved to me with a briefcase. He smiled broadly. "May I come on up?"

I nodded. He trudged up to the picnic table, wiping his brow with a white handkerchief. "Whew! I had to leave my car back there a mile. How did you folks get in?"

The four of us eyed this newcomer with suspicion and surprise. I replied, "We walked here, the same as you."

He pointed to the field. "What about the tractor?"

Dad knit his brow. "To be honest, I don't really know how Joe managed that. I guess he must have driven it over the abandoned gas line road somehow."

"Is that what chewed up your road?" The businessman set down his briefcase and shook his head. "That last steep hill looked like a war zone. I don't think anything will ever drive over it again."

There was a moment of silence as we reassessed Joe's feat. By charging to our rescue, he had apparently also risked the Niemi tractor on a dangerous, possibly one-way mission.

Then I remembered the necktie in our midst. "Isn't this a long way for a guy to hike to try selling us life insurance?"

The man chuckled and reached into his shirt pocket. "Would any of you happen to be J. Wesley or Elsie Jane Sullivan?"

I nodded toward my parents.

He handed my father a business card. "Henry Smythe, Taylor County assessor's office. We heard about your construction here and thought we'd update the tax rolls."

My father stared at the card, his face lengthening.

My mother nudged Dad on the shoulder. "Well go on. You were just shouting about how valuable you thought the place was."

"What I meant was, you just can't put a price on this kind of place."

The assessor took a clipboard out of his briefcase and flipped a few pages. "It says here you put an estimated value of $300 on the building permit in 1977."

"Well—" my father began.

"Actually, that's about right," I interrupted. "The original cabin only cost $100 for the materials, and if you don't count the stove or the furniture, the whole addition was about another $200."

"You found the logs for free?"

"That's right," I said. "We culled them from the forest to improve the stand. The windows are all second-hand cast-offs, and the shakes are from a cedar log that floated here in a flood."

"But this original permit was for a rustic storage facility. What I'm seeing here looks more like a house. That's a different assessment scale."

Dad snapped his fingers. "Don't you use comparative home sales in the area to determine value?"

"That can be a factor, yes."

"Well, the house next door sold just this summer. It's about this size, except with plumbing and electricity, and access to a real road."

"Oh? And where is it?"

Dad pointed across the pasture. "See that black spot? The new owners decided it was worthless and burned it down."

"So much for comparative home sales," my mother put in.

The assessor looked up at our cabin and smiled. "Still, this *is* a lovely spot here, isn't it?"

We didn't say a word.

The tractor clattered past on another pass. Joe waved, and I waved back, but with less enthusiasm. How on earth was Joe going to get his family's tractor home, I wondered?

That evening all of the thistles had been cut, and the clattering of the tractor stopped. My father and I walked along the edge of the pasture to see if Joe planned to face the 150-foot-tall gas line hill to take the tractor home. His father George was already at the base of the hill, checking the tractor's hose lines. He had rowed across the river with Laddie, the old farm dog. Laddie seemed thinner than I remember, and walked stiffly, but he wasn't wet, a sign that George now let him ride in the boat.

"Aw, Pop," Joe said. "It's no problem. Really." He swung onto the tractor seat and gunned the throttle.

George stepped back to join us and crossed his arms. "I could have killed that boy this morning," he said. "Normally he sleeps through breakfast, but today he was out of the gate at six with my tractor. Two hours later I saw him show up over here. The kid had driven twenty-five miles out to Highway 101 and back, just to get across the river."

"But you're letting him drive it up the hill now," my father said.

George tightened his lips in response.

Meanwhile Joe popped the clutch. The tractor jolted up the hill, engine whining. A third of the way up, where the grade steepened, the tractor ground to a halt, its gigantic rubber tires churning foot-deep pits into the slope.

Joe paused a moment, as if to consider his position, and then pushed a lever. The tractor's front bucket lowered to the road. He jammed two levers forward and the big scoop clawed into the dirt, pulling hard toward the tractor. This yanked the front wheels into the air, but it also allowed the big back wheels to inch up the hill an arm's length. There they began digging new holes.

Joe raised the blade, advanced it, and dragged the tractor another three feet up the hill. Then he repeated the operation again. Slowly, methodically, the tractor pulled itself crablike up the slope. Finally Joe and the tractor were on top looking down the other side.

The slope beyond was just as steep—about forty-five degrees—but it had been made more treacherous by the "war zone" of pits and ruts Joe created on his way in. At the bottom of the hill the road jogged sharply left to avoid the riverbank cliff straight ahead.

"That looks awfully steep," I said. "How will he keep the tractor from sliding out of control?"

George mused, "I suppose we could tie a log to the back of the tractor with a long cable. That way, when the tractor goes down the hill, the log would be dragging up the other side like a brake."

"How much is a tractor like that worth?" my father asked.

"About $14,000," George said.

None of us dared to speak the obvious: If the tractor began to roll, Joe might not be able to jump clear in time.

Down at the bottom of the hill the river lapped at the bank at high tide.

As we stared at the slope I could feel the moment of decision stretching thinner and thinner. The consequences of a miscalculation would be devastating. But Joe had been gradually edging closer to the brink. The front wheels inched onto the steepest part of the slope—and down. Now there was no turning back.

Joe dug the blade of the scoop straight down into the center of the roadbed while applying full brake. It was all he could do.

The tractor began to gather momentum, and for a moment it looked as though the hill was going to win this round. And then a pile of rock and dirt began to accumulate in front of the blade, slowing its speed.

"I hope that hydraulic line holds," George muttered.

Slowly, with the grinding roar of a steamship running aground on a gravel bar, the tractor descended the hill, scraping the road as it went.

At the bottom Joe looked back with a toothy grin. "And you got a graded road out of it."

George shook his head. He turned to walk back around the base of the hill on the river trail. "No one but Joe could have done that."

A few days later when I was putting the children to bed they demanded a bedtime tale.

"Put a magic dragon in the story, Papa," Karen begged, twisting in her sleeping bag excitedly. "No, wait! Put in a submarine."

"OK, a submarine."

"Bunny!" said little Ian sleepily.

"Do you want a bunny in your bedtime story, Ian?"

"Uh-huh."

"Well—" I had drunk two glasses of brandy that evening. I groped through the haze for a plot, lying on the loft's floor with my eyes closed. "OK. Here's what happened. One day Bunny Bob wondered why there were so many new weeds in the pasture, instead of the tender green shoots that he likes to eat. So late that night he decided to sneak away in his submarine and go ask the Great Wise Mole who lives in a secret cavern beneath the river."

"Ooh!" Karen squealed. "In the dark?"

Somehow I finished the story—a weird, rambling tale that nearly put me to sleep first.

Then, while Janell worked on a pen-and-ink drawing of a buttercup by lantern light, I wandered out into the pasture for a last evening bathroom break. With my fly open, and the chirp of crickets, and the muffled sound of heifers munching grass, I looked up to see Andromeda's trailing V of stars above the Niemi hill in the August sky.

Behind the second star, right where I always looked, was the galaxy I had never before seen.

I had been looking for the wrong kind of thing all along—a crisp telescope photograph of stars swirling down a drain. Even on the clearest night, the Andromeda Galaxy is nothing more than a faint white smudge. To the naked eye, our nearest neighboring galaxy, a million light years beyond every other light in the sky, is a blur so obscure it disappears if you stare straight at it.

I wished I could teleport halfway there to make it twice as clear. Then, when I turned around, our own Milky Way would no longer be a glowing band across the sky, but rather another small, blurry spiral. And if there were other lights in that black sky, they would be other galaxies only.

I was still gaping into the next galaxy when a ray of light streaked across the field's thistle stubble like a ground-level meteor. I zipped my fly and followed the beam to a man on his knees with a flashlight.

"Hi, Bill."

I recognized Wallace Boucher by his voice even before he tipped up his flashlight, skeletizing his angular features, backwards baseball cap, and black ponytail.

"Butch!" My head was still circling from the brandy. "What are you doing out here? It must be midnight."

"Shrooming." He held up a small plastic bag. "Hey, when I saw the thistles were gone, I knew there'd be a hell of a crop. But how'd you cut them all, man?"

"It's a long story," I said. "Have you been finding anything out here?"

Butch shook half a dozen tiny brown mushrooms from the plastic bag into his hand. The three-inch stalks were thin and scraggly, but the bell-shaped, peaked caps glowed like flesh in his flashlight beam. "Liberty caps. Psilocybin. See, the top's like a breast with a little brown nipple on top."

"Do they grow all over, or just here?" I asked.

"They like damp fields with cow pies. This one works."

"Why do you pick them at night?"

He shrugged. "It's when I'm off work."

"What happens if you eat them?"

Butch smiled. "You visit the Skookums, friend. Sometimes it's good, sometimes it's bad. It's always $50 an ounce. Don't go there unless you're ready for trouble. Are you?"

"Not tonight. I suppose this is one of your tribal traditions?"

"Yeah, it is. The Sahalie tribe isn't into eating magic mushrooms, but they love the rest of it."

"The rest of it?"

"Ripping off white people. Jeez, here I am, trying to sell you your own moldy cow shit for $50." Butch gave a laugh that sounded dangerously over the edge. Then he climbed atop a dark log nearby, sat cross-legged, and lit a hand-rolled cigarette.

I don't know why I waited after that. I guess I still had a question or two I wanted answered about his family and Clyde Moreland. Eventually a red dot glowed and his voice came from the sky.

"I suppose you know that Barry Bartola was shot?" Butch blew a smoke ring toward the stars.

"What? Are you serious?"

"Yeah," he said. "I try to keep these things in perspective, though. Death's just minimum wage when you do it for a living."

I shivered. If he was telling the truth, there had been another murder. "How did it happen?"

"Two rifle shots," he said. "First there was a twenty-two through his pickup windshield. That one grazed Barry's temple enough to spatter his wife. Sort of a warning. Then when he decided to step outside, he got a thirty-aught-six to the chest. Couldn't you hear the sirens from here?"

"No." I found myself remembering Barry Bartola. We had bought our rowboat from him at his marina years ago. Although I hadn't liked him much at the time, we had few enough neighbors in the valley. "Do you know who shot him?"

"It was self-defense, friend," Butch said. "Preemptive self-defense, maybe, like in 'Nam." A red light glowed as the butcher took another drag. "Bartola had been threatening Valerie Boucher ever since he found out she could block his road. He wanted to turn Skookum Rock into a Disneyland. Maybe he would've run her over to get through that gate. Maybe."

"That doesn't sound like self-defense to me," I told the darkness against the stars. "Shooting a man in his truck."

"That's why Valerie's in jail without bond. But things are never as simple as they seem. One puzzler is why she used two different rifles to shoot him."

"Was someone with her?"

"They haven't found anyone yet."

"Was it you?"

Butch let that one hang in the night air a minute. "No, not me. You see, I'm thinking of giving up the butchering business altogether. There's easier ways to skin cats."

"Then who fired the second shot?"

"Nobody's seen Val's boy these past three days. Little John's fifteen. For all I know he may be spooking around these woods, dodging Skookums."

I could hear Butch's plastic bag crinkling. My befogged brain was clearing. I decided to tackle him head on. "I've heard about the Bouchers. Your family was jealous of Clyde Moreland and wanted Skookum Rock. It sounds to me like they killed Moreland first, and now they've killed Bartola."

"Slow down, friend," the voice said. "First, Val's not part of my branch of the Bouchers. She just happens to have the same last name."

"That's an awfully strange coincidence."

"Hey, it happens. And anyway, killing people's no way to get back Skookum Rock. Whoever bumped off Moreland must have figured Bartola would get his land, because that's who ended up with a lot of it. No one in the tribe would have wanted that. Now that Bartola's dead, Skookum Rock goes to his mixed-up wife, or to his kids in California."

"I guess the Bouchers wouldn't win there either, would they?"

"No." The red dot flicked across Andromeda like a shooting star. Butch's shadow slid off the log and merged with the night. His voice came back across the pasture, "Things aren't as simple as they seem."

19

The Wileys

(June 1985)

> The forest was lush and fresh, as though it had been born in a rush of green brilliance under the rain.
>
> —Don Berry, To Build a Ship, 1963

My brother Pete revved his chainsaw to finish another cut. The alder tree gave a loud crack, tilted away, and fell down the hillside of salmonberry bushes with a crash.

"We go about things very differently, don't we?" he commented.

"Yes and no." I surveyed the dozen alder stumps on what had been Clyde Moreland's original homesite. Sunlight from a ragged blue hole in the forest canopy lit the hillside, probably for the first time in the three and a half decades since Moreland had moved his house and the trees had taken over.

Pete unscrewed the chainsaw's gas cap and sloshed the tank to see if it was low. "Well, you've been messing around building a cabin over here on the Sahalie for what, seven years? I figure it's time to come show you how to do it right."

"You mean, mess around?" I almost asked him who was going to clean up all the tree branches we had just felled across the trail below, but I was afraid I already knew the answer.

"No, build a cabin. After all these years you've got a crooked building that's full of mice. It doesn't even have a view of the river. I'll have mine up in three weeks, tight and true." He stretched and took in the view. "The old homesteader knew what he was doing when he built up on this hill. You can see everything from here."

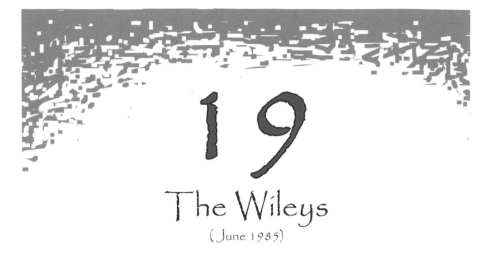

Pete and my father had been talking about building a guest cabin for several summers, but I had never really believed it would get past the sketches-on-paper-napkins stage. Why would the family need a second cabin on this remote property? And—this time I voiced my thought aloud—"Why do you have to do it so fast? It's not like we're running some kind of race."

Pete smiled. My brother is only fifteen months older than I. The two of us grew up with a competitive spirit. When we were teenagers we shared a newspaper delivery route on alternate days. I once boasted I could do the entire job by bicycle in sixty minutes. Shortly afterwards Pete got his drivers license, bought a motorcycle, and completed the route in fifty minutes.

"I can only spare three weeks' vacation for this, so I've got to be efficient," Pete said. He set a gasoline can on a stump and unscrewed its spout to refill the chainsaw. "But I think cabin building deserves the same kind of scientific method I've been bringing to the forestry over here. Dad and I are pre-fabbing the cabin frame out of plywood. He's working on that now in Salem. In four days we'll start assembling the finished panels here on the site."

"You're not going to dynamite a new road around the hill, are you?" I recalled Pete's plan to set of string of charges on the slope above the river.

"No." Pete frowned. "I got my dynamite handler's permit, but Dad says he'd rather we carry the building materials in by hand. If I slam my pickup hard enough on the old road, we'll only have to walk a few hundred yards."

While Pete refueled the chainsaw I looked again at the twelve-by-sixteen-foot rectangle he had marked with orange stakes. "The original cabin here was called the house on the stump. I guess this one will be the house on a dozen stumps."

"The stumps will rot away. I'm putting in pressure-treated foundation posts, soaked in chemical preservative."

"When do those go in?"

"Tomorrow." Pete screwed the gas cap back in place and raised the saw, ready to return to work.

"That's the solstice," I said.

"What?"

"Tomorrow is June 21. The longest day of the year. Why don't you come over to the log cabin for our solstice campfire? Susan will be there. She's bringing her kids for the weekend."

Pete paused, his hand on the starter cord. "A solstice celebration? Do you run around naked, chanting like druids?"

I laughed. "You can if you want. We usually just roast marshmallows, watching to see how late the sky stays light. Then I tell a ghost story."

"Ah, a ghost story. Like what happened to the first guy who built a cabin here?"

"That's the tradition. Want to hear it?"

He grinned and pulled the cord.

The next day I hiked out at noon to unlock the cable across the gas line road for Susan. I was lost in thought as I crossed the road culvert at Butterfield Creek, worrying about money. This was the fifth summer since Janell had given me a seven-year ultimatum to make a living from my freelance writing, and I was contemplating a desperate plan to research a risky book. Suddenly a large animal crashed away into the brush beside the road.

Instantly my thoughts snapped back to here and now, my heart pounding. Had I startled a bear? Although I knew that black bears do not eat people, it was hard to shake the thought that they could if they wanted. The crashing continued in the salmonberry bushes up the creek, seemingly loud enough for a rhinoceros. Now that I looked closer I could make out pathways trampled through the brush. At least one of the tracks resembled a pair of pointy four-inch parentheses. It looked like the hoofprint of an elk. Bull elk are great, shaggy animals that can weigh half a ton. They defend their territory by charging with their antlers.

I continued warily the final half mile to the county road and unlocked the cable. Ten minutes later Susan's little Ford Escort drove up Wilson Road in a cloud of gravel dust. The back seat was packed tight with gear and kids.

Susan rolled down her window and smiled. "Sorry if we're late."

"No, not at all. I just got here." I noticed my sister had cut her long brown hair to shoulder length. She was wearing new half-lens spectacles—perhaps reading glasses. They made her seem much older. Was she already forty?

Susan's husband Nick leaned across the seat. "We've been in this car over four hours from Olympia. If the kids don't get out soon they're going to riot."

Curly black hair and a full beard wreathed Nick's handsomely chiseled features, a reminder of his Greek heritage. But his Greekness did not extend far. He supplemented Susan's part-time counseling income by giving clients Chinese herbal medicines and massage therapy. The last I'd heard he was planning a trip to Asia to study acupuncture.

"The gas line road's too rough for your car," I said. "Just park here out of sight of the main road and I'll help you carry your stuff in the rest of the way."

A voice from the back seat piped, "Mom says we'll see lions and tigers and bears!"

"I don't know about the lions and tigers, but I'd give you even odds on the rest of that zoo."

The backseat voice squealed as Susan drove down the road to find a parking spot. I locked the cable behind them and caught up in time to help load their gear into backpacks. Susan's eldest, Mike, was happily chanting, "Bears, bears, bears," as he stuffed his jacket, water bottle, and toy panda into his backpack. He was a dark-haired, very talkative five-year-old, about Karen's age. His little sister Eva was a skinny, wide-eyed two year old of few words. Nick asked her, "Do you want to be carried in the backpack?" She replied, "No." Nick nodded and strapped her into the backpack.

"Didn't she just say 'No'?" I asked.

"Well yes," Nick admitted. "But 'no' is her second most favorite word. She uses it for almost everything, including yes."

"How can you tell what she means?"

Nick shrugged. "It used to be, we couldn't. Now we've learned to listen closer. 'No!' means no, and 'no…' is yes."

"I see," I said, although I wasn't sure I did. "And what is her most favorite word?"

My sister Susan answered, "Wiley."

"Wiley? What's that?"

Susan swung on her backpack and locked the car door. "It's the name of our neighbor's dog. Lately, every dog or cat she sees is a Wiley."

"Are we really going to see a bear?" Mike piped in.

Susan smiled. "We were just kidding about that, Mike." She turned to me. Her smile twitched slightly. "I was kidding. Weren't you, Bill?"

"Actually—" I paused, realizing I had their full attention. "I *did* hear something in the brush on the way here. Probably just an elk."

"Probably?" Susan asked.

"No," Eva announced enigmatically.

"Cool! Bear attack!" Mike took the toy panda out of his pack and waved it in front of us.

Nick frowned earnestly. "What do you think? Would it be best if we banged pots, or kept quiet and tried to sneak past?"

"Let's just hike in," I suggested. "The black bears here are pretty small and they run away as soon as they see people."

Despite this reassurance, Susan's family crept up the road behind me like stalkers on safari. I didn't want to seem worried—and I had pretty well convinced myself that the animal I had heard must have been an elk. Wasn't the hoofprint evidence enough?"

But then we edged around a corner in the road and there in the tall grass beside Butterfield Creek was the black, furry back of a very large animal. Even with its head down, I could see this obviously was not an elk.

Mike dropped his panda and stared open-mouthed.

Susan whispered through her teeth, "That's not what I'd call small, and it's not running away. Nick, *do* something."

Nick held up his hands and roared like an angry gorilla. Little Eva stood up in his backpack, clinging to his curly hair.

Down at the creek the large black animal lifted its head, blinked at us, and mooed.

"Wiley!" Eva gasped.

The rest of us laughed. Susan put her hand to her forehead. "A wily cow, anyway. How did it escape from the pasture?"

"I don't know," I said. "The Niemis said we should have thirty-one. Last time I counted, they were all there."

The black heifer kicked up its heels and trotted back into the forest. We continued our hike, passing Pete's beat-up pickup truck and following the river trail around the big hill. When we reached Pete's cabin site, he was digging a hole for a foundation post. He showed Susan's family the plans for his cabin, and they offered encouragement. Then we told Pete the story of Wild Cow and shared a laugh. After renewing my invitation to join our solstice campfire that evening, we left Pete to his work and hiked another quarter mile to the log cabin at the far end of the pasture.

When we approached the gate, thirty-one heifers were milling along the fence, tails swishing intently.

Eva stood up in her backpack. She pointed like a sailor in a crow's nest and cried, "Wileys!"

A moment later Karen appeared on the cabin porch, pointed at us, and cried, "Kids!"

Soon the four children were running off toward the creek, with Karen in the lead, to hunt for frogs. Meanwhile Janell, who had been planting a garden in a small tilled area just inside the fence, stopped to help Susan and Nick lay out their sleeping bags in the log cabin for the night.

When we returned to the front yard with tea and cookies we found our striped Siamese cat Kitsa pawing in the garden dirt. Janell groaned and shooed the cat away. "That beast of ours likes to pee in the garden because it's easy digging. The rows are going to come up so crooked it will look like the gardener was drunk."

"What did you plant?" Susan asked.

"Forty-day peas. That means they're supposed to be ripe in forty days."

Nick smiled. "I guess the cat thinks a forty-day pea means something else."

At this point the children trooped back from the creek, their shoes muddy, triumphantly carrying a bucket covered with a skunk cabbage leaf. "Look what we got!" Mike exclaimed.

"Are they Wileys?" I asked.

Eva looked thoughtful. "No…"

"Well let's put them in the wading pool for now. They all have to go back to the creek before the campfire tonight."

Karen and Mike tipped the bucket into the kids' plastic pool while Ian and Eva watched closely. The haul consisted of six rough-skinned newts, four frogs, and a snail. The newts promptly swam to the bottom of the pool, wagging their tails in graceful S-curves. The frogs paddled about the pool's edge, but couldn't find a place to jump out. I rescued the snail and put it back in the bucket.

"This one's named Goldie," Karen announced, pointing to a frog with broad yellow stripes on its sides. "The other frogs are Brownie, Biggie, and Littlie."

"What's the snail's name?" I asked.

"Snaily," Ian informed me seriously.

Mike grabbed one of the newts and held it up. "I caught three of the waterdogs. Look, they're orange underneath."

"That's a sign they're poisonous," I told him.

"Really? Cool."

"Orange is an easy color for predators like birds and raccoons to see. The only reason for a waterdog to be orange is to warn things away."

"Is it dangerous?" Mike asked.

"Not unless you eat it. Or kiss it. The skin's the poisonous part."

"Maybe it would turn into a prince if you kissed it," Karen suggested.

"Maybe, but you'd barf."

Mike nodded, eyeing the newt critically.

"Come on," I said. "Everyone has to wash their hands before you can have cookies." The kids crowded around the washbasin on the cabin porch. Then they charged toward the plate of cookies on the picnic table. On my way to join the adults in folding chairs nearby, I casually floated a small board in the wading pool, knowing the frogs would soon crawl onto it and jump to freedom.

"Don't eat it, Mike!" Susan said sharply, and for a moment I was afraid he had decided to sample a newt after all. Instead I saw that Mike had stolen the last cookie from his sister. He was about to put it in his mouth, but Susan had caught his shoulder. "Give it back to Eva."

Mike still held the cookie within biting range. He glanced to his mother. "What if I don't?"

Her grip tightened slightly. "I'll squeeze your shoulder."

"How much?"

"A lot. Give it back."

Mike weighed this option a moment before reluctantly handing Eva the cookie.

Susan let go of his shoulder. She looked to us. "Mike's a bargainer. The other day I told him to finish eating his salad. He told me, 'OK, I'll eat the salad if you give me two grapes and tell me an extra bedtime story."

Janell and I laughed, and one of the heifers at the fence mooed.

"What's with these cows, anyway?" Nick asked. "They've been standing here with their heads through the fence rails for ten minutes."

"It's in their neuron paths," Janell said.

Nick looked at her questioningly.

Janell explained. "Since they were calves it's been burned into their brains that fences mean food. They were hardly a day old when the Niemis put them in a stall. They learned if they stick their heads through the slats in the stall fence the farmer gives them milk from a pail. Later they're fed hay through a fence. Now they're trained."

"But you've dug a garden here. There's nothing but dirt clods on this side of the fence."

"Right. And I've reinforced the fence with barbed wire and extra rails," I said. "It takes a lot of determination to jam their heads through like this."

"I guess it's reassuring for them to think that the fence still provides," Susan mused. We watched the dozen heifer heads jockeying for position between the fence rails. "Still, you think one of them, someday, would wonder why you're giving them dirt to eat."

Karen galloped up with a couple of empty grain sacks and swished them in front of the heifer's black noses. They jerked back and waved their heads.

"Karen, that's teasing," I chided. "They think you're going to feed them grain."

Janell explained to Susan and Nick, "We got these sacks from the Niemis for hauling stuff. The burlap still smells like alfalfa pellets."

"I've got an idea!" Karen said. She called to Ian and Mike, "Come on!" She gave them each a bag and opened the gate wide enough for them to slip out into the pasture.

"Is that safe?" Susan asked, concerned. She caught Eva and held her on her lap.

"It's pretty safe," I said. "The heifers move when Karen orders them around. She's fearless." Still, I followed the children to the gate, where I could intervene if necessary. Karen obviously wanted to show off for her cousins. My first thought was that she was going to play at bullfighting by waving a grain sack in front of a heifer. Instead she put the sack over her head and mooed.

All of us laughed. The sack covered her to her knees. She really did look like a feed bag with legs.

The heifers pulled their heads out of the fence and stared at her, obviously dumbfounded. They edged forward uncertainly, necks outstretched, sniffing at this miraculous walking grain sack. Never before had they seen food that marched up to them.

When the heifers had formed a semicircle around Karen she reached down, picked up a stick, and began bopping them on the noses. The heifers jumped back and frisked around in confused wonder. It was weird enough to meet a walking grain sack, but to have it hit them on the head was absolutely bewildering.

"Enough, Karen," I said, laughing. By now Ian and Mike had put bags over their heads too, but they seemed to lack Karen's navigational sense. They merely bumped into each other. I herded all three of the grain sacks back inside the yard and closed the gate—just as the heifers galloped away in confusion, heading for saner parts of the pasture.

"Which way are the cows?" Ian asked from inside his grain sack.

"I want to chase them too," Mike's sack said.

Janell and Susan were silently laughing behind their hands at the two disoriented little boys—until Ian backed into the wading pool and sat in it with a splash.

Karen took off her gain sack and clapped her hands. "Yes! We caught another critter!"

Janell pulled Ian out of the pool and began taking off his wet things. "But this critter we get to keep."

20

The Ghost Story

(June 1985)

> Everybody with second sight says this place is haunted.
> —Halldor Laxness, *Independent People*, 1946

On the evening of the summer solstice my brother Pete showed up with four paper bags. Susan's family and my own were sitting around a bonfire I had built in a pit near the garden.

"What's a party without fireworks?" Pete asked. "I bought some for each of the kids. Hope that's OK." Without a pause he passed out the bags to the wide-eyed children. "You can light them when it gets dark, but I have to do the rockets myself. I got them at the Sahalie Indian reservation where they're almost legal."

Karen, Ian, Mike, and Eva began excitedly pulling brightly packaged sparklers, poppers, and fountains out of their bags.

"This is the solstice, not the Fourth of July," Susan commented.

Pete shrugged. "Bill said anything goes. Besides, I figure there must be a reason they open those fireworks stands in June."

By this time Mike had convinced the children to dump their fireworks into four piles on a blanket so they could compare their loot. He began negotiations at once. "OK, I've got an idea for a deal. Eva, if you give me one of your Killer Bees, I'll trade you three colored sparklers and a Ground Bloom Flower."

Pete pulled up a folding chair. "By the Fourth of July I'll be nailing the roof on my cabin." He looked to me. "So how's the famous writer doing? Any spectacular projects lined up for the summer?"

I hesitated, unsure how my brother and sister would react to the plan I had dreamed up. "Actually, I'm thinking of hiking."

"Hiking? Where?"

"Across the state."

Pete looked puzzled. Susan leaned forward with a worried expression. "That's hundreds of miles. Why would you do that?"

I looked to Janell for help.

"It's one of his book ideas," she explained. "I'm not exactly wild about it either. It means he'll be gone for two months from August to October."

"I'm still not sure I follow," Susan said.

I tried to explain. "You know how Congress just designated two dozen Wilderness Areas in Oregon? I figure if I hike through them all, I can write two books—a nuts-and-bolts guidebook and an adventure story based on my journal."

Pete whistled. "Wow, what a scheme! Do you think you can really pull it off?"

"I don't know." I put another log on the campfire, sending a shower of sparks into the deepening blue of the twilight sky. "I'm planning to start at the westernmost point of Oregon, at Cape Blanco, and go all the way to the easternmost point in Hells Canyon. From the Pacific to Idaho, the route I've mapped out is over a thousand miles."

Susan shook her head. Her husband Nick asked, "What will you do for food?"

"I'm putting together nine boxes to mail ahead to checkpoints along the way. I figure my backpack will still weigh fifty or sixty pounds. I've been warming up by hiking ten miles a day with a pack full of firewood." I shrugged. "I don't know. Can it be any harder than building a log cabin by hand?"

"Yes, and more dangerous too," Susan said, frowning. "What happened to that other writing project you were working on?"

I sighed. There had been several other book projects. Two years ago I had written a how-to book on building garden carts and bicycle trailers—and it had sold 11,000 copies—but because I had signed the first contract the publisher offered, I had earned only $1500. That had not been enough to reset the clock ticking away on my deadline to earn a living as a freelance writer. Janell had given me seven years, and five of them were already gone. Last year I had written a historical novel. Most likely, this was the writing project Susan meant. "I sent the manuscript of my novel to an agent, but it's like dropping a book into a black hole. It seems you never hear anything back. I need something else to work on, and I've always liked backpacking."

"Good," Pete said. "Then I'll count on you to help pack in the plywood panels for my cabin next week."

"That wasn't what I had in mind." I glanced at my brother sideways. Was he needling me or was he serious? His entire cabin project put me on edge. Sometimes I thought he was building it as a challenge.

Certainly it felt like an intrusion on the pioneer lifestyle Janell and I had crafted for our summers. We were both stubborn enough that a collision of wills would make sparks fly.

"Hey, is it dark enough yet for fireworks?" Karen interrupted.

We looked at the sky. A pale blue glow lit the horizon almost all the way around us, the luminescent shore of a vast sky-lake overhead. Already a first planet shimmered from the depths.

"It's not quite ten o'clock, but I think we could light a few," Pete said. He took a matchbox from his pocket. "Who wants to go first?"

The four kids looked at each other. Ian clutched a bright yellow Killer Bees package in his hand. "If you light them, do they burn up?"

"Yes, that's what fireworks do," Pete said.

"I'm gonna keep mine," Ian announced.

Pete shrugged. "How about you, Eva? You want to light yours?"

"No," she said uncertainly.

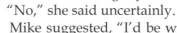

Mike suggested, "I'd be willing to light one of my color sparklers if everybody else shoots two of their poppers and roasts me a marshmallow."

"One sparkler?" Pete scoffed. "I thought you kids wanted to see fireworks."

"We're still trading them around, Uncle Pete," Karen explained. "We want to keep ours and watch you shoot off your rockets."

"Weird," Pete said. But then he got out his arsenal of Sahalie fireworks and started lighting rockets. The first red explosion sent our cat streaking into the cabin for cover. The second rocket slipped—perhaps not entirely by accident—and screamed low across the pasture. It detonated like a clap of lightning twenty feet above the heifers. They kicked up their heels and stampeded toward the river.

"Oops." Pete grinned. "I'd better be more careful." He began firing his rockets in twos and threes, more nearly overhead. We oohed and aahed for each of the fiery sky flowers. The last and largest rocket spiraled into the sky, frantically whistling higher and higher. When it vanished among the stars we all held our breaths, expecting a giant fireball. But nothing happened.

"Huh," Pete said. "That one cost twenty bucks. A guy on the reservation sold it to me under the counter. He said it was the best of all."

I smiled, remembering what Butch had told me last summer about the Sahalie tradition of dealing with gullible outsiders.

"Maybe it's OK to end with a mystery," Janell commented. "That last rocket sounded a bit like the spiral bird. We never see them either."

"A spiral bird?" Nick asked.

"We don't know what they really are, but we hear them calling from the salmonberry bushes all the time. Bill says they're actually Skookum spirits."

The solstice night was now dark enough that the dwindling campfire cast flickering orange shadows on our faces. " I leaned forward and spoke in a low, ominous voice. "The vengeful Skookums are lurking in the woods even now."

"Ghost story!" Karen exclaimed, clapping her hands.

"Wait," Pete said. "First tell me about these Skookums."

"Oh, it's an old legend that the Sahalie Indians tell," I explained. "They say evil spirits lived at Skookum Rock until they were driven out. Now they wander around looking for revenge."

"Skookum Rock?" Susan asked. "Isn't that where a guy was murdered last year?"

"That's right. Barry Bartola got shot when he tried to drive through a private gate on the way to Skookum Rock. Bartola owned the rock and wanted to build an RV park there. At the trial, the lawyer claimed Bartola was violating a sacred Indian site."

"So was he really killed by Skookums?" Pete asked.

"Maybe." I never had figured out how Valerie Boucher and her son had won acquittal. According to Butch's version of events, Bartola's wife had witnessed the whole thing. Bartola had been shot twice, and the Bouchers had been standing at the gateway with two rifles. Maybe the jury couldn't decide which of the Bouchers had aimed the fatal bullet. Rather than convict the wrong person, the jury might simply have decided to let them both go free.

I mused aloud, "There's also a connection between Barry Bartola and Clyde Moreland, the old homesteader who lived here."

Pete raised his eyebrows. "Other than that they were both murdered?"

"Yes. Before Bartola owned Skookum Rock, it belonged to Moreland."

"Aha!" Pete shot a dark and meaningful glance toward the children. "I think we have enough information to start your ghost story now."

"Uh oh," Eva said.

Ian clutched his Killer Bees a little closer.

"Make it really scary this year, Papa!" Karen squealed.

Susan held up her hand. "Don't overdo it. Eva's only two."

"Just the facts, ma'am," I said innocently. "All I do is tell what happened to Clyde Moreland. It's sort of a tradition. Each year Janell and I learn a couple of new clues about the case and I put them into the story."

Janell gave me a wry smile. "At least it usually *starts* with the facts." She opened a bag of marshmallows and began putting them on sticks for the children to roast.

"Right." I pushed back my sleeves. "So the story starts in 1917, when Clyde Moreland was a young man studying law at Portland State University. He wasn't doing that well in school, so when the United States declared war on Germany he joined the Army. They gave him a rifle and sent him into the trenches in France. In the first battle, a shell with poison mustard gas exploded nearby. It burned his lungs so badly that he was sent to a makeshift hospital in a French village for three weeks to recover. And that's where he met someone who changed his life."

"A beautiful Belgian nurse!" Pete exclaimed, leaning forward into the circle of firelit faces.

"What?" I demanded, impatient at this interruption. "The truth is, he met a Frenchman named Boucher."

"No! Didn't you know about his wife Josephine?" Pete asked, feigning incredulity.

I put my hands on my hips. "Clyde Moreland never married."

"That's what people here thought, because it was a *secret* marriage," Pete said mysteriously.

"Really?" Karen asked. She was holding a stick over a bank of glowing coals, slowly roasting her marshmallow to a puffy golden brown. "What was Josephine like?"

At this point I realized that Pete had commandeered my tale—yet another example of our sibling rivalry, I suppose. If Pete could show he was better at inventing stories, he would cheapen my freelance writing efforts. I decided to bide my time until he ran aground. Then I would step in and pick up the pieces.

"She was rich," Pete continued. "Josephine came from a family of wealthy diamond merchants in Antwerp. As soon as Clyde had recovered enough that he could be discharged from the Army, he eloped to Monaco with Josephine. There they bribed a drunken monk to marry them in the cathedral at midnight."

"That sounds pretty reckless," Susan objected. "Wasn't she worried that Clyde was marrying her for her family's money?"

"Yes, she was," Pete said. "Before the ceremony she made him sign an agreement that he'd give all her money back to her family if she died childless."

Karen took a bite of gooey marshmallow off her stick and spoke with her mouth full. "So what happened?"

"They went back to the Monte Carlo hotel, where they ordered champagne and jellied eels from room service."

"Yuck," Ian said, watching Pete with large eyes. Meanwhile the stick Ian had been holding sagged into the fire, and his marshmallow burst into flames. He began frantically waving the stick.

Pete nodded. "Clyde thought eels were yucky too, but Josephine insisted they were a delicacy back home in Antwerp. Then they got into a big fight about whether they would live in Belgium or Oregon. Clyde stomped out, went to the casino next door, and lost $20,000 playing roulette on her credit. When he came back, she was dead."

"Dead?" Janell asked. "How?"

"Poisoned by eels past their pull date."

It was time to step in. "Pete, that's not a ghost story. If you're going to scare anybody, you've got to tell them about the loophole Clyde found in the marriage contract." I knew if Pete asked 'What loophole?' I'd be back in the saddle again.

"What loophole?" Pete asked.

"Well, Clyde had studied to be a lawyer, right? When he realized he couldn't pay back his $20,000 gambling debt without her money, he took a closer look at their contract. It really did say that he'd have to give back all her money if she died childless. But it was supposed to be paid to her uncle in Antwerp on the day of her burial."

"So?"

I lowered my voice. "So Clyde didn't bury her. He had her body put in a glass coffin filled with helium. The mortician assured him she could last that way indefinitely. Only her eyes would have to be replaced with something more permanent. Clyde dressed Josephine up in her white wedding gown and draped her favorite diamond necklace across her throat. Then he had the mortician replace her eyes with giant blue sapphires from her earrings."

I could see the children move closer to the fire to keep from shivering. The marshmallows were forgotten. My sister Susan gave me a warning glance. I hurried on.

"Once Clyde convinced the authorities that he got to keep Josephine's money as long as her body stayed above ground, he moved back to Oregon. But it's hard to live in Portland with a corpse in a glass coffin. Before long he decided to move to a homestead out here on the Sahalie River where people would ask fewer questions. The last of Josephine's money went to outfit Clyde's new farm. He bought horses, a plow, dairy cattle, and chickens. He built a little cabin on a stump right where Pete is building one now. He even invited all the neighbors up and down the valley for a housewarming. But none of them guessed what he was hiding in the little locked shed behind the house."

I felt as if I had rescued the story after Pete's detour. I gave him a look that said as much.

"Well, that's not a very scary ending," Pete said, rising to my unspoken challenge. "You didn't even tell about the farm foreclosure."

Pete was doing exactly what I had done to him. Still, he was stealing the stage so smoothly I really didn't have any choice but to ask, "What foreclosure?"

"I thought you'd never ask." Pete picked up the story with a smile. "When the Great Depression hit, Clyde's crops failed three years in a row. Finally the county sheriff came up in a boat and handed him a foreclosure notice. Either Clyde had to pay $5000 in back taxes or he'd lose the farm. At first Clyde panicked, because he'd spent all of Josephine's money. But the thought of Josephine reminded him of something she still had: a $5000 diamond necklace."

Susan groaned. "Oh, no."

"Oh, yes," Pete said grimly. "While the sheriff waited in the cabin, Clyde took a hammer and slowly approached the locked shed. He'd never loved Josephine very much, but over the past fifteen years he'd started to hate and then to fear this corpse he couldn't bury—this thing behind the house. When he unlocked the shed, there she was, staring at him through the glass coffin, as beautiful as the day they were married, but with a new, demonic glare from the sapphire eyes. He concentrated on the diamond necklace at her throat, raised his hammer, and smashed the glass."

Pete raised a stick over his head and brought it down into the embers of the campfire. All of us jerked back. "A whoosh of air rushed through the broken glass. Josephine began to sag in the coffin, her skin suddenly wrinkling. Terrified, Clyde grabbed the necklace, dashed outside, and slammed the shed door. Then he staggered back into the cabin with the necklace in his trembling hands, bloody from the glass. The money saved the farm, but Clyde didn't talk much after that. People said he had a haunted look, and whenever the wind moaned in the trees at night, he would stare out the window in terror, as if he expected to see a pair of glowing sapphire eyes."

For a moment we stared into the fire in silence. Then Susan announced, "All right, that's it. Eva, have you heard enough?"

A very small voice answered, "No."

"Are you ready to go to bed?"

"No!"

Susan gathered the little girl up in a blanket. "I think that means yes."

Janell turned a flashlight on, momentarily dispelling the spooky mood. "Come on, Ian, it's past bedtime for you too." She and Susan walked up to the log cabin with the two sleepy-eyed children.

When they were gone Nick pushed the fire together to burn the last of the wood. "Actually, that was a pretty good story, Pete. But you forgot to bring in the Skookums."

"And you left Clyde Moreland alive," I added. "It's supposed to be a murder mystery. You have to make us afraid that something horrible is still out there, looking for its next victim."

Karen raised her hand excitedly, as if she hoped to be called on next. "I know, I know!"

"What, Karen?"

"I know how it ends! After Clyde Moreland sells the diamond necklace the farm keeps losing more money, and the next time the sheriff comes for the taxes, Clyde has to go back into the shed to get the sapphires!"

"Yeah," Mike said, chuckling. "But by then her corpse is all rotting away, with, like, green flesh hanging off of her bones."

"And afterwards the Skookums come and take over Josephine's body, so she's a zombie, stomping around trying to get her eyeballs back." Karen giggled. "That's why Clyde Moreland moves his house across the river. Because he wants to get away from her, you know?"

"Until a rainy night in 1962," I added darkly, "When Moreland was shot to death by his own military rifle out in his yard."

Nick cast me a sidelong glance. "That part really happened, didn't it?"

"Yes, it did. But there was one hideous fact the district attorney never revealed at the inquest."

"What's that?"

I curled my fingers into claws and lowered my voice. "When the police found Clyde Moreland's corpse, both of his eyeballs were missing."

The next day, concerned that Pete and I really might have frightened the small children with our tale-telling competition, I asked Ian how he had liked the Clyde Moreland story.

"It was OK," he replied. "But you should have put a bunny in it."

21

A Different Cabin

(July 1985)

> All hands that are well employed in cutting logs and raising our winter cabins. The fleas were so troublesome last night that I made but a broken night's rest.
>
> —William Clark, The Journals of Lewis and Clark, 1805

My brother Pete planned his cabin to be as different from mine as possible. This must have been challenging, given that the remoteness of our Sahalie property made modern construction techniques difficult. We still had no road access. Electricity and plumbing were out of the question. And even though a natural gas pipeline ran underground through our field, it was a long-distance transmission line a foot in diameter, under such pressure that it could be tapped only if you first built an entire utility substation.

Nonetheless, Pete tackled his cabin project with the zeal of a missionary building a demonstration house for the elucidation of benighted jungle natives. Money was not a problem for Pete, as it was for Janell and me. Where we had thinned trees from the nearby forest to get free logs, Pete bought plywood and two-by-fours from a lumber store in Salem. Where we had used local rocks for the foundations, Pete hauled in concrete blocks for footings. Where I had left eighteen inches of air space below the first log to prevent rot, Pete bought wooden piers treated with expensive chemical preservatives and buried them in the dirt.

But Pete really did assemble his cabin in just three weeks. And as it went up day by day, Janell and I began to realize that speed was not the only advantage Pete's design had over our low-tech pioneer style.

Log cabins, by their very nature, tend to be dark inside. If the openings for windows or doors are too large, they weaken the structure of interlocking logs. Freed from such constraints, Pete brightened his cabin with a sliding glass door facing the river, picture windows in sliding aluminum frames, and additional triangular windows in the sleeping loft. Perched on a hill amid alders, the cabin's glass walls lent it the airy feel of a tree house.

Another perhaps surprising drawback of log cabin construction is that the heavy log walls really do not provide good insulation. With no dead air spaces, solid logs transmit cold or heat quickly. On the rare occasions we visited in winter, our log cabin was chilly even with the stove going full blast. And although I had mortared every imaginable chink with cement, mice somehow still managed to keep slipping in.

Pete, on the other hand, had needed merely to fill the small cracks between his plywood panels with latex caulk to make his cabin virtually airtight. No mouse or mosquito could find its way in. Even a modest fire in a small box stove heated the room so quickly he needed to open one of the screened windows.

Throughout the construction process, Dad pitched in with hammer and saw while Mom provided support with kettle and broom. I stopped by on my daily warm-up hiking regimen to help carry loads of building materials in from Pete's pickup.

As the allotted three weeks drew to a close, Pete nailed on a roof of composite asphalt-and-fiberglass shingles and rolled out a floor of sheet vinyl. Then, on the last day before they had to leave, Pete and my parents invited us over for their housewarming. Janell brought home-baked rolls. My mother provided potato salad and apricot Jello. Pete opened a half-case of canned beer for the celebration.

Karen and Ian quickly discovered the ladder Grandpa Wes had built to the sleeping loft overlooking the main room below. A nicely crafted railing with mahogany slats allowed the children to play on the sleeping bags up there without danger of falling. Janell admired the propane system Pete had rigged up. Narrow copper tubing connected a replaceable five-gallon tank under the house with a gas light fixture overhead, a four-burner range, and even a small propane refrigerator. I was impressed with the deck outside the sliding glass door. Cantilevered over the hillside on tall posts, the eight-by-sixteen-foot platform made the cabin seem much larger, but still managed to preserve its tree house ambiance.

To be sure, evidence of the cabin's hasty construction was everywhere. The outside plywood shell was still unpainted. Inside, the décor consisted of mismatched cabinets Pete had found at a factory seconds sale. He had nailed the cupboards, seemingly at random, onto the walls' otherwise bare two-by-four studs. Folding chairs and planks on sawhorses completed the furnishings. But it was astonishing how much had been accomplished in so little time.

"Will you be staying here a lot?" Janell asked.

My father looked to Pete. "I'm afraid I've used up my vacation for this summer. How about you?"

Pete tipped back his chair and put his feet up on the deck railing. "I plan to do this whole vacation thing differently." He tilted his beer can toward me. "Each June, you guys bum a ride over here and stay here the whole summer. Now me, I see this as a place for quick getaways whenever I want—even just for a day or a few hours. That's why I've joined WULAC."

"What's WULAC?" I asked, opening a beer for myself.

"The Willamette Ultra-Light Aircraft Club."

"An aircraft club? You're getting a pilot's license?" Dad asked, eyebrows raised. He had served as the co-pilot of a B-17 bomber in World War II, and sometimes grew wistful about flying.

"No, no. You don't need a pilot's license if your aircraft weighs less than 500 pounds, including yourself and your gear. So what you do is mount a lightweight engine and propeller on a hang glider. Then off you go. You can fly wherever you want. As long as you stay under a 500-foot ceiling, of course, so you don't get in the way of regular airplane traffic."

My mother frowned. "This whole thing sounds awfully dangerous."

Pete shrugged. "That's why I'm training with a club that knows the rules. I figure I'll be able to take off in the field behind my house in McMinnville and land an hour later here in the pasture at the Sahalie."

"To fly here from McMinnville you'd have to cross the entire Coast Range," my father objected. "That's sixty miles of uninhabited forest. What happens if you run out of gas?"

"I won't."

"What if there's a storm?"

Pete popped open another beer. "It's a hang glider. I'll ride it out."

My mother gave the rest of us a worried look. I knew what she was thinking. This new scheme of Pete's was even more reckless than his plan to blow up a road route with dynamite charges, and she had less leverage to stop it.

"Don't worry, Mom. He probably won't get over here much anyway," I said.

"What do you mean by that?" Pete asked, an edge to his voice.

I should have backpedaled, retreating to an innocuous comment about the demands of his work and the shortage of vacation time. But the can of beer had made me incautious, and our old rivalry spoke with its own voice. "You didn't really build this cabin as a getaway, did you, Pete? You built it to prove a point. To teach us log cabin builders a les-

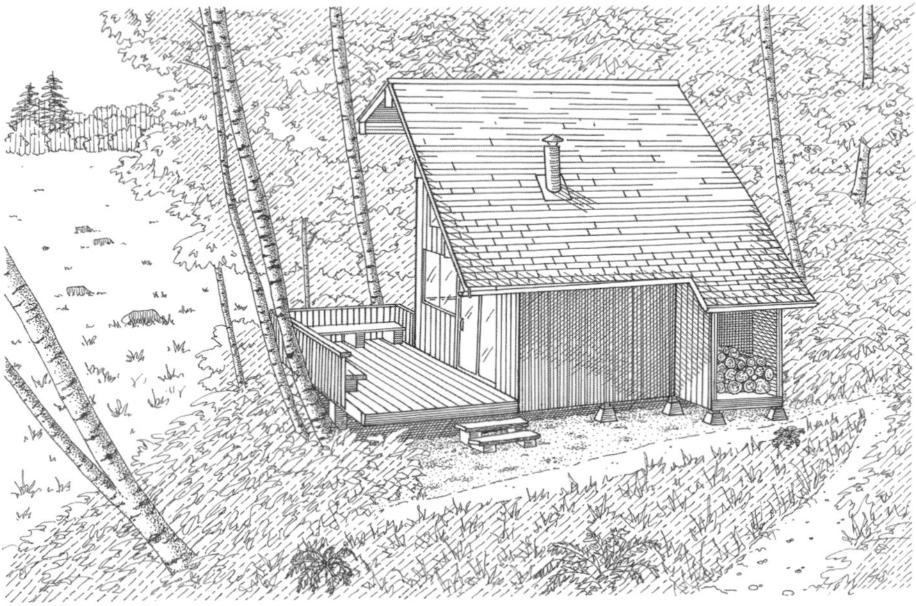

son. Now that you're done you're not likely to stick around."

At once I could feel the mood shift against me. My father shook his head. "Pete and I built this cabin together, Bill. It was as much my idea as his, and we certainly didn't do it to criticize all the work you've done over here."

"That's right," my mother added. "It was supposed to bring the family closer together. Now there's room for everyone to come visit at once."

Pete added, "Up to now, Mom and Dad have had to camp out in a backpacking tent when they're here. Now they'll have a comfortable place to stay. We thought you and Janell might want to use the place too."

"Really?" Janell asked.

"Of course you already have a cabin," my mother said, "But you might want to come over to store milk in the refrigerator or to bake a cake in a real oven."

Janell nodded, considering these advantages.

I realized that I had made a stupid mistake by criticizing Pete's motives. I was about to apologize when Pete said, "See, Bill? You've got a lot of lessons left to learn."

"Like what?" I asked. There was a tone of challenge in both our voices.

"Like what the land here is really about. I plan to use this cabin as a base for intensifying my forestry management plan. We're sitting on some of the most valuable commercial timberland in the world, and you've been neglecting it."

I looked to my parents. "Is that why you bought this property? To clearcut the forest?" After eight summers of living at the Sahalie, I had become possessive about the trees. It hurt me to see them cut, even though they did not belong to me.

My mother bit her lip.

"Well, not all at once, no," my father replied. "We don't need the money right now. But property like this is a big investment. And Pete's done a lot of research about selective logging."

Pete continued, "This place could be a valuable piece of Mom and Dad's retirement plan. That's why it's important to upgrade the value of the forest. Right now, twenty-five percent of the trees here are alder. Twenty-five percent! After all the summers you've been here, and after all my work on improvement projects, the forest is still full of weed species."

"Maybe that's good," Janell said quietly. We turned to her. "I read an article in an environmental magazine that says scientists recently discovered that alders fix nitrogen. Alders have an orange fungus that grows on their roots. For years nobody knew why the fungus didn't seem to be hurting the trees. It turns out the fungus is symbiotic, creating natural fertilizer. Now they're saying a healthy forest needs alder once in a while to fix nitrogen, just like a wheat farmer has to rotate in a crop of clover every few years."

Pete rolled his eyes. "I read an article like that too. But no forester is going to wait thirty years for weeds to grow fungus. Alder logs are only worth half as much as Douglas fir at a mill. If the forest needs nitrogen, the most cost effective plan is to get rid of the alders, buy fertilizer, and spread it by helicopter."

"Is that your idea of a getaway vacation?" I asked angrily. "Coming over here to chainsaw alders, and then spray chemical shit on the stumps?"

"That's enough, both of you," my mother tried to break in.

But Pete was already laughing. "Here's Mr. Back-To-Nature complaining that I like to work even when I have time off." He pointed a finger at me. "Your problem is that you don't have a job at all. For the last umpteen years you've been leeching off your wife's daycare paycheck."

Janell gasped. "Preschool is *not* daycare! And Bill works harder than anyone I know. He's written two books and dozens of articles and designed bicycles carts so people won't have to use cars, and now—." She broke off angrily.

"And now what?" Pete narrowed his eyes. "Now he's going to show the world what it means to be a crazy hippie. He's going to hike a thousand miles across Oregon so he can hug every tree in the state."

"That's cute, Pete." I banged my fist down on the bench. "And you think you're Mr. Practical, piloting a motorized hang glider across the Coast Range? You're the one who's crazy!"

"Stop it!" Dad commanded, his face red.

My mother had covered her ears with her hands. In the silence that followed she lowered her hands, glaring imperiously at Pete and me. "This is not how our family behaves. Both of you are competent, lovable people. When you put your energies together, you can accomplish almost anything."

Out of the corner of my eye I could see Karen and Ian, pressing their faces against the glass of the loft's triangular window. I lowered my head, ashamed that I had set such a poor example for my own children. "I'm sorry I raised my voice. I didn't mean to talk like that."

"It was my fault too," Pete said quietly. "I let things get out of hand."

"From now on," our mother declared, her voice ringing with the same iron authority that had kept us in line as children, "this entire Sahalie property is going to be a safe haven for everyone in the family. As long as I live, no one at either of these cabins is allowed to argue in anger."

And so it was. In our family, when Mother spoke in That Voice, it was law. The argument between Pete and me would smolder quietly on, as dangerous and irreconcilable as ever. But Mother's edict would keep it from bursting into open flame again for years.

Janell and I did not have many visitors for the rest of that summer. Pete and my father really had used up their vacation time, and Susan had already come for the solstice. After our radio's batteries gave out, Janell and I found ourselves gradually growing hungrier and hungrier for news from the outside world.

Each morning it was my job to get up and light a fire in the stove. This involved lifting a cookplate lid, throwing a few sheets of crumpled newspaper inside, laying kindling on top, and lighting a match. But the process often took more than half an hour because of the newspapers. We had already used up our recent newspapers as fire starter. In fact, I had begun rummaging up ancient newspapers from the bottom of our storage can, some of them five or six summers old. Still, it seemed impossible to crumple them without at least reading the comics and the front page. Before long I would be engrossed in other articles as well.

One day Janell came down the spiral stairs, her hair tousled, and saw there still was no fire to cook breakfast. She asked with a yawn, "So what's the news?"

"There's been another bombing in the Middle East, I'm afraid," I said, shaking my head. "A big hurricane's headed for Mississippi, and there's a finance scandal in Congress."

"It figures. Anything upbeat?"

"Well, they've unearthed a new mummy in Egypt."

"Really? When was that?"

"Uh—" I look at the top of the page sheepishly. "Actually, June of 1978."

"Oh. Well, save the article for me anyway. Maybe you could start the fire with the classified ads." She wound the clock on the shelf above the kitchen sink. Then she compared her wristwatch. "What time do you have, Bill?"

I looked at my pocket watch. "Eight twenty. Why?"

"Our clock says eight, but my watch says it's nine."

"Maybe we should compromise," I suggested. "Let's call it eight thirty."

"Might as well." She began resetting the clock, but then stopped as if she had remembered something. "You know, last night I had a dream about our neighbors in Eugene, the Softiches."

I looked up from the newspaper. "What about them?"

"Well, Kay said they've decided to move to Portland."

"Oh?" At one level I knew this was not even gossip; it was merely a dream. But in a sense, it was still news. Our neighbors had been threatening to move for years. "Did she say what part of Portland?"

"Between Gresham and Troutdale, I think."

"That makes sense. They have a cousin out there they visited once, and it's close to a community college where Joe might be able to find work."

"Sure, but what a dull suburb, and the wind in winter is intolerable. Besides, it means Kay will have to quit her job at the pediatric office. I think they're making a mistake."

I nodded agreement. "Maybe we should invite Joe and Kay to come visit us here."

This switch back to reality stopped Janell for a moment. "Maybe we should. We could use some company. Now that Pete's cabin is done they could stay there. Do you think Pete will come flying over the hills one of these days to visit?"

"I don't think his motorized hang glider scheme will really get off the ground. But I bet we'll see his pickup again. Despite our argument."

"I wish we hadn't done that," Janell said. "I feel like it's our own fault if we're lonely this summer."

Karen's feet creaked on the ladder as she climbed down in her pajamas. "Is the mush ready yet?"

At this point Janell took the newspapers away from me and began crumpling the classified section for the fire. Then she stopped. "Hey, look at this. Here they're offering an apartment in downtown Eugene for only $150 a month!"

Karen and Ian dealt with the shortage of visiting kids by collecting pets. By turns we had containers of snakes, polliwogs, and caterpillars on the porch—until Janell or I judged that the animals had served a long enough sentence and deserved parole. Shortly after we had made Karen give up the last of these pets, she discovered that the entire area around the log cabin was populated by trolls. Before long both she and Ian were able to locate the trolls—usually in dark corners, but often right out in the open. At this point the children began carrying long, heavy sticks as magic wands.

"Why do your wands have to be so big?" I asked.

"So I can whack the trolls on the head," Karen explained. "It hurts."

"The wands wouldn't have to be magic to do that."

"Mostly we use them to turn the trolls into things."

Ian confided, "I turn them into trucks."

Karen grinned. "I turn my trolls into leaves and grass and twigs. See, Papa? They're all over!"

And they were.

This was also the summer that Ian learned to use the husicka by himself. Although he was nearly three years old, he had not yet been toilet trained. It didn't help when we pointed out that his cousin Eva had already mastered this skill. Eva had been afraid of our bathroom because it didn't flush. To overcome this barrier, Susan had hung a can of rocks beside the outhouse hole and convinced Eva that rattling the can provided the necessary flushing noise.

Ian's problem was that he simply didn't care. He didn't want to stop whatever he was doing to go to the outhouse. The turning point came when he learned to dress and undress himself. One day we simply decided to make changing wet pants *his* problem, rather than ours.

That afternoon Ian shuffled up to Janell while she was weeding in the garden. He announced, "Mama, I'm wet."

"Fine," she said. "Deal with it."

"What do you mean?"

"You know how to change your clothes. Go put on dry pants, dump the wet ones in the diaper bucket, and wash your hands. Then maybe you'll go potty in the outhouse next time."

With the downcast look of a bad dog told to leave home, Ian slowly shuffled back to the log cabin. I was working at the table inside, sorting through a stack of natural history books to collect information for my hike across Oregon.

"Papa, I'm wet," Ian announced to me.

"So I've heard." I pointed to the spiral stairs. "Your mother said you should deal with it yourself."

He crawled up to the bedroom, pouting. For nearly half an hour I could hear his heart-wrenching sighs as he slowly pulled out the clothes drawer and put on dry pants. From time to time he would gaze painfully out the window to see if Mama or I wouldn't help him after all.

Finally Janell threw down her trowel and marched up to the log cabin.

"Don't tell me you're giving in?" I asked.

"No." She held out a small clump of greenery. "It's just that I've been weeding these plants out of the lettuce, and now I realize I don't know what they are."

"They're weeds, right?"

"Yes, but what kind? They're not on my plant list." She took her botany books from the bookshelf and spread them on the table.

Over the past few summers Janell had identified more than 120 different species of plants at the Sahalie, from giant willows to tiny buttercups. Each year it became harder to discover new plants for her to add to her list. Usually she was pleased when she found a new addition. But this one had been growing right under her nose, and she seemed irked that she had spent half an hour pulling it out of the garden without knowing what it was.

"Chickweed," she announced at length. She read from the book, "A wild salad green, used by native tribes. High in vitamin C."

"Chickweed, huh?" I put a sprig of the tiny-leaved plant in my mouth.

"Don't eat it!"

"Why not? Aren't you sure of your identification?"

"Well, yes, but—"

"Then it's a salad green." I chewed thoughtfully. "Actually it tastes better than the lettuce we're trying to grow. Probably has more vitamins too."

She frowned. "Then why did I bother to plant the damned garden? I feel like Pete, weeding all the wrong things."

A small, sorry voice from upstairs whined, "Mama? Can you help me?"

I mouthed the words, "Don't do it."

She sighed. Then she walked to the door. "I'm sorry, Ian. You can come see me in the garden when you've got dry pants."

"Are you going to keep weeding, then?" I asked.

She shrugged. "I guess I'm going to gather salad greens. The stuff we actually cultivate grows so slowly here, chickweed may be the only crop we get."

For me the loneliest part of the summer was the thought of what lay ahead. On August 18 Janell's parents were scheduled to meet us at Wilson Road and drive us back to Eugene in their camper. And on August 21 I would catch the night bus to Port Orford, the closest town to Cape Blanco—the westernmost point of Oregon, where I would begin my long solo hike through the wilderness.

The next-to-last day at the log cabin was the hardest of all. The sun cut through the fog just after breakfast, leaving puffy white wisps dragging across the forested hills behind the pasture. The cat yawned and curled in the sunbeam on the rug, putting her paws over her eyes with a contented sigh. The window box was full of marigolds and geraniums we would have to leave to wither. The garden was speckled with the pea blossoms and bean flowers of vegetables we had planted too late to harvest. The cows grazed past as I watched from the breakfast table.

Upstairs Karen was worriedly packing her toys in her little backpack. I knew she was anxious about kindergarten. She would start school in a few weeks, while I was gone. She had enjoyed setting her own schedule at the log cabin. To her, kindergarten sounded like an entire year of following other people's orders.

Outside, Ian was running about the yard with his usual grasshopper-before-winter indifference. But then I heard him stop and say, "Oh no. Do we have to leave the Biemis and all the dear sweet cows?"

Janell spread out her inventory lists of log cabin food and supplies on the kitchen counter. She updated them carefully, pulling out every can and bottle from the cupboards, repacking, resorting, and rearranging for winter.

After breakfast I rowed across the river to get milk and mail at the Niemis for the last time. When I returned I brought Janell a fat letter from her co-teacher at the preschool. She sighed. "I think I'll jog around the field a few times before I open it. I'm not ready to think about work again yet." She looked out across the pasture. "I wish we could keep everything just the way it is now."

"Everything? You'd want to always have the garden half grown, Pete's cabin unpainted, and a wild cow roaming the woods?"

She laughed. "Even all that, I suppose. But you know what I mean. The kids are playing in the hammock. The water's boiling on the stove. I wish there were some way to lock it all up and keep it safe."

"What I do is take a mental picture of the pasture from the log cabin window. Then I call it up whenever I want to remember summer."

She nodded. "We have a difficult year ahead of us, with your 1000-mile hike and Karen's kindergarten and my job. Let's hang onto that snapshot."

22

The Break-In

(June 1987)

Simplify, simplify.
—Henry David Thoreau, Walden, 1854

Every June I worried what we would find when we hiked into the Sahalie for the first time of the summer. This year in particular, after surviving the bewildering adventures of my months-long hike across the state, I wanted everything at our log cabin to be the same.

Instead, all of my nightmares seemed to be coming true. Already, trudging in through a dismal rainstorm, we had been sickened to discover that the Willamette Pacific Lumber Company had clearcut a square mile of hillside adjacent to our Sahalie property. All that remained on that forest was a ghastly battlefield of stumps, bulldozed caterpillar lanes, and slash piles. Winter windstorms, finding nothing but stumps to slow them on the scarred slopes, had slammed into the woods on our side of the property line, bending and snapping many of our trees. We had to stop every few hundred yards on the riverbank trail to fight our way through the dripping branches of another wind-felled hemlock.

We slogged past Pete's cabin without stopping, eager to reach the haven of our own log sanctum. But when I saw our cabin from the pasture, my heart froze.

"Why is the cabin door open?" Karen asked.

"Let's find out." The padlock hung from a splintered board beside the dark doorway. Grimly we climbed the porch steps.

Ian, not quite five years old, clutched the wet stuffed bunny he had carried in.

Janell set down her wet backpack and the cat carrier. Tight-lipped, she stepped inside the doorway.

"Oh shit," she whispered.

My heart thumping, I followed her into the dark front room. Even before my eyes adjusted to the gloom, I was hit by the sour stench of rodent nests. Then I saw the floor—books and debris strewn about as if the room had caged a tornado. The kerosene lamp was gone, and on the walls—

"Janell, the tools!" A rush of rage almost choked the words. "They've taken my grandfather's tools!"

"God, no! That's awful, Bill!"

"And the bottles from Clyde Moreland's homesite are gone too!" I pointed to the empty shelf.

"Maybe we should have boarded up the windows so people couldn't see what was in here."

"I didn't think burglars would come in all this way," I said, incredulous. "Who would do that anyway? This stuff was really only valuable to *us*."

"Whoever it was must have figured they could sell old tools and bottles as antiques."

The cat meowed miserably from the porch. Outside, Ian's voice said, "I'm letting Kitsa out of her box, OK?"

"Why did they make such a mess?" Karen asked.

The intruders had emptied every drawer and shelf onto the floor. They had dumped a jigsaw puzzle onto the table, scattering pieces across the room. "They probably thought we'd hidden money somewhere." I added bitterly, "They sure picked the wrong house for that."

"Why didn't they at least close the door?" Janell demanded. "It smells like mice have been coming in for months. I bet there are nests everywhere by now."

The cat prowled past us, sniffing. Her ears were alert and her eyes wide. She stalked into the kitchen doorway and suddenly jerked her head up, her tail twitching.

Uneasily, we followed the cat into the other room. Janell, in the lead, clapped her hand over her mouth with a small cry. I half expected to see some giant wild animal cornered against the far wall. But there was nothing. Nothing at all. Just a strangely empty—

"Oh my God," I breathed.

Janell collapsed on a chair as if she had been shot. "My stove! They took my woodstove."

The black stovepipe still hung down from the ceiling, but all that remained beneath it was a pile of ash and a few sooty bootprints.

"How on earth could they do that?" I asked, numb. "That thing weighed hundreds of pounds. They had to carry it most of a mile."

"Damn them!" Janell cried.

I put my arm around her shoulder. The tools had been my proudest possessions, and the woodstove had been hers. We had carved a home from the woods with my grandfather's ax, adze, and crosscut saw. That inheritance had meant more to me than money ever could. Janell had not inherited her antique woodstove, but I knew she had grown to love it as an adopted child. The old enameled stove had filled the house with the tantalizing smell of baked bread and cookies. It had gathered the family on dark evenings for festive bowls of fresh hot popcorn. It had dried diapers and lifted spirits through the dreariest of rainstorms. It had been the warm heart of our Sahalie home. The burglars who had ransacked the log cabin had done more than steal our few small treasures. They had violated our family.

Karen climbed the ladder to the kid's bedroom and wailed, "My Legos! They took my whole pirate island!"

"I'm sorry, Karen." A cold gust from the storm outside creaked the broken door open wider, swirling papers and ash across the corner where the stove had stood.

"Don't cry, Mama," Ian said bravely.

"I'm not crying." Janell straightened, wiping her eyes with the back of her hand. "After all, it could have been worse."

I looked at her doubtfully. After seeing the ghastly clearcut, the wind-felled trees, and now the gutted cabin, I wasn't sure I agreed. "How?"

"Well, they didn't burn the place down. They didn't take the wooden chairs you made, or the trestle table we built. We can sort through the stuff they dumped on the floor. Some of it we'll want to throw out, but most of it is just fine."

"I bet they left the old box stove I stored under the cabin," I suggested. "It's small and rusty, but I'm sure it still works."

Janell looked at the empty corner of the kitchen with a sigh. I knew what she was thinking: Our old box stove might be able to heat the room and boil water, but it would never replace the elegant enameled wood range, with its oven and warming rack.

Kitsa rubbed against Janell's leg. Janell petted the cat and managed a smile. "As long as all of us are here, we've got the most important things." She hugged me and Ian, her eyes closed.

We decided to straighten up the place enough to have lunch. Then we would make a list of everything that was missing. After that I would go into town for the afternoon to report the robbery and buy the most important things we lacked. If we couldn't make the log cabin habitable by evening, we would move temporarily to Pete's cabin.

While I dragged the old box stove out from its storage spot under the cabin, Janell began putting drawers back where they belonged. I had just set the little stove in place—using a rock to replace a missing leg—when

Janell exclaimed, "Oh! This drawer's alive!"

Both kids and the cat came to watch a young family of five furry field mice scurry frantically around the drawer, trying to hide among the chewed remnants of our dishtowels. Apparently the mice were too young to jump out, but they were too quick for Janell to catch by the tail.

"Wait, I know a trick." She held one end of a paper towel tube near a corner of the drawer. Before long one of the mice raced into this small dark tunnel, looking for refuge. At once Janell clapped her hand over the open end of the cardboard tube. "Got one!" She shook the mouse out into a tall, smooth-sided bucket where it couldn't escape. Then she began fishing for the rest of the mouse family. One by one they hid in the alluringly dark tube and wound up in the bucket. When she had them all, she took the bucket far up into the woods and set them free.

By then I had connected the stovepipe and lit a small but cheering fire. "It looks like our cast iron pans were stolen too," I said. "Add that to our list."

"At least we still have a coffeepot to heat water." Janell took an oven mitt from its peg on the wall, put her hand inside, and squealed.

"What is it?"

"Another mouse." She jerked her hand back and folded over the top of the mitt.

"A mouse was trying to make a nest in a hanging glove?"

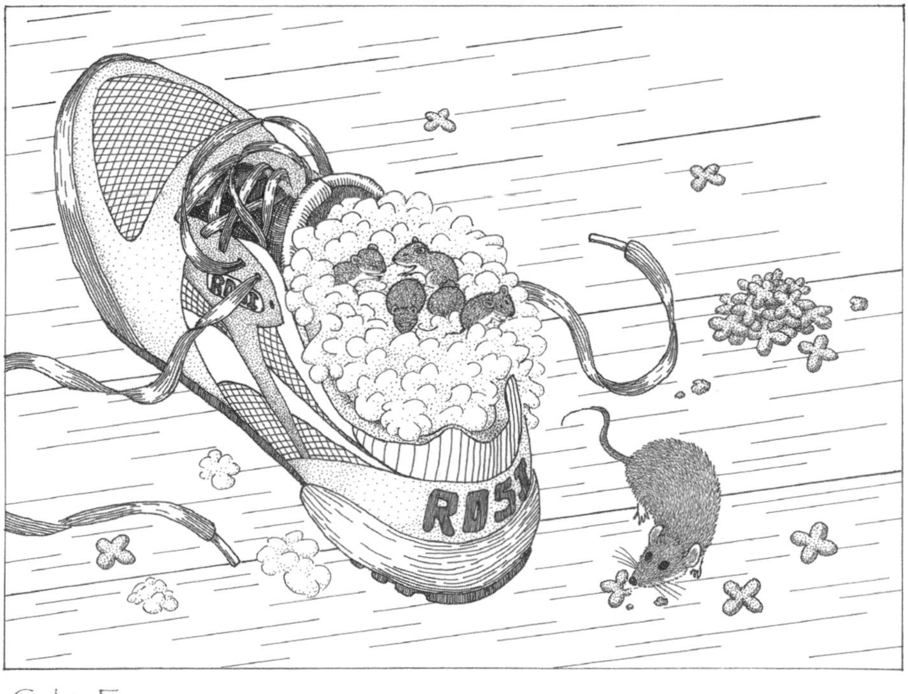

"I think it just got started."

"Well, take it outside, and let it start over in the woods."

She had hardly left when I heard a thump and a squeak from the front room. "Papa!" Karen cried. "Kitsa's got something in the tool closet."

I was wearying of the rodent battle, but I went into the other room and pulled the cat out of the tool closet's bottom shelf. She had a large, stunned-looking deer mouse in her mouth. I carried Kitsa outside and pried open her jaws. At once the mouse leapt to the ground and scurried under the porch—probably heading straight back to its nest, I thought. I went back inside, knelt by the tool closet, and pulled out the ball of dry moss the mouse had collected at the back of the shelf. I was about to put it into the woodstove when Karen caught my hand.

"Look, Papa! Mouse babies!"

Sure enough, wriggling in a hollow in the moss ball were three tiny creatures. Their eyes and ears were still closed, but they waved their heads about searchingly. They obviously were not newborns, because they were not pink and ugly. Already they had a thin coat of dark gray fur—white on the bellies—and extremely delicate, long whiskers. Exposed to the light, they began to squeak, convulsing slightly with each effort.

"They're cute!" Karen exclaimed.

Ian touched one with his finger. "Where's their mama?"

"I made Kitsa let her go. She ran under the porch."

"Can we keep them?" Karen asked.

"Karen, this cabin is already lousy with mice."

"You're not going to kill them, are you?" she demanded, outraged.

"Look, we'll just put the whole nest under the porch. Then the mother will hear them squeaking and take them away to a new home. Someplace far away from our house, I hope."

After lunch the rain had let up, so I took the list we had made and hiked out the muddy river trail past Pete's cabin to the far side of the gas line hill, where we had left our car.

Yes, we owned a car. This was still a strange concept for me. For ten years Janell and I had lived without a car of our own. Instead we had ridden bicycles, used public transportation, and borrowed other people's vehicles when necessary. It had been part of our 'living lightly' mantra: The single most damaging thing an average person can do to the planet is to drive a car. We vowed not to buy one.

Stiffening that resolve was our increasingly desperate shortage of money. Despite all my hard work and many promising leads, the seventh and final year of my career deadline as a freelance writer was ticking to a close without a significant financial breakthrough.

But a few months ago my oldest brother Mark had offered to give us a car for free. He had bought a four-wheel-drive Subaru for a ridiculously low bid at an auction of repossessed vehicles. The first owner had disconnected the odometer cable, so no one knew the car's exact mileage. The door was dented and the windshield had a crack. For a while Mark drove the car to his job at the Tektronix laboratory, but the commute really did not demand this sort of high-clearance stump jumper, and I suspect his fellow engineers snickered at his bargain. When he went to buy a replacement car, the salesman told him the beat-up Subaru had no trade-in value at all. The car was utterly worthless. Mark says he thought of me and the Sahalie right away.

Karen had dubbed our Subaru the "silver submarine." As I drove out the gas line track toward Taylorville, I realized just how appropriate this moniker was. First I had to gun the car over a gravel hill in the lowest possible four-wheel-drive gear. Then I had to shoot it across the narrow Butterfield Creek culvert, plow it through a vast mud puddle, penetrate a stand of seven-foot-tall grass, and finally ford a foot-deep stream that had been diverted across the gas line roadbed by beavers.

When I finally reached the safety of the gravel county road and drove on into Taylorville, the Subaru looked like the Vehicle From the Black Lagoon. People stared as I pulled to a stop in front of Jim's True Value hardware store. Mud coated everything but the twin arcs left by the windshield wipers. Slugs and caterpillars clung to the hood. Long stalks of grass trailed from the bumpers like the tentacles of a swamp beast.

I slammed the door, stomped the mud from my rubber boots, and walked to the public telephone to report the burglary. The only pay phone in this part of town is on the sidewalk between a surfboard rental shop and The Filthy Lapdog, a coffee shop where a neon light blinks, "Fresh Coffee & Bait." I put a quarter in the slot, dialed the sheriff's office in Bayview, and explained about our loss. Eventually I was connected to a deputy who sounded curious enough about the incident that he agreed to meet me at the gate on Wilson Road in an hour.

Then I walked back to the hardware store and picked out two kerosene lamps, some cast iron pans, an ax, and the other things on my list. As I was waiting for the cashier to ring up these purchases, I noticed a woodstove in their window display. The stove had been there several years—mostly as decoration, I assumed—but now I recalled that Janell had always walked slowly past this particular window, admiring the shiny, nickel-plated curlicues on the oven door.

The cash register rang up the frightening total of $309.45, dinging its bell as excitedly as a pinball machine announcing a new high score. Still, as I wrote out the check, I managed to ask in a casual voice, "So what are you asking for that wood cookstove in the front window?"

The cashier sent a stock boy to check.

"$2199.95," he shouted back

I winced.

"Wait—it's on sale. Ten percent off."

I wished I could buy the stove for Janell. I wanted to make her happy with a grand surprise, to prove that we could make the cabin as cozy as before. But how could I? Two thousand dollars was about what we had left in our savings account. In my seven years as a struggling freelance writer I had gradually dragged her to the brink of desperate poverty. I had promised not to plunge us over that dark edge. Disappointed and disheartened, I turned away from the display window and wheeled my shopping cart of pans and lamps out to the silver submarine.

The gray-haired sheriff's deputy eyed me suspiciously as he drove up to the Wilson Road gate. "Your name Sullivan?"

"Yes. Thanks for coming."

He got out of his patrol car but did not shake my hand. "Ron Stromness. Where's the house?"

I nodded toward the overgrown gas line track. "It's about a mile south. We can drive partway in my Subaru if you want. After that there's just a trail."

He shook his head. "I thought I'd seen every house in the county in the past thirty years. You really don't have a road all the way into your place?"

"No, the thieves must have carried everything out by hand."

He sized up my car. "I guess maybe I'll walk too. What's all that stuff in your backseat?"

"I bought a few things to replace what was stolen." I opened the door so he could see. "As long as we're hiking in, maybe you could help carry some of it?"

Without a word he took my new ax from the car and started walking down the track.

We didn't speak for the next half hour. Occasionally the deputy cleared a branch from the trail, swinging the ax without breaking stride. Before long his pant legs were soaked from the wet leaves of trailside brush. Strands of lichen hung from the round brim of his hat. When we reached the log cabin I held open the door. He leaned the ax against the porch, ducked into the front room, and touched his hat brim. "Afternoon, Mrs. Sullivan. I'm Ron Stromness, Taylor County Sheriff's Department. I hear you've had a burglary."

Karen and Ian were cowering behind the kitchen door, watching the deputy with big eyes. I expected Janell to tell him her name was actually Sorensen. Instead she said, "Yes, they took my stove and most of our antique tools. I'm afraid it might have happened several months ago. We only come here in summer. I've saved some jars and glasses they might have handled. Can you take fingerprints?"

"Yes ma'am, but it's not usually much help after so long." The deputy used a handkerchief to hold a canning jar up to the light of the window. "No, judging by these smudges, they used gloves."

"The bootprints are big, so they're probably men," I suggested. "And it would have taken at least two of them to carry our woodstove that far."

"Hm. Any suspects? Neighbors? Acquaintances? Who knew about your cabin?"

I looked to Janell. "It wouldn't have been the Niemis. Lucas Hamilton knows about the cabin, but he must be ninety years old. Of course there's Mrs. Nelson. She sometimes keeps delinquent boys at her farm."

"But she lives across the river and she doesn't have a boat," Janell objected. "What about the butcher?"

I shook my head. Although Butch was unpredictable, it didn't seem possible that he could have done such a thing.

"I know!" Karen exclaimed, stepping out from behind the door. "I bet it was the Skookums!"

"Oh?" the deputy asked. "Where do they live?"

I smiled. "Out in the woods. They're spirits from an old Sahalie legend. You know, as in Skookum Rock?"

"I see." He frowned. "Well, if we discount evil spirits, I'd say this looks like the work of drug users. They get desperate for cash. They probably figured they could break in here without anybody seeing them."

"How did they find out about it?" Janell asked

"Willamette Pacific just opened up a whole section behind your place last winter. The loggers might have noticed the cabin and mentioned it to their friends. Is there a trail up to that new logging show?"

"There's an old deer path that went up into the forest, but now it goes straight up a hillside of slash."

"I bet that's the way they went. I'd recommend putting up 'No Trespassing' signs and installing a loud burglar alarm."

"But we don't have power," I objected. "And nobody would hear the alarm anyway."

"Then just barricade the windows and doors when you leave. The burglars had to work so hard for so little here, they probably won't be back." He wrote something on a business card and handed it to me. "Here's my name and the case number. Give me a call if you think of any more leads."

"What are you going to do?" I asked.

He shrugged. "Not much I can do. Keep an eye on the antique stores, I guess."

"Do you think I'll get my stove back?" Janell asked.

He was already on his way out. "No ma'am, I'm afraid it's long gone. They probably sold it at an estate auction in Nevada months ago."

Apparently the deputy thought his investigation here was over. He strode across the pasture toward the river trail. I followed along, partly because I needed to carry another load of supplies back from the car. After a few minutes he glanced back at me on the trail and asked, "So what do you do out here all summer? I mean, for a living?"

"I write."

"You write?" He shot me another suspicious glance. His attitude had begun to make me uneasy. Suddenly I realized he might think we were involved in the drug business ourselves. That would explain why we had chosen such an isolated location for our cabin. Even the break-in must have looked like a raid by rival drug traffickers. The puzzling part would be why we had reported our loss at all.

"I write books and articles," I explained. "Maybe you saw the cover story I did for *Oregon* magazine about my hike across the state?"

"You!" He pointed at me, open-mouthed. "I saw you on TV! Last month, I think it was Channel Six in Portland. You're the guy who walked through all the wilderness areas, aren't you? Man, what an adventure!"

I nodded. It had been a grand adventure, exploring a route through rainforest, alpine meadows, and desert canyons for two months. In the Diamond Peak Wilderness I had accidentally poisoned myself with mushrooms. In Southern Oregon I had been held at gunpoint by a marijuana grower. I had ended the trek by hiking forty miles a day through Hells Canyon, trying to outrun October snowstorms.

"They said on TV that you were writing a book about it."

"Two books, actually, but they might not come out for ages, if at all." That was the problem with freelance writing. It was a waiting game, full of speculation. A publisher in Seattle had given me a contract to write a guidebook to Oregon's outdoors, *Exploring Oregon's Wild Areas,* but I had spent the entire $3000 advance preparing the book's maps and photography. Meanwhile I had sent the journal about the hike, *Listening for Coyote,* to my agent in San Francisco. But that was the same black hole that had swallowed the manuscript of my historical novel. I had not heard from my agent in months. The truth was that I had reached the end of my seven-year experiment. In the fall I would have to follow through on my promise to Janell. I would have to get a more reliable job. I really might end up as a clerk at K Mart.

"A writer!" The deputy chuckled as he walked ahead of me on the trail. "You'll laugh, but I had you pegged as a drug racketeer. I meet all kinds out here on Wilson Road. Last year it was a murderer. Or maybe two."

"Were you involved in the Bartola case?"
"I was the first law officer to respond."
"Seriously? Are you allowed to talk about it?" I was more than a little interested in finding out if the Bartola murder was connected to Clyde Moreland's death.
"Sure, now that the trial's over." The deputy walked beside me, suddenly garrulous. "I was driving down Wilson Road when I see a pickup parked crooked about where your gate is. Mrs. Bartola is hysterical, wailing over her dead husband. There's blood all over her truck. I call for backup, then I drive on out to the end of Wilson Road. At Valerie Boucher's gate there's a mob scene with people and rifles everywhere. I didn't know what the hell was going on."
"But Mrs. Bartola was an eyewitness to the shooting. She must have seen who killed her husband."
"She was pretty rattled," the deputy said. "By the time it came to trial the Bouchers had hired this big-name lawyer Munroe. He grilled that old woman on the stand for three days, pouncing on every inconsistency in her story. He even suggested she might have shot her own husband and pinned the blame on Valerie Boucher."
"Is that possible?"
"Sure, and he might have been shot by Skookums too. No, either Valerie or her son must have pulled the trigger. Maybe both. They didn't want him to barge through their land to get to Skookum Rock. Still, it's murder, and it's a shame they got off scot-free."
"Why did they?"
He shrugged. "They had a slick lawyer. He portrayed Valerie as this poor single mom struggling to defend her land against an unscrupulous developer. Then he told the jury they couldn't know for sure who fired the fatal shot. If they convicted either Valerie or her boy there was a chance they'd be sending an innocent person to death row."
By this time we had reached his patrol car at Wilson Road. Before he got in I asked, "Do you think there was a connection between the Bartola shooting and the death of Clyde Moreland, the old homesteader on our place?"
"The Moreland suicide?" The deputy stroked his jaw. "That was twenty years ago. But there was something fishy about it, now that you mention it. Moreland owned a lot of land, so people looked at his will pretty closely after he died. One of the two witnesses who signed Moreland's will was Barry Bartola."
I whistled. The connection was close enough that it gave me goosebumps. "Who was the other witness to Moreland's will?"
"I don't remember exactly." The deputy got in and started the car. "But I've got a feeling it might have been another of these slick lawyers."

Only after the deputy had driven away did I think of Lucas Hamilton.

When I got back to the log cabin Janell had already straightened up the house somewhat. She and the kids were huddled around the box stove.

"Uh oh, it's Papa," Ian said, crouching over as if to hide something.

"What's up?" I asked.

Guiltily, Karen held out a tiny mouse in her cupped hands. "The mother mouse didn't come back for the babies. They were squeaking really loud under the porch. Mama said we could keep them."

"Just until they're big enough to live in the woods on their own," Janell added quickly. "We've been trying to feed them warm milk."

"This one is named Eater because he eats so well," Karen announced.

"Mine is Face Washer," Ian said, "Because he wipes milk all over when he drinks."

With a laugh I asked Janell, "Does your mouse have a name too?"

I think she blushed, but it was too dark in the room to tell for sure. "Bumbler. This one doesn't know what to do with the milk yet."

I smiled and went to fill the new lamps with kerosene for the evening. The thieves really had not stolen the spirit of our summer retreat. The heart of our log cabin was something more important than a stove.

23

The Mouse Babies

(July 1987)

> Dreamily he fell to considering what a nice snug dwelling-place it would make for an animal with few wants and fond of a bijou riverside residence, above flood level and remote from noise and dust.
>
> —Kenneth Grahame, The Wind in the Willows, 1908

The mouse babies had crossed the line from pests to pets, but I wondered whether they could survive in our care. Janell was as determined as the children to save them.

The children warmed the mice carefully in their hands. They offered them milk—first from their fingers, then with a wet piece of cloth, and finally from an eyedropper. That first night I watched doubtfully as the comic, wriggling babies flailed around in the milk. They did not seem to be drinking much. Eater got so excited by the smell of milk that he squeaked and lost track of what he should be doing. Face Washer got his paws wet and rubbed them all over, but how was that helping? Bumbler lunged around in the milk puddles, waving his head to no apparent purpose.

Finally we dried off the mice and put them in a coffee can lined with polyester pillow stuffing. Karen punched holes in the plastic lid for ventilation. When the mice fell asleep, exhausted from the long day, I took out the *Book of North American Mammals* and verified that these were not beady-eyed field mice, but rather deer mice, large-eyed forest dwellers. As adults, they would live beneath a rotten log and eat fir seeds. According to the guide, they would take two months to mature and could live to the age of three. When we went to bed Janell set the alarm clock for 4am so she could get up for a middle-of-the-night feeding attempt by lantern light.

In the days that followed, Eater, Face Washer, and Bumbler became the mouse stars of our own Sahalie pet drama. At their feeding performances four times a day they crawled up the children's sleeves. They lost their footing and rolled onto their backs. They nosed about squeaking. They slept. But eventually they also learned to drink milk. And so they grew larger, furrier, and if possible, even cuter. Our cat Kitsa watched this show with such intense curiosity that we carefully kept the babies in their lidded coffee can between feedings. Whenever the can emitted squeaking or scratching noises, Kitsa pricked her ears and paced, her tail twitching.

Three weeks later we were sitting at breakfast, feeding the mice flakes of oatmeal, when I saw my parents hiking up the trail toward the cabin. My brother Pete walked along behind them, carrying a shopping bag in his hand.

Karen flung open the window. "Grandpa! Grandma! Uncle Pete! Come see what we've got!"

Grandpa Wes waved. "Hi, Karen. What have you got?"

"Mice! In the cabin!"

My parents exchanged puzzled looks. When I met them at the front door my father asked, "This is good news?"

"Actually, it's the best news we've got. When we arrived here three weeks ago we found the door open. Someone broke in last winter."

"Did they take anything?" Pete asked. He set his shopping bag on the floor.

"They stole Grandfather Sullivan's tools," I admitted. "And somehow they managed to drag away our cookstove."

"What!" my mother gasped. "How could they take your stove?"

"I don't know. I've hooked up the old box stove and bought some new—"

"Look at Eater!" Karen interrupted, holding out a mouse in her hand. "Isn't he the sweetest thing?"

Ian came up behind her, petting a fidgety mouse with his finger. "This one's Face Washer. Because he washes his face."

My mother stooped to admire the mice. "How did you catch them?"

"They're babies," Karen said proudly. "The mother mouse didn't come back so we're raising them ourselves."

I explained, "We found a lot of mouse nests in the mess the thieves left behind. It took a week to clean everything up."

Janell leaned out of the kitchen doorway. "Would you like some coffee? We're just finishing breakfast."

"Sure." My father brightened at this suggestion. I brought extra chairs into the old portion of the cabin and Janell poured coffee.

My mother cradled her coffee cup in her hands. She shook her head at the rusty box stove in the kitchen corner. "I'm going to miss your beautiful old cookstove."

Janell sighed. "I miss it too. A lot."

"It's a good thing the thieves didn't find my cabin," Pete said. "Of course, my door had a much better lock." Did his voice have a tone of challenge, or was I just imagining it? Since our argument two years earlier, I had become cautious around Pete.

"Have you told the police about the break-in?" My father asked.

I nodded. "A sheriff's deputy hiked in to look for clues, but he said there wasn't much he could do. He suggested we barricade the windows and doors when we're gone. I've started building heavy shutters, using steel straps and lag bolts."

"Sounds like a worthwhile project." My father sipped his coffee. "I guess we've got our work cut out for us too. Pete's got a new plan."

I set down my coffee cup, concerned about what Pete's plan might entail.

Dad continued, "And your mother's scheduled me to spend the next three days out in the pasture, pulling tansy." He gave Mom a wink. "But I thought I'd take her out for a quiet little boat ride first."

"Boat ride!" Karen and Ian both jumped up. "Yeah, a boat ride! Can we go? Please?"

"Well, I don't know," my father said. He had obviously envisioned this boat trip as a romantic outing alone with Mom. I knew that their first date together had been in a canoe. They had been students at the University of Oregon in 1943. Although Dad had capsized the canoe on that outing he still retold the story fondly because Mom had had the courage to agree to a second date.

"Please?" Karen begged.

"Oh, come on, Wes," my mother said.

"All right," he grumbled. "I guess I can row you all."

"Yippee!" Ian squealed.

Janell gave Ian a stern look. "You have to put the mice away first. And Karen, you'll need to get the life jackets."

I gave Dad the key to the rowboat padlock. "We haven't gone on many boat rides this year."

"Why not?"

"Dairy inspectors won't let the Niemis sell unpasteurized milk anymore, so instead of rowing across the river to get milk, we drive into town once a week."

"That's too bad," my mother said. "I worry about that farm now that Dolores has passed away."

I nodded. Mrs. Niemi had died of heart failure in December. My parents and I had driven to Taylorville for the funeral just before Christmas. George and the rest of the Niemi family had been red-eyed and speechless. We had given them a ham dinner in a box. I felt guilty that we hadn't visited the family much since then.

Karen bounced up with the life jackets. Soon she and Ian were yipping and squealing as they led my parents across the pasture toward the boat landing.

Janell and I were left with Pete. An awkward silence hung in the air. My brother sat in a corner, swirling cold coffee in his cup.

"So Pete," Janell said. "What's this project you have in mind?"

In reply he set down his coffee cup, went to the other room, brought back the shopping bag, and emptied it onto the table. Before us was a pile of electronic fittings, batteries, buzzers, and two handset telephones.

"I thought we could use a little more communication out here," he said.

I nodded slowly. "Yes, that's always good. But telephone service won't be easy. The nearest connection is at the Niemi farm. The phone company will charge a fortune to string a line across the river."

He shrugged. "I wasn't thinking of connecting to the outside world. Just an intercom between the two cabins. If one of us presses the buzzer, the other picks up the phone and talks."

"That's a great idea!" Janell said. "It takes ten minutes to walk from one cabin to the other, and I'm always wanting to check in with you or your parents. Do you have enough wire?"

"A quarter mile. I'm wondering if we can string it through the woods where it won't be in the way?"

"I'm sure we can," I said. "Let's go look."

With the camaraderie of two boys on a backyard expedition, Pete and I set off into the woods. We both knew that scouting the exact route of the telephone line was not the important thing. What really mattered was that Pete and I were once again working together.

And so we ended up wandering deeper and deeper into the woods, exploring one detour after another. Pete found a deer trail that ducked beneath a giant fallen log. I explored a route that led to a grotto with a hidden pool. Finally we ended up near the back corner of the property, on a mossy knoll perched between two forks of the creek.

For a long time I stood there with my brother. A thousand greens cascaded down the glen, through oxalis, sword fern, mossy branches, hemlock, and the translucent dapple of alder leaves. The foot-wide creek gurgled prodigiously, as if trying to sound much larger that it was. A spiral bird looped its mysterious call through the branches. A winter wren trilled. I wished I had brought my journal. I wanted to capture the harmonies of the Sahalie forest that Pete and I were sharing.

"You know," Pete said, "if we had thinned this part of the forest properly a few years ago, it wouldn't have been hit so hard by the windstorm."

I looked at him, suddenly realizing we might not be on the same wavelength after all. "You're thinking about forest management? Can't you see how beautiful it is here?"

"Sure, but it's so close to the neighbor's clearcut that the wind bent over a lot of the hemlocks. It would look better if I came back with a chainsaw and cleaned them up."

He was probably right. The wind-damaged trees really did not look very tidy. Some of their crowns had bent almost to the ground. "What will you do with them if you cut them down?"

Pete shrugged. "There's enough wood here to fill a log truck or two, but without a road, we can't get it to market. The logs will just rot on the ground, I guess."

Suddenly I had an idea. "I'll help you clean up the trees if we cut them into ten- and twelve-foot lengths."

He scratched his head. "You're not thinking about building another log cabin, are you?"

"Maybe a little one, with a single room. It would only take a few weeks to put together."

"But why?"

How could I explain? "I know this will sound strange, but I'd like a quiet place where I can go to write."

"Out here?" Pete stared at me. "What's wrong with the cabin you've got?"

I sighed. "I can't concentrate when the kids are running around. And I may have to give up writing altogether when we're in town. This may be the only place I'll still be able to write."

"What about that adventure book you were doing? The one where you hiked across the state? I thought you sent the manuscript to an agent."

I looked down. "I gave her the Niemis' phone number. Joe said he'd row over if they got a call. Nothing."

Pete pursed his lips. He squinted up at the bent hemlock trees. "Ten- and twelve-foot lengths, you say?"

Janell was outside hanging laundry on the clothesline when Pete and I returned from our exploration. "Did you find a route for the telephone line?"

"That was the easy part," Pete said. "The real project will be cleaning up the windstorm damage. And Bill's talking about building another cabin."

"Really?" Janell looked at me uncertainly.

"Just a room where I could write." I flushed, a little embarrassed that I hadn't discussed this with her first. I gave her a let's-talk-about-it-later look.

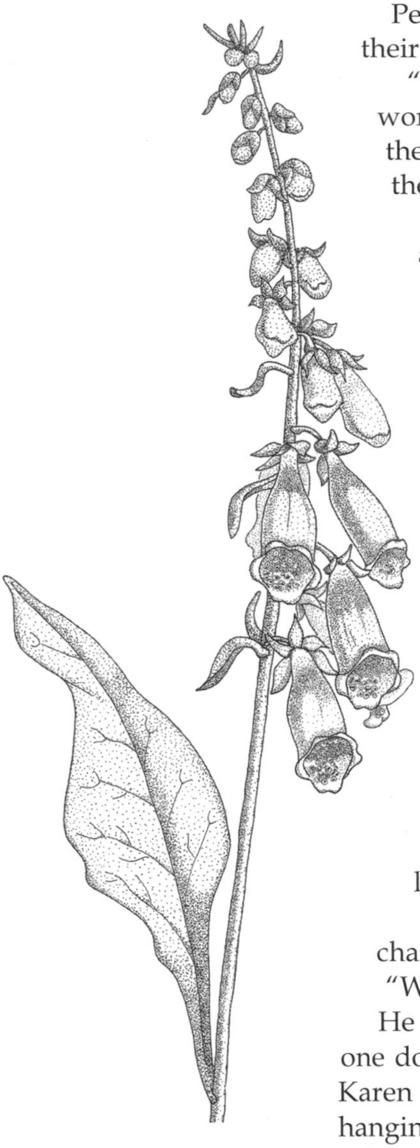

Pete asked, "Aren't the kids back from their boat ride yet?"

"No," Janell said. "And I'm starting to worry about your parents. I've been hearing the shrieks of excited little children from the direction of the river."

"Here they come," I said, pointing across the pasture.

Sure enough, Karen and Ian were galloping through the grass from the boat landing. Grandma Elsie followed more slowly, carrying the life jackets. Last of all came Grandpa Wes, holding what looked like a blue rag in his hand.

"Grandpa jumped in the river! Grandpa jumped in the river!" the kids cried as they ran up to the log cabin.

When Grandpa Wes finally reached the gate I realized the rag in his hand was actually a pair of wet boxer shorts. He handed the undergarment silently to Janell. She considered this a moment, and then hung it on the line to dry.

My father sat down heavily in a lawn chair in the yard.

"What happened?" I asked.

He shot me a dark glance. "I rowed everyone downstream for about half an hour. Then Karen saw a branch of red vine maple leaves hanging over the river. She and Ian simply had to have those pretty red leaves."

Grandma Elsie explained, "They wanted to give them to Janell. I thought it was sweet."

"Yes," Grandpa Wes said, his voice still low. "So I rowed over to the branch, took out my Swiss Army knife, and started sawing away. But you know, vine maple branches are tough. After a while the knife slipped out of my hand. It sank in about three feet of water and settled in the mud."

"I saw it down there," Karen said. "It was red."

"That was my favorite pocketknife," Grandpa Wes went on. "I stuck my arm in after it, but it was just out of reach. I used the oars to lift it up within a couple inches of the surface, but then it slipped again. That time it sank in about five feet of water."

"I told him to forget it," Grandma Elsie said. "He can always buy another knife."

"But I've had that one for years. And I'd already gotten my arm wet. So I stripped to my shorts and went after it."

"Grandpa made a really cool splash," Ian said.

My father looked down. "It's not as easy as you think, diving in the river. The water was murky and everything was out of focus without my glasses."

Karen said, "I suggested he skootch the knife up to shallower water with his toes."

"Finally I got my knife. I almost tipped the boat trying to crawl back in. Then a cold wind came up while I was changing back into my clothes. And of course the kids wouldn't let me row home until I'd gotten that darned branch of crazy red leaves." After Grandpa Wes had recounted this part of the story he suddenly looked around. "Hey, where *is* the branch, anyway?"

"Oh that?" Karen shrugged. "We left it back at the boat landing."

Silently Grandpa Wes opened his mouth, rolled his eyes to the sky, and curled his fingers into claws.

Janell hid a smile with her hand. "Karen? I think it's time you and Ian went inside to feed the baby mice."

"Sure, Mom." The kids bounded up to the porch and opened the door. Kitsa had evidently been waiting to be let in, because she trotted in behind them.

Grandpa Wes was just starting to tell us something else about our children when he was interrupted by a wail from the cabin. Karen appeared in the doorway, her eyes wide. "The mouse babies! They're gone!"

"What!" Janell dropped her clothespins and ran to the door. I was right behind her.

Inside, we found Ian holding the empty coffee can on his lap. "Ian!" Karen shouted, "How could you forget to put the lid on?"

Ian looked frightened. "I was in a hurry to go on the boat ride. I didn't think they could jump out." Tears welled in his eyes.

"That's all right, Ian," Janell said, taking the little boy in her arms. "We'll get them back."

"I didn't think the mice could jump that far, either," I said. "They're not supposed to be mature for another few weeks."

Grandpa Wes stooped in the doorway. "I'm afraid it looks like your mice are precocious."

"Oh no!" Karen said. "Will they be all right?"

"They'll be fine," Janell said. "They must be somewhere right here in the cabin. We just have to find them before Kitsa—"

We all stopped. Where *was* the cat? Karen and I went to the kitchen door to look. Karen clapped her hand to her mouth. "Oh! It's Eater. He's in the cat food bowl!"

I didn't see the cat, but it was true that a deer mouse was sitting in Kitsa's feeding dish. Perhaps because it was gnawing on a piece of dry cat food, Karen had decided this must be Eater, and not Face Washer or Bumbler.

"How are we going to catch him?" Karen whispered.

As if in reply, a shadow streaked out from under the table. Kitsa pounced on her dish, scattering cat food in all directions. I grabbed the cat and pried open her jaws. The mouse dropped to the floor, dazed.

"Eater!" Karen swept up the mouse in her hands. "Oh what a bad, bad cat!"

I held the cat in my arms. "Kitsa didn't mean to be bad, Karen. We've trained her to eat from her food bowl. What is she supposed to do if she finds a mouse in it?"

That afternoon Janell and I drove into town to buy a live mousetrap. Although Eater had managed to survive his adventure, we didn't want to risk having Kitsa catch the other mouse babies when we were not watching.

The hardest part of the trip for me was walking past the woodstove in the display window of the hardware store. I saw Janell slow down, drawn by the pull of this beautiful cooking instrument. Sunshine glinted from its chrome handles and racks. Janell is not materialistic; she wants so few things. It killed me that I could not buy her this one indulgence. Then she took a breath and marched past the window without a word.

At the back of the hardware store a white-haired clerk stopped shelving pots to show us the three different mousetraps he stocked. One of them, a green plastic cage, had a label that claimed the trap caught mice alive. "But to tell you the truth," the clerk confided quietly, "It doesn't work very well. If I were you, I'd ask at the pet store down the block."

Once again we had to pass by the alluring cookstove in the display window. When we reached the pet shop the woman there told us she didn't normally sell mousetraps. But she added, "I do have a little wind-up thing I use when the gerbils get loose. I suppose I could sell it to you for $35 and order another for myself."

"How does it work?" I asked.

"It uses rodent psychology." She fetched what looked like a sheet-metal shoebox from behind the counter. The box had a wind-up key on one side and a tunnel-like hole through the middle. "Mice can't resist crawling through little holes. You wind up the trap and set it on the floor against a wall. When a mouse goes into the hole a spring flips the mouse aside into a chamber. There's room for about a dozen inside, and the spring is good for at least that many."

"You don't need bait?" I asked.

"No."

"And the mice aren't hurt?" Janell asked.

"No, just a little startled."

"We'll take it," Janell and I said together.

When we got home we wound up the trap and set it against the log wall behind our rusty little stove. I doubted that a mouse would really want to crawl into a tin hole, and in fact, nothing happened that evening. But during the night I dimly heard a thunk or two. Shortly after dawn Karen scrambled down the ladder to the kitchen as eagerly as if she were checking her stocking on Christmas morning. Her excited voice summoned the rest of us downstairs. We set the tin box on the table. Through the little holes on the side we could make out a cluster of mice, twitching their whiskers and sniffing.

"We've got at least seven in there!" Karen said.

"Which one's Face Washer?" Ian asked.

"It's hard to tell," I said. "And you know what? I think that means you've succeeded."

"Succeeded?" Janell asked.

"That's right. The baby mice you saved have grown up. They're as big as adult mice now. It's time to set them free in the woods."

"Eater too?" Karen asked. She got the coffee can and peered through the holes in the lid, biting her lip.

"Especially Eater. If he keeps eating cat food, he'll end up *being* cat food."

Ian sighed. "I don't care how big they get. It's hard to let our babies go."

Janell blinked at her son and nodded.

As soon as we were dressed we took the mice up into the woods behind the cabin. It was a solemn procession that chill, foggy morning. In the lead, Karen clutched Eater's coffee can. Next came Ian, holding a small bag of oatmeal. Janell followed, bringing the tin box. When I thought we had gone far enough that the mice could not find the way back, I pointed out a hollow log. "This looks like a good home for deer mice. It's dry inside and there are lots of fir seeds nearby."

Ian emptied his little bag of oatmeal on the dry duff inside the log. Then he reached into his coat pocket and added a small handful of cat food.

Janell knelt beside the log. She set down the tin box and slid open its metal panel. Instantly the mice shot out of the opening, scampering away in all directions.

"None of them stopped to eat my food," Ian complained.

"They'll come back after they've calmed down," I said.

Karen still clutched her coffee can. "Are you sure I can't keep Eater?"

I nodded. "We're not his real family. Eater needs to live with his brothers and sisters."

Karen swallowed. Slowly she opened the lid.

Eater leapt out of the can and scurried across the log. But then he turned, his nose twitching. I could see his little round ears, his big, black eyes, and a bit of his fawn-colored belly.

"I'm sorry, Eater," Karen said. "This is your home now."

The little mouse jumped into the hollow log, snatched a piece of cat food, and vanished.

24

Beaver in the Refrigerator

(August 1987)

> At our family log cabin on the Sahalie, we have trouble with beaver in the refrigerator.
>
> —J. Wesley Sullivan, The Oregon Statesman, 1985

Summer tilted toward fall, and still there was no word from my literary agent. I began preparing myself for the humiliating mental shift from freelance writer to job applicant. Unless I found steady work when we went back to Eugene we would no longer be able to meet our health insurance premiums. We would not even have enough money to enroll Ian in the four-year-olds' class at Big Little School, where Janell taught part-time.

Every other Monday I rowed across the river to double-check that my agent had not left a message with the Niemis. For the final trip of summer Janell and the kids came with me to say goodbye to our neighbors. We had also been invited by Mrs. Nelson, the elderly woman a mile downriver, to drop by for a light lunch.

I got up early that morning to begin building a fire. Our rickety old box stove was so inefficient that breakfast took more than an hour to cook. Large sections of the stove's sheet metal back had rusted away altogether. I had temporarily patched the holes with a cookie sheet and baling wire, but the stove still smoked so badly that we had to leave a window open when the fire was going.

When Karen got up I asked her to fetch the jug of milk from the creek. A few minutes later she ran back into the house, empty handed. "Papa! We've got beavers in the refrigerator again!"

This cry brought Janell and Ian hurrying downstairs. It had been two years since animals had disturbed the bottles and jars we keep cool in the creek. The last time, Grandpa Wes had found tooth marks on a nearby tree and decided the intruder was a beaver.

"Did you see it?" Janell asked.

"No, but the milk's gone."

"Gone?" I asked, surprised. The plastic milk jug had been nearly full. It must have weighed six pounds. "Can a beaver carry a milk jug?"

"I don't think so," Janell said. "Let's go check it out."

The four of us ventured down to the creek. The milk jug had indeed disappeared, but a jar of cream and six beer bottles had merely been tipped over, as if something large had waded past.

"Our visitor must have liked spaghetti too," Janell said. "Last night I put out a container with leftovers."

"Very strange." I searched through the bushes around the creek, expecting to find the crumpled or slashed milk jug nearby. I found nothing. "You know, I think this might have been a human thief."

"Human?" Janell asked, startled. "We haven't seen anybody on this side of the river for weeks."

"Who else could haul away a heavy plastic milk jug? That handle was designed for a human hand. Maybe the people who broke into the log cabin have come back."

"Oh, God!" Janell put her hand to her mouth. I could tell she was remembering the mess the thieves had left in the cabin, and the void where the woodstove had been.

"The deputy said they might be drug users," I said.

"Wait a minute," Janell said, putting her hands on her hips. "If they're drug users, why did they leave the beer? In fact, why would anyone choose to take old spaghetti?"

"Hmm." I thought about this and nodded. "I suppose you're right."

Janell shook her head. "No, It must have been an animal. Something that came here in the dark looking for things it could smell. It ignored things in glass or metal."

"Maybe it was a bear!" Karen exclaimed. "Let's go look in the bear stump. I'll bet we'll find everything there!"

Karen dashed off toward a hollow stump where she and Ian sometimes pretended a bear had its den. The rest of us followed. When we reached the stump, however, it was empty.

"I don't think it could have been a bear," I told her. "A bear would have torn open the containers and left them behind."

"Well, what about a nutria? Or a raccoon?" Janell suggested.

"Or a Sasquatch? Or a Skookum?" I teased.

"Could it have been a salamander?" Karen asked.

Janell looked at Karen doubtfully. "I think a salamander would be too small."

"Maybe a herd of salamanders?" Karen suggested.

Suddenly Ian put his hands to his mouth. "I know! Tigers!"

I put my arm around his shoulder. "It's all right, Ian. Tigers don't like spaghetti. But you know what? I think it might have been a giraffe."

We all laughed, and even Ian seemed relieved. But as we were walking back to the cabin he pulled me aside earnestly.

"Papa," he said, "I don't think it could have been a giraffe for two reasons."

"Oh? What are your reasons?"

"Well first, giraffes don't live around here. And second, you'd see the milk dripping from its mouth."

We still had not solved the riddle of the beaver in our refrigerator when we rowed across the river to see the Niemis. The tide was at its highest. The river seemed to be holding its breath before changing directions. My oars dipped into the broad, green pool. Then they dripped two rows of widening circles.

"It must be hard for the Niemis this year, with Dolores gone," Janell mused.

"Very hard," I said. "I guess Christmas was the worst. Dolores bought Christmas presents for everyone in the family just before she died. She hated shopping, but she'd always been Santa Claus. Imagine how the family must have felt on Christmas morning when they opened those gifts."

"Good God, I can't." Janell looked up at the Niemis's riverbank. A half dozen Holstein cows looked back, chewing cud. "I've always had the feeling Dolores kept their farm from falling apart. Weren't the dairy inspectors threatening to shut the whole thing down?"

I nodded. Last fall the inspectors had issued an ultimatum: The Niemis would have to install a hundred thousand dollars worth of improvements or else they would have to quit the dairy business altogether. It was far from certain that their archaic farm machinery could be modernized in time.

I tied our boat to a tree and carried the kids up the steep bank one at a time. We walked together up the road toward the weathered green farmhouse. When we reached the farmyard, however, Janell gripped my arm. Ahead, on the deeply shadowed porch of the house, stood the silhouettes of George and Dolores.

Impossible! And yet there she was, talking with Mr. Niemi. He was as old and bent as I remembered, but she stood straight, wearing the same apron and holding the same tin milk can that had been her trademarks in life. Like a vision from a purer world, Dolores seemed young and strong, miraculously freed from the long illness that had swollen her legs and crushed her heart.

Then the two of them noticed us and took a step forward. At the edge of the porch the sun caught Mrs. Niemi's face, and she became someone else. She became MaryLou.

George broke into a big grin. "Well looky here, it's the whole Sullivan clan. Haven't seen you over here for a while, Janell. Do you know my daughter-in-law MaryLou?"

"Uh, it's been a few years." I could tell Janell was quickly trying to recall MaryLou's place in the Niemi family. Two years ago MaryLou had married the younger Niemi son, Jack, and they had moved away. MaryLou had brought a young daughter into that marriage. I had forgotten whether she and Jack had had a child of their own since then.

"It's good to see you again, MaryLou," Janell said. "Don't you and Jack live in Cloverdale?"

"Well, we did at first," MaryLou said. "Jack wanted to try his hand at a dairy somewhere else for a while, you know how it is? But after his mother passed away we decided to come back here."

"And boy, have they made big changes," George chuckled, running his thumbs under his suspenders.

MaryLou leaned inside the front door, "Cherie! Junior! We've got visitors!"

Almost at once two children popped onto the porch. Cherie was Karen's age—six years old—but was taller and had a dark complexion. She wore a pair of denim overalls and one pink ballet slipper. "Our dog Major ate a kitten," she announced to Karen. "There's three left hiding under the house. Wanna see?"

"Yeah!" Karen ran with her.

MaryLou snagged Cherie by the back of her overalls. "Where's your other slipper?"

"Mom!" Cherie sang the word painfully, stretching it into two syllables.

"You're not supposed to wear them outside."

"Aw, Mom!" Cherie wriggled loose and escaped around the house with Karen.

The other child, a blond boy of Ian's age, said simply, "I'm gonna fix a truck." He took a heavy wrench from a toolbox on the porch step and strutted toward a junk car in the driveway. Ian followed, mesmerized.

MaryLou shook her head and said simply, "Kids." Then she asked us, "Do you folks have time for coffee?"

"We're on our way to Mrs. Nelson's place, but we can stop for a minute." We followed her and George inside.

George put the milk in the refrigerator and stood by the kitchen table. He aimed one of his thick, work-worn fingers proudly at a large framed photograph on the wall. "Well, what do you think?"

It was an aerial photograph of half a dozen metal-roofed buildings arranged in an S-shape along a brown-and green bluff. "It looks like your farm," I said.

"Yup. Last winter a pilot flew by, taking pictures of all the houses and farms in the valley. Afterwards he drove around selling enlargements for a hundred dollars apiece." George clicked his tongue. "I know that's a lot, but I reckon it's paid off. Since Jack came back we've stood around this picture lots of evenings just planning how things are going to be."

MaryLou distributed cups and poured coffee. "We didn't have much choice about most of the changes. The state doesn't want manure running off into the river anymore, so Jack's pouring cement for a giant sewage tank. Everything will get pumped there and spread in the woods with sprinklers."

"There'll be a new hay shed, and a covered courtyard," George beamed. "This farm's not going under. We're going Grade A."

"That's great news," Janell said. She looked around the kitchen. "It looks like you've been straightening up in here too."

MaryLou sipped her coffee. "I told Jack I had to have a new washing machine first thing. And I wasn't going to have Joe hanging around the house, so we got him a trailer up by the highway. Now I'm going through the cupboards, throwing out rancid walnuts and ten-year-old jars of home-canned fruit."

Her off-hand comment about Joe caught my attention—and not merely because she had thrown out the elder Niemi son like a jar of bad tomatoes. Joe was the one who had promised to let me know if my literary agent called the Niemi farm. Suddenly I realized this might be why I hadn't heard about my book manuscript.

"I don't suppose you've gotten a telephone call for me?" I asked, trying not to sound too eager. The truth was, this was pretty much my last chance.

"A telephone call? For you?" MaryLou looked at me sideways. "Why on earth would somebody call you here?"

I let out a long breath and stared into my coffee. I could almost see my hopes drowning in that black pool. Sullenly I threw in my agent too. My seven years of freelance writing were sinking into oblivion. Dimly I heard Janell and MaryLou continuing the conversation, talking about children. George tried to tell me about some kind of automatic grain-feeding device. My thoughts were elsewhere, submerged and dark.

Finally we were outside, rounding up the kids. Janell had to convince Karen that we couldn't take a kitten home. Ian and Junior were playing Fix the Truck so intently that it was hard to interrupt. Junior played this game by banging his wrench on the hood of a derelict car. Then he stopped and called, "OK, *now!*" Ian, sitting in the driver's seat, responded by wiggling all the levers he could reach. Next Junior shook his head, banged the wrench on the hood again, and asked, "OK, how about *now?*"

In the end I had to lift Ian out of the car, and he cried, and we said our goodbyes while he was still crying. I carried him a quarter mile along the road to Mrs. Nelson's farm before he gulped down his sobs and walked by himself.

By the time we neared Mrs. Nelson's farm Ian had forgotten his troubles—and I had emerged from the depths of my own self-pity enough that I could look at the situation with more perspective. Perhaps I needed a lesson in gumption from Mrs. Nelson. In her ninety-two years she had survived floods and murder scares and countless hard times. She would scoff at the setbacks I faced.

I also recalled that Mrs. Nelson scoffed at the behavior of her relatives' children. I began to worry what she would think of Karen and Ian.

"Kids, we're going to visit Mrs. Nelson for lunch," I told them at the farm gate. "She's usually very nice, but she's ninety years old. I want you to remember three rules at lunch."

"OK," Karen said. "What are the rules?"

"First, don't put your fingers in your nose."

Karen glared at Ian. He squirmed.

"Second, no fighting."

This time it was Ian who glared. Karen shrugged.

"Third, no matter what the food tastes like, don't say you don't like it."

"What if it's yucky?"

"Then don't say anything. Understood?"

"OK, Papa."

An old Jersey cow sauntered up from the barn to meet us. A black calf frisked along beside her. We passed the garden, a sparse array of cabbages, potato plants, and weeds. A half dozen white ducks fluttered off the house porch, quacking.

Mrs. Nelson answered the door with a big smile. "So these are the children you've told me about? Aren't they a fine-looking pair!" Mrs. Nelson herself looked unchanged from the first time we had met her, almost ten years ago. She still wore no glasses. A fine hairnet corralled her white hair. A cooking apron covered her long housedress. I did notice, with some surprise, that this otherwise fastidious woman was wearing one blue sock and one green.

Then she ushered us into the dining room for the "light lunch" she had promised, and I realized why her socks were mismatched. She must have gotten up in the dark that morning to start work on such an enormous farm feast. Steaming platters of food crowded the table, hardly leaving room for our plates. She had baked six pans of cinnamon rolls and a dozen dinner rolls, all from homemade yeast dough. She had sliced and grilled ten salmon steaks. She had dug, peeled, boiled, and mashed a huge pile of potatoes, and tossed in a lump of sweet cream butter the size of my fist. She had picked and shelled a heaping casserole dish of fresh green peas—and then had boiled them almost to mush to make sure they were done. She had filled an entire enamel washtub with lettuce, green onions, radishes, and tomatoes for our salad, and prepared a pitcher of ranch cream dressing from scratch.

"And of course, homemade pickles," Mrs. Nelson said, setting out a dish filled with bright green and red vegetables.

We loaded up on all this hearty food. To me it seemed a farewell banquet—one last big feast before fall, when our money would run out and I would have to start applying for jobs. The kids zeroed in on the cinnamon rolls, and I'm afraid we let them. The salmon was so flaky and delicious I took thirds. Mrs. Nelson did not hold back either, using a dinner roll to load her fork and mop her plate.

When we had finally slowed down, and I feared I was about to burst, Mrs. Nelson announced, "Well now, here's home-canned peaches for dessert." She ladled up five bowls of peaches from a Mason jar. "And some custard." She set a cup of homemade pudding in front of each of us.

Karen eyed the custard warily. It looked delicious, but I knew she had never tasted this kind of dessert before.

While her spoon hovered above it, I whispered, "Remember the third rule."

Karen thought about this a moment. I had forbidden her from complaining about anything she ate. She set down her spoon. "Mrs. Nelson?" she asked. "Can I eat my custard outside?"

"Well now," Mrs. Nelson said. "I suppose you could, since it's dessert."

Karen went into the next room for a minute. When she returned, a spoonful was missing from the custard. Silently, she set the cup beside her plate.

"Did you like it?" Mrs. Nelson asked.

I could sense the tension building within Karen. Would it be worse to lie to this elderly woman or to break Rule Number Three?

"Could I have the rest of your dessert, Karen?" I asked.

She nodded with relief. "Yes, Papa."

"All right then, you kids are excused."

Karen and Ian ran out the front door. We could hear their excited voices as they chased the ducks across the farmyard.

Janell and I thanked Mrs. Nelson profusely for the lunch and insisted that we would do the dishes.

"Just let me put away a few things first." Mrs. Nelson covered the food—enough leftovers for seven men—and found places for it in her refrigerator. Then she brought coffee back to us in the dining room. "You know, when I saw that jar of raspberry jam you'd left on my doorstep last summer, I thought to myself, finally you've got neighbors who know what it means to be neighborly."

"You don't have all that many neighbors out here," Janell said.

"Oh, there are plenty of people in the valley, but some of them, you've just got to wonder how they were raised." She sat down and sipped her coffee. "You know the Farles, across the river and down a stretch?"

We shook our heads.

"Well they moved in there as newlyweds thirty years ago. I remember I rowed over there first thing with some dried salmon and a bushel of pears. As a nice welcome, you know." Mrs. Nelson humphed. "Mrs. Farle took that gift without so much as a thank you, and I'll be darned if she's returned the visit yet. So that was that."

"You mean you haven't talked to her in thirty years?" Janell asked, amazed.

"Honestly, would you?" Mrs. Nelson set down her cup.

"I suppose you knew Barry Bartola, the fellow that got shot?" I asked. As long as our coffee klatch seemed to be focusing on neighbors, I figured we might collect a few more clues for our on-again, off-again murder investigation.

"Did I know Barry Bartola?" She sat back. "That's just what that bigshot defense attorney asked me. He came out here hoping for some dirt that would help his case. As soon as he walked in the door I knew I had a pretty big fish on the line, so I thought I'd play him a while. I sat him down and began describing Barry Bartola as a fine-looking, well-mannered, neighborly man. 'Just like a prince,' I said. 'That was Barry Bartola. In the daytime.'"

She laughed. "That broke up the attorney. He asked me, 'How about in the nighttime?' Well, what can I say about a boy who breaks into my shed, kills my dog, and tries to steal a whole raft of my logs? When it got dark, Bartola was perfectly amoral. No, it took forty years, but he finally got what he had coming to him."

"What do you know about Bartola's land?" I asked. "A lot of it used to belong to Clyde Moreland. How did Bartola wind up with it?"

Mrs. Nelson narrowed her eyes. "I've wondered about that myself. First Clyde died, shot in his own yard. Then Barry, shot in his truck. It's enough to make a person nervous. Maybe the trial would have dug up more if the case hadn't fallen apart."

"Oh? How did the case fall apart?"

"Didn't you hear? Munroe found out the county sheriff and the district attorney were crooked. They'd been dividing and selling contraband from drug busts. The jurors wouldn't believe anything the state said after that."

I raised an eyebrow at Janell. The truth about the two murder cases still seemed just beyond our grasp.

On the long walk home from Mrs. Nelson's farm, Janell must have noticed I was slipping back into despondency. "Why don't you ask the Niemis one more time?" she suggested. "Maybe your agent called while we were having lunch."

"Not much hope of that, is there?" I said. But then when we were walking past the Niemi farmhouse I couldn't resist. I stopped and tapped at the door after all.

MaryLou did not seem surprised to see me. "You know, Bill, what you said this morning got me thinking. We really haven't gotten any phone calls for you. But I did find a letter mixed in with the bills. The handwriting was so bad I could hardly read it."

I tore open the little white envelope and tried to decipher the scribbled card inside. It was from my agent! She had lost the Niemis' telephone number and wanted me to call her as soon as possible!

"Can I use your phone?" I asked. "My literary agent wants me to call her in San Francisco."

"Oh! Won't that be expensive? Anything past Seaview is long distance."

"Please? It's important. I'll pay back whatever it costs."

"Well, I suppose." She led the way into the living room. A dog sat scratching itself on a threadbare carpet. A bare light bulb hung from the plywood ceiling. She pointed to a dark corner, where an old black dial telephone sat crooked atop a pile of equipment catalogs.

With my heart in my throat, I dialed the number on the card.

After the fifth ring there was a click. "Pomada Larsen Literary Agency. Elizabeth here."

"This is Bill Sullivan in Oregon. You wanted me to call?"

"Good Lord, Sullivan, is that really you? Where on earth have you been for the past month?"

"I'm sorry, I've been at this log cabin out in the woods. I thought I told you."

"Then you haven't seen the newsstands?"

"No. Why?"

My agent laughed. "Are you sitting down? That article you wrote about your hike was picked up by *Sierra Magazine*. They splashed it on the cover of a quarter million copies nationwide. With that kind of publicity, I sent your book manuscript out to sixteen publishers simultaneously. We've got three offers, and we need to make a decision fast."

"*Three* offers?" I sagged onto a couch.

"Yes, but the most enthusiastic one is from Pat Golbitz at William Morrow. She's the editor who published *A Walk Across America* by Peter Jenkins. It's already past five o'clock in New York, but she may still be in her office. Call her as soon as we hang up, OK?"

She gave me a number, and we hung up.

MaryLou was watching me nervously. "That was three and a half minutes. We've never used long distance before."

"I'm afraid I need to make one more call."

"Another! Not to San Francisco again?"

"No, actually, New York."

"Oh my." She bit her lip.

I dialed the numbers and waited as the connection crackled across a continent. Then a woman's voice said, "Golbitz."

I swallowed. "Ms. Golbitz? This is Bill Sullivan, the author of *Listening for Coyote*. My agent Elizabeth Pomada said—"

"Your agent should be drawn and quartered. She refused to give me your number. Don't you have telephones out there in Oregon?"

"Uh, not everywhere. You see, I live at this log cabin without electricity. We have to row across a river and hike up a road to get to a phone."

"You're kidding."

"No, I'm calling from a dairy farm on the Sahalie River."

There was a silence from New York. Then she said, "All right, maybe we can use that in the PR. Now, about the book. I love the way you've written it, and I know you've got other publishers interested, so I've offered your agent a pre-emptive bid of $25,000. On the condition that we close the deal with you immediately."

I gasped. "Twe—twenty-five?" This was more money than I had earned in my entire life!

"As an advance, of course. Do we have a deal?"

I nodded, and then realized she couldn't hear a nod. "Yes. Yes, that sounds fine."

"Good. I'll work out the details with your agent. And Mr. Sullivan? Thanks for writing this book." Then she hung up.

In a daze, I lowered the receiver onto the phone.

The very next morning I drove into Taylorville and bought the $2000 woodstove on credit. By evening I had hauled the parts in along the river trail and assembled everything inside the log cabin's kitchen. Then I hammered the assembly bolt threads flat so that the stove could never be disassembled. Even if burglars broke into the cabin again, the warming rack, claw feet, and decorative chrome trim now made this elaborate stove far too large to fit through the cabin doorway.

After the kids had gone to bed, Janell and I turned down the kerosene lantern. She sat on my lap and watched a coffeepot simmer on the beautiful new stove. Orange firelight flickered in the chrome bells of the air intake vents.

"This is perfect, just like this," Janell said.

"You don't want to use the advance to buy a new car? Or a sailboat?"

"No, just my stove. I don't want anything else to change."

I held her closer. "Neither do I."

I was about to kiss her when I noticed a movement outside the dark window.

"What's wrong?" she asked.

"Shh." I nodded to the kitchen window. "Someone's outside. At the cooler."

"That's where I put the food from the creek," she whispered.

In the faint light outside the window I could just make out a small dark hand lifting the lid of the cooler cabinet mounted on the cabin's back wall. "That's not a human hand," I whispered, growing more alarmed.

"It doesn't look like a beaver either." Her voice rose uncertainly.

Suddenly the lid banged shut. A burglar's mask with narrow-set, beady eyes stared in the window at us. Two small hands held up a stick of butter.

"Hey!" Janell jumped toward the window. The burglar leapt to the ground and scrambled toward a tree.

I grabbed a flashlight and aimed it out the window. On a branch thirty feet high, licking the stolen butter, was a large raccoon.

"I think we need a new refrigerator," I said.

"No, the one we've got is fine," Janell said. "We just need a burglar-proof latch."

25

To Elsie With Love

(June 1991)

> Today, Elsie, on our golden anniversary, this book is dedicated to you.
>
> —J. Wesley Sullivan, To Elsie With Love, 1993

"I wonder what Kitsa makes of her two lives?" my father mused, watching our cat's pink nose sniff inquisitively at the holes of her cardboard carrier. My parents were helping us move into the log cabin for the summer. Dad and I had stopped to rest on the steps of Pete's cabin while Mom, Janell, and the kids caught up.

"What do you mean, two lives?" I unlocked the sliding glass door of Pete's cabin and glanced inside to make sure nothing had been disturbed over the winter.

"Well, for nine months of every year she lives like an ordinary domestic cat in Eugene. How many other cats live on your block?"

"Fourteen, at last count." Pete's cabin looked OK, but as always I was struck that he had never really finished it after his initial burst of construction six years before. Now when he visited the Sahalie, he spent his time calculating the forest's timber volume, not working on his cabin. The walls were still bare two-by-four studs. The mismatched cabinets were still stacked along the walls. It was true that Pete had installed an intercom between our two cabins, but our communication had dangerous gaps. His argument with me about logging the property remained as unfinished as his cabin.

"I imagine a lot of the other cats are larger than her?"

"What?" I closed the door and returned to my father. "Oh sure. Kitsa only survives in Eugene because she's smart. And still pretty fast, for her age."

"What a frightening existence." Dad sighed and looked out across the pasture, a soothing sea of green. "And then she gets in a cardboard box and finds herself miraculously transported each summer to Cat Nirvana on the Sahalie. Here she has everything she could want. A log cabin with nooks where she can sleep. Small wildlife to satisfy her prowling and pouncing instincts. For three months each year Kitsa escapes the world of ordinary cats to reign as queen of all she surveys."

I put on my pack. "I think that's why people need a summer getaway too."

Grandma Elsie and the kids marched into view on the river trail. Karen ran ahead to join us on the porch. "How many cows do we have this year? I don't see any!"

"Maybe we'll find them on the other side of the field," I suggested. As we hiked the steep path down into the pasture I lagged behind to give my mother an arm. Mom was seventy, but I worried that she appeared to have aged dramatically in the past year. Her hair had turned completely gray, she had lost weight, and she walked with a slight stoop. I wished I knew what was causing her sudden decline.

"There they are!" Karen exclaimed, pointing to a cluster of Holstein heifers.

"Looks like the Niemis must have had a white bull last year," my father commented. The young cattle were in fact mostly white, their fur marked only by occasional black spots and squiggles.

"They look kind of goofy," I said. An inquisitive heifer nervously reached out her nose toward us. She was entirely white except for two black circles around her eyes. "Especially this one."

"I'm going to call her Sunglasses," Karen announced. "Let's name them all."

"Then this one should be called Necktie." My father pointed to a heifer with a black splotch at her throat.

"And this one's Mousie," Ian said. I had to study the heifer a moment before I recognized the black spot on its side as a distorted Mickey Mouse hat.

Janell caught up with us, a grocery bag in her arms. "Could that one be Lizzie?"

Slowly, painfully, a bony old cow made its way through the herd of young heifers. Her ear tag was gone and her legs were stiff, but the pattern of spots on her back awoke old memories from our first summers at the Sahalie. Our tame old friend hobbled forward to Janell and lowered her head.

"It's been fourteen years," I marveled. "The Niemis must have finally put her out to pasture."

"Don't they usually butcher dry cows?" my father asked.

"Grandpa!" Karen complained. "Ian and I are vegetarian now. Don't talk about killing animals."

Janell scratched the fur on Lizzie's nose. "I'm glad they let her come back for one last summer. Lizzie never wanted to leave this side of the river. Now she's home again."

Kitsa meowed from inside her box, an eerie wail of warning. My father carried the box on toward the log cabin. "I think this cat's been in here too long without a bathroom break."

The rest of us followed. When we finally caught sight of the log cabin I noted with relief that the shutters were intact. But I also saw that a maple tree on the hill had started leaning toward the cabin during the winter. It would need to be cut before it fell and damaged the roof.

"Why are the children vegetarian?" my mother asked, apparently still stuck on Karen's remark.

"We told you, Mom," I said. "A lot of the kids in their grade school are vegetarian. I guess because we live near the university."

"So Karen and Ian are copying other children?"

"It's not just that. They don't want to eat meat from a steer they've known personally. They treat the cattle here like pets."

Janell added, "It didn't help when our freezer broke down last summer. By the time we got back to Eugene we had two hundred pounds of rotten meat in the basement. The whole house smelled like roadkill for a month."

"Oh, that does sound bad." Mother wrinkled her nose.

While I got out the keys to unlock the front door, Dad opened the cat carrier. Kitsa rushed out, stopped to sniff in all directions, and then strutted down toward the pasture, her tail high.

"Hail Queen Kitsa ," Dad said. "The monarch of the Sahalie has returned to reign over her savannah."

"To fertilize her savannah, more likely," Janell said. "Kitsa likes molehills out in the field because the soft dirt's easy to dig."

I struggled with the keys, trying to find the right one.

"Kitsa's pooping!" Ian announced.

Finally I opened the lock.

"Uh oh, here come the cows," Karen said.

I looked up. Our herd of heifers had drawn themselves up into a line as if for a cavalry charge. Cattle instinctively chase cats, dogs, and other four-legged intruders. It is as if cows remember, deep in their bovine brains, a time long ago when they needed to charge as a herd to defend against wolves or saber-tooth tigers.

At first the cattle trotted slowly toward Kitsa. The cat perched awkwardly atop a molehill, her tail in the air. Then the heifers lowered their heads and broke into a run. Kitsa held her ground, determined to finish her business, but the hooves were thundering closer. At the last possible moment she kicked a rooster tail of dirt behind her, shot across the grass, and dove under the fence.

I opened the door just in time for a bolt of Siamese lightning to streak into the safety of the log cabin.

"Long live the Queen," my father said, and we all laughed.

We divided up chores to prepare the cabin for the summer. I went from window to window, unfastening the shutters. My mother swept out the dust and dead flies that had accumulated over the winter. My father started scything the tall grass in our front yard. Janell carefully unpacked and reinstalled the cookplates and firebox door of her chrome-plated woodstove. She took these essential parts to Eugene each winter to make absolutely sure that no one would attempt to steal her prized range.

Once the fire was going and enough of the shutters were removed that we had daylight in the cabin, Janell gave the children their moving-in presents. Each year we gave them a toy on the first day to help entertain them at the cabin. They tore open the wrapping paper excitedly.

"Cool! I got the *Enterprise!*" Karen showed off a model kit of a galaxy-class starship.

"And I got a Klingon battlecruiser!" Ian exclaimed. Janell spread newspaper on the kitchen table and helped them start gluing their plastic spaceships together.

When I finished with the shutters I found Mom rearranging the books on the living room shelf. "I brought some extra books," she said, "so you can have an entire section by Sullivans."

In addition to *Listening for Coyote*, the journal of my hike across Oregon, she had brought copies of the two outdoor guidebooks I had published more recently. She had even brought a computer manual Pete had written about his real estate program, although it seemed out of place at a log cabin without electricity.

"This is still my favorite," she said, pulling out *Jam on the Ceiling*, a collection of my father's newspaper columns. After Dad had refused to put together this anthology himself Pete and I had done it for him secretly as a Christmas surprise. I had edited hundreds of Dad's old columns into a manuscript and Pete had used his computer expertise to format it into a book. We had named it *Jam on the Ceiling* after his most famous column—the story of a disastrous weekend when he attempted to make homemade strawberry jam while my mother was out of town. Finally we had wrapped up one copy, labeled it "For Dad," and tossed it under the family Christmas tree. Dad had been dumbfounded when he unwrapped the book and discovered he was the author.

"It shows what you and Pete can accomplish when you work together instead of arguing," my mother said. She set the book on the shelf with its face out.

"Well I blast you back with photon torpedos!" Karen shouted, zooming her horribly beweaponed starship past us in a dogfight with her brother's Klingon cruiser.

"Maybe you two could play upstairs," I suggested. "Why don't you go find the cat?"

"Yeah!" Ian said.

"Warp five to the Planet of Fleas," Karen said, heading for the spiral staircase. "Engage!"

Moments later Kitsa bolted down the stairs, looking hunted. She paused at the porch door, her tail twitching. Perhaps she remembered her recent encounter with the heifers, because instead of going outside she trotted into the kitchen and climbed onto a high shelf behind the woodstove. There the Queen of the Sahalie sprawled, out of reach of cow hooves and photon torpedos, warming her paws beside the heat-shimmering stovepipe.

Later that week, after my parents had returned to Salem, I took a bow saw up the hill behind the cabin to deal with the little leaning maple tree. I didn't want it to fall on the cabin. By now I had enough experience felling trees that I was confident I could easily aim this sapling out of harm's way. I targeted an open spot between the cabin and the outhouse and began sawing out the undercut notch.

But the little tree's trunk was curved in a funny sort of way, and it surprised me by leaning onto my saw, pinching the blade. The saw sat there, absolutely stuck. To get the blade loose I had little choice but to chop through the trunk higher up with an ax. This freed the saw, but it also made my previous targeting efforts worthless. With dismay I watched the tree tilt toward the cabin roof. I grimaced and twisted to one side, as if my gymnastics might yet change the tree's direction.

The treetop hit the roof with a leafy *whoomph* and bounced slightly. Almost immediately our cat shot out of the kitchen window. A moment later Janell poked her head out and yelled, "Nice aim!" Smoke began drifting out the window around her.

I dropped the ax and scrambled down the hill to the cabin. I quickly determined that the leaves of the treetop had cushioned the blow enough that the roof itself was largely undamaged. The trunk however, had managed to hit the stovepipe dead center, ramming it down three feet until the flattened cap was flush with the roof.

Inside, the kitchen was a hell of soot and smoke. The stovepipe had ripped loose on its way down, leaving the stove pumping black smoke like a trapped locomotive.

"Jesus, Janell, are you all right?"

She was on her knees, using a ladle and an oven mitt to scoop red-hot coals from the firebox into a washbasin on the floor. Sparks flew up about her smudged face as she worked. "I was baking cookies," she said through gritted teeth. "Then all of a sudden somebody felled a tree on my stove."

"I'm sorry! I honestly didn't think it would hit the cabin."

"Oh you didn't? Then it was a big surprise for you too?"

Karen's voice asked from the other room, "Can we help?"

I carried a bucket of flaming firewood out past the wide-eyed children. "I think you two can help best by staying outside in the yard a few minutes. Papa made a big goof."

For the rest of the morning I scrubbed soot out of the cabin. Janell took the cookies to Pete's cabin to finish baking them in his propane oven. That afternoon I cut the tree off the roof, removed the mangled stovepipe, and put a bucket temporarily over the hole.

By the next day, when we were driving into Taylorville to buy new stovepipe, I was already able to view the fiasco as a hidden opportunity. "You know, as long as I have to repair the roof, I might as well add a gable to the kids' room. A gable with a window would give them more headroom, more light, and a view of the pasture."

"Gee, you could write a whole book about it," Janell suggested, her tone suspiciously bright. "How about calling it, *Remodel Your Home With Falling Trees*."

Although Janell's resentment about the tree incident lingered for weeks, the resulting roof repair project turned out to be immensely popular with the children. Building the gable involved cutting, barking, and flattening a number of small, kid-sized logs. One corner of our front yard became a construction site, where I prepared the logs while Karen and Ian ran around on them, balancing and jumping and participating in general.

Because Karen was older than her brother, and very verbal, she tended to boss him about when they played. One day Ian jumped over a log and threw a wood chip toward the pasture.

At once Karen admonished him, "No, Ian! You're not supposed to do it like that. *You* did it like *this*." She demonstrated by staggering over the log with her tongue hanging out. Then she threw a wood chip at her feet with her face screwed up in confusion. "You're *supposed* to do it like *this!*" Karen returned to normal, leapt gracefully over the log and threw a wood chip like a baseball pitcher.

Ian, ever silent, aped her motions as best he could.

Karen still complained, "No, Ian, you did it like *this*," and she started her demonstration over again.

Finally it got to be too much for me. I asked Ian, "How come you do what she tells you?"

Ian shrugged silently.

I went on, "I bet if you hit yourself over the head with a stick she'd say, 'No, Ian!' Then she'd clobber herself on the head with a stick, and say, "*You* did it like *this!* You're *supposed* to do it like *this!*"

Both kids laughed. But Ian still didn't say anything.

Later that day Janell and I were reading in the kitchen while the kids played a game upstairs under the unfinished gable. From what we could overhear, it seemed they were pretending a family of magic otters was battling Ian's stuffed bear with rainbows.

"Hey, it's my turn!" Karen said in her usual bossy tone.

To my surprise Ian dared to reply, "It is not."

"It is so!" Karen retorted.

"Is not."

Frustrated perhaps by his unexpected defiance, Karen announced, "Well, you're a dope."

"No, you are," came the brave little reply.

"No, you are!"

"I am not."

"Are so."

"Am not."

"Yes, you are!"

Ian responded, "Oh yeah? Then prove it."

Karen paused as she puzzled out this challenge. "Prove what?"

"That I'm not a dope," Ian said.

And for once Karen was struck completely silent.

A few days later Ian hiked with me to the boat landing. I needed to ferry cedar posts across the river from the Niemis so I could repair our fence. I loaded a dozen posts on *Earnest's* deck, perched atop the heap, and paddled across canoe-style. Ian sat in the backseat with his orange life jacket, staring down into the river.

"Look how deep the water gets," I said. "Right at the bank here it goes down as deep as a house."

We landed and climbed up the bank. He turned to watch the green water slowly backing up with the tide.

"Funny, isn't it?" I said. "You'd expect noisy whitewater rivers to be deep, but they're not. The Sahalie hardly moves, but it's twenty feet deep."

"Yeah," he said.

"There's a saying," I added. "'Still waters run deep.' But the saying is really meant to be about people, not just rivers."

I went on with my work, stacking fenceposts. Ian, however, remained on the bank, silently staring out into the impenetrably green Sahalie.

Never had we seen so many hummingbirds and yellowjackets as that summer. I had to rope off an area beyond the woodshed because the bees had built a nest in a hole in the ground. As long we stayed clear, they zoomed in and out of their den without bothering us much.

The hummingbirds, however, were closer to home, fighting over the flower box directly outside our kitchen window. While we sat at breakfast, calmly spooning up grapefruit, the thumb-sized birds outside would swoop and dive bomb each other, buzzing and squeaking fiercely. Even when I cranked open the window they battled on, almost within arm's reach, vying for supremacy over the potted geraniums. As soon as one of the birds temporarily established air control it would frantically dart about, stabbing flowers and even unopened buds with its needly beak in search of nectar. If a second hummingbird attempted to join in, a spectacular aerial dogfight invariably ensued. Often both combatants would lose, with one bird zooming away over the house while the other spiraled off to the clothesline.

One morning Janell opened our bird book on the breakfast table. After a minute she gave me a puzzled look. "They're females."

I checked the book's illustrations. She was right. The fierce hummingbirds we saw fighting—some shimmering green or blue, others with a regal red dot on their throats—were all females. "I wouldn't have thought female hummingbirds would be so mean."

"They must really want nectar." Janell watched out the window as a hummingbird zipped from the clothesline to the fence and back. Suddenly Janell picked up the binoculars that we kept on the windowsill. She adjusted the focus and smiled. "Aha!"

"What is it?"

She handed me the binoculars. "Look closely at the barbed wire beside the gate. One of those barbs is a baby."

"You're kidding." I focused on the fence. A tiny green bird, no bigger than a fingernail, was clutching the wire. It pointed its tiny needle beak one direction and then the other. It wiggled its tiny fuzzy wings. As I watched, the mother buzzed up and hovered. A giant by comparison, she refueled the baby with her beak.

"That's incredible." I put down the binoculars. "Let's show the kids."

"Let's make sure the cat stays inside."

For the rest of the morning our cabin served as a blind while we watched the baby hummingbird. It sat on its wire fully six hours that day before it finally buzzed erratically across the pasture toward the river.

What was wrong with my mother? Toward the end of summer my parents returned for a weekend. Dad was as ebullient as ever, laughing and joking with the children, but when he looked the other way, I thought I noticed a dark shadow cross Mom's face. She seemed so frail and quiet! I asked if anything was wrong, but she merely shook her head.

On the first day of the weekend we had a picnic in the yard, with a watermelon, corn on the cob, and a bottle of sparkling apple cider. "Forty-nine years," my father announced, leaning back in his lawn chair. "At our next wedding anniversary, your mother and I will have been married almost half a century. Did I ever tell you about our first date?"

Of course he had, but it was new to the children, and they giggled when he described tipping Grandma Elsie's canoe in the University of Oregon's Mill Race.

The sun shone through dappled alders. A hawk circled above the pasture. It was the kind of glorious afternoon at the Sahalie that made me wish time could stand still. My father took a deep breath, savoring the scent of deep grass and wood smoke. He closed his eyes and sighed, "It doesn't get any better than this." Did the corner of my mother's mouth twitch before she turned aside?

"Look, here comes the cat," she said.

In the door of the cabin, Kitsa blinked at the sunshine and yawned.

"Well," Dad said, "the Queen of the Sahalie finally awakens."

Kitsa paraded before us, crossing the yard. Karen tried to grab her, but the cat jumped past.

"You can't stop Kitsa when she's on her way to a throne," Janell said.

The cat looked about, choosing a direction. Then she walked straight into the roped-off area behind the woodshed.

"Not there, Kitsa." I stood up.

"What's behind the rope?" my father asked.

"A yellowjacket nest." I hesitated to go after the cat, afraid that I would disturb the nest myself.

With the aloof demeanor of royalty, Kitsa perched directly over the soft dirt of the nest's entrance hole and lifted her tail.

I began backing away. "I think we should go inside."

Suddenly a swarm of angry yellow insects buzzed out of the earth. Kitsa leapt in the air. When she hit the ground, her fur was standing on end. Yellowjackets arced about her like incoming missiles. She twitched, put her ears back, and streaked across the yard toward the cabin door.

The rest of us hurried after her—except for Ian, who for some reason was simply standing there in the yard, watching the bees zoom about him.

"Ian, come on!" Janell cried.

The little boy stood perfectly still. Suddenly he jerked his leg, frowned, and said, "Ow."

I dashed back down the steps, swept him up in my arms, and carried him inside. Then I yanked off his shoes, picked him up, and gave him a shake. A yellowjacket fell out of his pant leg and flew to the window.

"Why wouldn't you come when I called?" Janell demanded. "Didn't you know how much a bee sting hurts?"

"No," he said, his lips tight. Obviously the pain in his leg was intense, but he refused to cry. "I was doing an experiment."

It was several months later, at Easter, before the truth emerged about my mother. Janell and I had taken the kids to Salem for the traditional egg hunt in the backyard of my parents' apartment. Afterwards Dad asked me to go for a walk with him, alone. As we strolled among the oaks of the neighboring city park he announced, "I'm going to write a book."

"A book? About what?" I asked.

He gave me a sad smile. "That's what I asked too."

"I don't understand. I thought you didn't like writing books. Pete and I had to put your last one together."

He sat on a park bench and stared at his hands. "I guess I'd better start at the beginning."

"I guess so." I sat beside him, worrying already that this might not be good news.

"Two weeks ago I took your mother out to dinner to celebrate our forty-ninth wedding anniversary. At first she was cheerful. Then I realized it was only an act."

"Is something wrong with Mom?" I asked.

He held up his hands and looked away. "She told me she'd been to the doctor that morning for a physical. She passed all the usual tests just fine."

"And?" An ominous fear began spreading through me.

"And then she asked the doctor about a problem she has with her car."

"What?" I looked at my father. "A doctor's not a mechanic."

He lowered his head. "Her problem was that she sometimes gets in the car and just sits there. She doesn't know what to do. She says it's like she simply forgets what comes next."

"That could happen to anyone," I objected.

"Anyway, the doctor said he'd give her a little quiz. Sort of a game. He asked her to list the letters of the alphabet backwards, starting with Z." Dad slammed his hand on the armrest, shaking the park bench. "She couldn't do it. She couldn't get past Z. He asked her what was the capital of Italy. She couldn't remember. He asked all kinds of questions—obvious things that she used to know. But she didn't have any of the answers."

"Then it's not just forgetfulness?"

He shook his head. "The doctor said it's dementia. Probably Alzheimer's."

"What!"

"He said it's going to get worse. She's gradually going to forget everything." My father covered his eyes with a hand.

"There's got to be something we can do," I said.

He wiped his eyes. "That's what I said too. And you know what she answered?"

I shook my head.

"She asked me a favor, as a present for our anniversary. Of course I told her I'd grant her anything."

"What did she want?"

"She wants me to write me a book about our marriage." My father took a deep breath and looked out among the oaks. "She asked me to write down everything, starting with the very first time we saw each other. Everything. So that she'll never forget, no matter what happens."

26

The Sahalie Spirit

(June 1994)

> The winds which passed over my dwelling were such as sweep over the ridges of mountains, bearing the broken strains, or celestial parts only, of terrestrial music.
>
> —Henry David Thoreau, Walden, 1854

I was angry and alone, carrying a small square box of ash along the trail to the Sahalie. Never had the misty rainforest seemed so gray. The call of an unseen spiral bird leaked from the gloom like a cry from the netherworld.

My mother had not deserved this humiliating death. Over the past three years a horrible, mind-eating disease had stolen her from us, thought by thought. She should have lived to watch her grandchildren grow up, go to college, and start their own lives!

At first Mom had been able to fight her way through the fog. Many an evening my father stayed up with her, reading aloud from his book, *To Elsie With Love*. Then she would smile, and the tension of her mental battle seemed to ease.

By the third year, however, as the disease shut down more and more of her brain, almost everything made her fearful - noises, strange people, timetables, expectations, even inactivity. She began venting her anger at my father, a man already weary from his role as caregiver. She would call him Gus or Chris, or fail to recognize him at all, saying, "I'm supposed to know him, but I don't." Her confusion was typical of Alzheimer's, but it hurt nonetheless.

Finally, bed-ridden and exhausted, she withdrew from the world, first closing out her apartment, then her friends, then her family—and finally the arduous task of breathing.

By the time I stopped to rest beneath an ancient spruce tree, my anger at losing my mother had yielded somewhat. I needed to accept her passing and face my task. I opened the gilt cardboard box and lifted out a plastic bag the size of a pouch of brown sugar. With a jolt of both grief and horror, I recognized chunks of white among the gray powder. Bits of bone.

Alas, Mother! Was this all that remained of the caring, loving woman who had held our family together all those years? At forty-one, I was the youngest of her four children. Perhaps that had left me the least prepared. I had been shocked when, a month after Mother's death, the other children suggested we drop the custom of gathering in Salem on Christmas. We would no longer exchange gifts. Our family had grown old. Things fall apart; the center cannot hold.

Hesitantly, I untied the plastic bag. No one had wanted to come with me this day. Even Janell and the kids were waiting in Taylorville until I was done. Perhaps I should have listened when my eldest brother Mark suggested I wear gloves. Mark's new in-laws were Chinese. They had been amazed that Elsie wanted her remains scattered at the Sahalie, instead of being properly interred. Mark's mother-in-law had called him twice to warn of the dangerous spirits this folly might unleash upon us.

I scooped up a handful of ash and strewed it into the woods on either side of the trail, like a farmer broadcasting seeds. What legacy would spring from this ground, I wondered? In life, Mom had made the Sahalie a refuge of family peace by the sheer force of her will. She had forbidden the family from arguing about whether our thirty acres of Sahalie forest should be logged. Now that she was gone, changes were in the wind.

My father did not believe in silencing dissent. An open, honest man, he wanted disagreements discussed and resolved—the sooner the better. And so he had announced that his four children should decide how to manage the Sahalie property now, before the summer was over.

But how could we agree? Would we cut the forest or not? What would become of the cabins? And would the decision tear us even farther apart?

I walked slowly around the pasture from Pete's cabin to mine, spreading a fairy-dust memorial to my mother's peacekeeping.

"This may or may not be a good place to raise trees," Janell said, helping a crowd of children crank out pasta dough in the log cabin kitchen, "But it's definitely a good place to raise kids."

In fact, Janell and I were pouring a lot of effort into kid-oriented activities that summer. How else would we keep Karen and Ian interested in life at a remote log cabin? Karen was fourteen, an awkward Middle School age when peers and showers and good hair days were critical.

Ian was twelve, just emerging from Grade School into a world where everything seemed to be growing like crazy, including him.

Together Janell and I had made a list of our top three projects for the summer: 1. Arrange for lots of other kids to come visit. 2. Feed them constantly. 3. Do something to improve bathing facilities.

Altogether we had booked nineteen cousins and school chums to stop by, in twos and threes, over the next two months. Parents seemed delighted to get their children out of the house and into our unofficial Sahalie summer camp. The current batch of visitors consisted of Lisa, a long-haired, blonde eighth grader with a turned-up nose and an equally turned-up wit; and Trevor, a dark-haired sixth grader with a fascination for food and secret weapons.

Trevor's first words each morning were "What's for dinner?" Once we had settled this issue—while the kids packed away a long and large breakfast—Trevor and Ian would go to work in the front yard. There they cobbled together scraps of metal and wood into fierce-looking but relatively harmless "thistle whackers." They used these machetes to slay the Canadian thistles in the pasture. When he thought we weren't listening, Trevor fantasized about creating a potato cannon, using a pipe, a can of hairspray, and a match, in order to lob vegetables at the dairy cows across the river.

Lisa and Karen, meanwhile, had invented a game they called Limited Vocabulary. By turns, each of them was restricted for half an hour to a vocabulary of only seven words: No, What, Why, Oh wow, Maybe, and Hmm.

"I'm going to make the perfect noodle," Ian announced, holding up a sheet of green pasta dough.

"Oh wow," Lisa said sarcastically, rolling her eyes. "Why?"

Trevor snickered as he laid his noodles in crosses on a cookie sheet. "I'm making pistol pasta. It's shaped like swords and machine guns."

"Look, I'm braiding mine," Karen said. "Want to mix colors?"

"Hmm," Lisa replied. "Maybe."

My particular assignment for the summer was to do something about the bath situation. Bathing had always been a problem at the Sahalie, partly because the river itself was too cold and murky for swimming to be much fun. One year my father had rigged up an outdoor shower at the cabin, using a bucket, a rope, and a pulley hung from the eave. But the shower had several drawbacks. It was hard to heat enough water on the wood stove. Hoisting the heavy bucket required two people. And the person who actually took the shower had to stand outside naked, exposed to mosquitoes, cold winds, and the scrutiny of passersby on their way to the outhouse.

For many years we had been reduced to bathing in pioneer fashion—taking turns scrubbing ourselves in a washtub on the kitchen floor. As in *Little House in the Big Woods,* the children would get to wash first, then Mama, and finally Papa. Not only did I wind up with cold, brackish water, but I had to contort myself into bizarre yoga positions to fit various parts of my body into that little tub.

Sometimes I gave up, drove the family into Taylorville, and jumped with them into the public swimming pool to get clean.

This summer, however, spurred by the demands of an increasingly fastidious teenage daughter, I had come up with a radical new bathing plan: I would build a solar hot tub.

The idea came to me when I heard that my brother Mark in Beaverton was dismantling his experimental solar water heating system. In the late 1970s, inspired by articles in the *Whole Earth Catalog,* Mark had built four solar panels. Each panel consisted of a network of copper tubes in an insulated plywood frame. The top of each panel was a sheet of glass scavenged from an old sliding door. Mark had mounted these homemade panels on the roof of his suburban Beaverton home. Then he had connected them to his existing water heater with a pump. For years the system had worked well, substantially reducing his electricity bills on sunny months. But one winter the pump failed, the pipes froze, and water wound up pouring through Mark's roof. He had been ready to haul the panels to the dump when I offered to take them off his hands. I patched up three of them and arduously hauled them in to the log cabin for my hot tub project.

Of course a key part of my project was still missing: a suitable tub. Our old washtub was far too small, and we couldn't afford to spend thousands of dollars on an official Jacuzzi-type pool. Surprisingly, I spotted a promising vat in an ad for a ranch supply store in Taylorville.

When we went to the ranch store the clerk that met us wore a cowboy hat and pointed boots. He sized up Janell and me skeptically. "So you folks want to buy a cattle watering trough? Well, how many head are we talking about here?"

"A family of four," I said.

"A family of four?" He puzzled over this a moment. "That's a mighty small herd of cattle. I reckon you could get by with the hundred-dollar model." He showed us an oval, 150-gallon tub molded from half-inch-thick, recycled black plastic. Large white letters on the side announced, RUBBERMAID AGRICULTURAL DIVISION.

"Could I try it out?" Janell asked.

"Try out a watering trough?" He took off his hat and scratched his head. "Just how would you do that, ma'am?"

Janell stepped into the empty tub, sat down, and made herself comfortable. "Yes, I think this will do nicely."

Although I suspect the clerk thought we were lunatic refugees from some urban asylum, he sold us the trough, a black garden hose, and a bag of hose clamps. Then I hauled everything in to the log cabin and laid it out in the front yard. Without electricity, of course, I couldn't use a pump to force hot water from the panels to the tub. Instead the system would have to rely on convection—the tendency of hot water to rise. So I positioned the tub at the edge of the yard and set the three panels below it, on the slope down toward the pasture. Then I connected everything with pieces of black hose, filled the tub with water from the creek, and hoped that the sun would eventually come out from behind the clouds.

When the sun finally emerged the next day I measured the water temperature with Janell's candy thermometer. The outlet hose was slowly sucking chilly, 50°F water from the bottom of the tub. Once the water had made its way through the tubing in the three solar panels, however, it reemerged at a scalding 170°F at the top of the tub.

After five hours the sun disappeared behind the trees. I stirred up the water in the tub, tested the temperature with my hand, and invited the troops to try it out.

"Girls first!" Lisa cried. She and Karen had evidently anticipated the grand opening of the pool. They ran out of the cabin, already wearing swimsuits.

Karen dipped a toe into the water and said, "Oh wow!"

"It's 108 degrees," I warned.

"No!"

"Yes. And you can't use soap in the tub, so you'll have to wash your hair later."

"How?" Karen asked.

"In a wash basin."

"What!"

"There's plenty of hot water."

"Hmm," Karen said. "Maybe."

The girls climbed into the tub, splashing and giggling. "Boys have to wait!" Lisa taunted.

Ian and Trevor sulked on their way back to the cabin. They whispered conspiratorially. A few minutes later, when I was in the kitchen with Janell, I noticed the boys creeping like commandos through the grass toward the hot tub. Ian had a toy shark in his hand. Trevor carried a giant squirt gun attached to a water tank on his back.

With a nod I drew Janell's attention to the boys outside, stalking ever closer to the unsuspecting girls. Janell raised an eyebrow and closed her book.

I scooted back my chair. "It's my turn to intervene."

Janell stopped me with her hand. "Those girls have been plaguing the boys for days."

"But— " Squeals and splashes erupted outside.

Janell smiled and reopened her book.

Time was running out for the four Sullivan siblings to decide how to manage the Sahalie forestland. Finally we agreed on a summit at the log cabin on a Saturday in mid August. Pete arranged for a professional forestry consultant to hike in and offer advice. My sister Susan, who had always been the family's best mediator, promised to be on hand. Her role became even more important when Mark sent word that he would leave the decision to the other three of us.

On the chosen Saturday Janell and I nervously straightened up the cabin and the yard. Pete arrived first, hiking up to the log cabin in jeans, a business shirt, and a baseball cap. I barely had time to show him the solar hot tub before Susan's family arrived in a noisy mob.

Karen and Ian rushed out to greet their cousins. Susan's children really had changed a lot in the past few years. Eva, who once had known only the words "No" and "Wiley," was a talkative imp. Mike, the garrulous bargainer, had become a quiet, lanky teenager.

Susan dropped her backpack on the picnic table and sank into a lawn chair. "We tried to call ahead from the other cabin, but the intercom must be broken."

"Oh, sorry," Pete said. "I think it's something with the buzzers."

Susan's husband Nick hiked up to join us. "Your television's broken too," he said.

"What television?" I asked, puzzled.

Nick held his hand out to the empty pasture. "You know, the cows. They're gone. What are you going to watch from your window without the Cow Channel?"

Janell and I laughed. "You're right," she said. "We used to watch the heifers a lot. I wish the Niemis would put some over here again."

"Why don't they?" Susan asked.

I shrugged. "I guess they got tired of swimming them over."

"Fair enough," Nick said. "We were getting tired of all that beef we got as rent."

"Mama?" Eva asked, pulling Susan's arm. "Can we do the airplanes now?"

Pete perked up. "What airplanes?"

Susan gave a disparaging wave. "Oh, I brought a book of paper airplane patterns for the kids. But we probably don't have time to make them now."

"Sure we do!" Pete said. "The forester isn't coming for another hour."

Susan reached for her pack, opened it, and took out *The Big Book of Do-It-Yourself Paper Airplanes*. All four of the children crowded around.

"I want to make The Tube," Mike said, pointing to a black, circular paper plane pictured on the cover.

"I'll help each of you make one," Susan said.

"I've got an idea," I said. "Why don't we have a contest for the kids? We could have two prizes, one for the plane that flies longest and one for the plane that flies farthest."

Susan groaned. "Why do Sullivans have to be so competitive?" But by then the kids were already asking about the prizes and discussing which planes might win in the two different categories.

Karen chose the Valkyrie, a sheet of paper folded into two overlapping triangles. Ian opted for the Falcon, a sleek, dart-shaped missile. Eva hesitated a long time before making her choice. Finally she asked her father which paper airplane he thought might win. Nick suggested the World Record plane, a slow, rectangular model that held the indoor flying record. Susan tore out the appropriate pages from the book. Janell got cellophane tape and paperclips from the cabin.

Soon the kids were test-flying their entries for the Great Paper Airplane Contest. I could tell that they were throwing their planes much too hard. The planes dived violently, bending their noses. The kids added paperclips, hoping to improve performance. Because breezes tended to distract Karen's plane into circuitous flights, she argued that loops and curves should count toward the overall distance. After some debate, the others overruled her; length of flight would be measured solely in a straight line toward the pasture fence.

Finally the four children lined up beside the picnic table to throw their airplanes for the contest. Susan, always the diplomat, was chosen judge. The other adults shouted encouragement as, one by one, the kids launched the Tube, the Valkyrie, the Falcon, and the World-Record Plane. When the last plane had crashed into the grass Susan announced that Karen and Mike had tied for the longest time aloft—just under three seconds. Ian and Eva tied for the longest distance—just short of the pasture fence. As a result, all four children shared cookies as prizes. The adults applauded and everyone was happy.

Still I couldn't help suggesting, "Now that the kids are done, I wonder if I could submit an entry, just as a demonstration?"

Susan shrugged and tore out a blank sheet of airplane paper from the back of her book. "Go ahead."

"What's yours going to be called, Papa?" Karen asked.

"Let's call it the Sputnik." I stood up, wadded the paper into a tight ball, and threw it overarm. The ball rocketed into the sky for three full seconds and landed ten feet past the fence.

"Wow, Papa!" Ian said solemnly. "I guess you would have won both prizes."

"Maybe not," Pete said. "You haven't seen the Stealth Bomber yet." He took Susan's book, tore out a sheet of paper, and folded it into a wedge-shaped plane. With the windup of a pitcher in slow motion he lofted it onto the breeze. It sailed for the count of five and landed in a thistle twenty feet beyond the fence.

Susan shook her head. "You two are impossible."

Pete's professional forester turned out to be Tom Norton, an old family friend who had been assistant Scoutmaster of my Boy Scout troop in Salem. In his role as forester he wore a silver hardhat and an orange vest with countless bulging pockets. He hiked around the property with me and Pete and Susan, marveling at our cabins and our forest. I had prepared myself to be skeptical of Pete's forester, but Tom was so friendly, and so forthright, that I found it impossible not to trust him.

"You have to be realistic," Tom said when we reached the back corner of our property, on a trail near the little cabin I had built for my writing. "You can't afford to haul logs by helicopter, and it won't pay to go the old-fashioned route, using horses to drag logs down to the river. You need a road if you want to sell timber. So you've got to ask yourself, do you really want a road?"

"Yes," Pete said. "It's the only way to manage the forest."

"No," I said. "We like the isolation. A road would make us more vulnerable to burglars and vandals."

Susan sighed. She dumped her jacket on a mossy log and sat on it. "Is it even possible to build a road here?"

Tom tilted his head. "I think so. The river route is too steep, but Willamette Pacific built a road to the ridge behind you when they clearcut their property. You could pay them access rights to extend a logging road down here."

"How much would that cost?" I asked.

"Maybe $15,000," he said.

Pete peered up through the trees at the clearcut, a green jumble of salmonberry bushes and ten-foot-tall fir saplings. "And how much would we make by selling our timber along a road like that?"

"Right now, with the market low and your forest still pretty young, you'd probably make about $40,000."

"That means we'd have $25,000 profit," Susan said. "If we split it four ways, it would be a nice chunk of change, but it wouldn't exactly be like winning the lottery." She stood up and grimaced; despite her jacket, her pants had gotten wet from the log.

"You don't have that many acres you can cut," Tom explained. "A lot of your property is pasture, and state law requires that you leave buffers along rivers and creeks."

"Wait a minute," Pete objected. "The timber here is worth more than that. I've spent fifteen years thinning out alder trees. Now most of the forest is hemlock. Hemlock's more valuable, right?"

"Fifteen years ago it was." Tom took a tape out of his orange vest and measured the diameter of a hemlock tree. "Nowadays mills mostly just care about the total volume of wood fiber. If you've got big alder trees the mills sometimes pay a premium. They peel them for plywood veneer."

I slapped my forehead. "All this time Pete's been chainsawing alders and making a mess for nothing."

"Well, I wouldn't say that," Tom objected, putting his measuring tape back in a vest pocket. "Thinning really does help the other trees grow better. The hemlocks you thinned for your log cabin didn't hurt either. In another ten years this forest will be worth a lot more."

"How much more?" Susan asked, putting on her damp jacket. I worried that she cared so much about the money.

Tom shrugged. "It's hard to say. The markets change. People change. Who knows what the world will be like ten years from now?"

No one had more questions for Tom. We hiked out with him as far as Pete's cabin and said goodbye. Then Pete and Susan and I sat on folding chairs inside the unfinished cabin. Susan tried to use the intercom to ask how her children were doing at the log cabin, but the buzzer still didn't work, so she sat and stared at her hands. Although we said nothing, we all knew it was time for a decision about the management of the Sahalie forest.

Pete opened a can of cola from his propane refrigerator. "Look, I know markets change, and the science changes, but we've got to do the best we can. It's our duty to try to keep this forest growing and healthy."

"And you'd do that with a chainsaw?" I asked.

"I'd do that by managing it. A forest is like a garden. If you don't take care of it, you'll end up with a mess."

I shook my head, paced to the window, and looked down through the trees at the river. "Nature is not a mess. There are probably a thousand species all balanced together in a forest like this. You only care about the four or five you can sell."

"The bugs can take care of themselves, and you know it." Pete waved his cola at me. "You live in a house made out of wood. You write books printed on paper. How can you stand there and tell me it's a crime against Nature to cut trees?"

"Did I say that?" I turned to Susan. "Is that what I said?"

Susan put her hand to her forehead. "Let's not get into personal attacks, OK?"

I faced Pete. "Every other part of this valley is a giant tree farm. There's clearcuts for miles and miles, everywhere you look. Can't we leave this one little corner, just these few acres on our property, to let the Sahalie forest do what it wants?"

"You mean, to let it do what *you* want," Pete objected. "Our parents bought this property as an investment, not just so you could sit in your cabin and daydream. Don't you think the rest of us have a right to profit from it too?"

I sat down in a chair by the unlit woodstove. "Pete, compared to Susan and me, you're already rich. For us, five or ten thousand dollars is a lot of money. For you, it's nothing. Why do you care about the money so much?"

"How many times do I have to explain it to you? Money is not the only issue. I care about the forest, the property, the future—all of it."

"All right, that's enough," Susan said, scooting back her chair so she could look us both in the eyes. "It's getting late and I have to drive to Olympia tonight. Let's see if we can't settle this whole business. I want to hear your suggestions for how to manage the property. Pete, you go first."

Pete finished his cola and threw the can into the sink. "Simple. I'd build a road down from the ridge and log enough of the forest to pay for it. Then I'd plant the pasture with spruce trees."

"You'd turn the pasture into a tree farm?" I asked, amazed.

"Why not? We're not renting it out for cattle anymore."

"But that pasture is the view from our cabin. And think of Clyde Moreland, the old homesteader. Do you know how hard it must have been for him to clear that land?"

"The pasture is an old clearcut," Pete said. "I thought you hate clearcuts."

I turned aside, angry that Pete was right. If we wanted to restore the Sahalie forest to its original condition, we ought to plant the pasture with spruce trees. But I had grown used to our broad, green field. I remembered marveling at its tall grass when we first carried our gear through it to the log cabin site. I recalled the heifers stampeding across it the day we heard the volcano blow. I remembered Ian whacking thistles with his homemade machete, and my mother pulling tansy plants.

I sighed. "The pasture is full of history."

"History?" Pete scoffed. "You never even found out if Clyde Moreland was murdered. All you've got are ghost stories."

"Hold it," Susan said, raising her hands to demand silence. "We're not done yet. I want to know how Bill would manage the property. Go ahead."

I sank back into my lawn chair beside the cold woodstove. Suddenly I felt drained. "Well, I guess we could plant a few spruce trees around the edge of the pasture. That would help to hold the riverbank. Maybe we could thin the forest a little, mostly for firewood. But I don't want a road, and I don't want intensive logging. This is a summer retreat. It shouldn't have to look like a commercial tree plantation."

I looked to Susan. Pete was looking to Susan too. We both knew she had the deciding vote. For better or worse, Dad had left this decision to us, and our brother Mark had asked not to be involved.

"So what's the verdict?" Pete asked.

Susan let out a long breath. "I don't see much of a choice, really. The forester said he'd let our trees grow another ten years before logging. I'm no fan of cutting trees, but if they were worth a lot more than they are now, I might be interested."

"What does that mean, exactly?" I asked.

She looked at me and shrugged. "It means I think we should manage things your way for ten years. Then we can decide if we want to change things later."

Pete slammed his hand on the table and stood up. "That's it? You don't think we should do a damn thing for ten years?"

Susan took his arm. "I'm just trying to keep our options open. If we build a road and cut the forest, we can't ever go back to the way it was before."

Pete shook his arm loose. He looked around his unfinished cabin. "In that case there's nothing for me to do here. Maybe I can find timberland somewhere else." He took his coat off a nail on the wall and opened the sliding glass door.

I stood up, suddenly afraid that winning this battle could lead to a terrible loss. "You're leaving? Just like that?"

"Just like that. No reason for me to come back for ten years, if at all."

"What about the cabin here? You can't just walk away from it."

"Watch me," he said. "Do whatever you want with the damn cabin. There's nothing here I want anymore."

Pete flung his coat over his shoulder, strode down the steps, and hiked out the trail along the river. He never once looked back.

Susan and I walked out on the deck, watching him go. I felt as if my stomach was tearing inside me. This was the brother who had been my friend, my nemesis, my almost-twin for forty-one years. How had I lost him?

"Damn it!" Susan said. "I did that all wrong."

"It wasn't your fault." I sat down on the bench and looked out across the pasture. The shadows of evening were stretching across the grass toward the river. "Mother once said there was a spirit of the Sahalie. Maybe that's why she wouldn't allow Pete and me to argue here."

Susan drew back. "What, don't tell me you put Mom's ashes here? Right here, at this cabin?"

"No. I wish I had."

27

Brain-Dead Poker

(July 1995)

> Banish wisdom, discard knowledge, and the people will be benefited a hundredfold.
>
> —Lao Tzu, Tao Te Ching, circa 400 BC

Lightning flashed a blue scar across the darkness. The sound of rain drummed from the dry forest branches that formed a hall over our heads.

"Tacky." Janell shook her head. "Very tacky."

As we watched, a green glow lit a mouth-like shape on the trunk of a gnarled tree beside us. The bark-covered lips opened, and the tree began speaking in a rumbling voice. "The Sahalie tribe has a legend that powerful spirits of great cunning live in the ancient forest. These are the Skookums, spirits who rule the night and fly on the winds of day. They smile on players of fortune who enter their realm. Here, dreams can be real and wishes can come true."

A sudden clap of thunder shook the ground. I flinched, but Janell merely clicked her tongue. "Honestly, this is too much."

Black double doors ahead of us began opening automatically, revealing a kaleidoscope of flashing, colored lights beyond.

"Enter!" the tree boomed. "And welcome to the Skookum Rock Casino."

We walked into a dim, cavernous room with neon signs and blinking slot machines. "All right," I said, "I'll admit the entrance is a little overdone." I had talked Janell into visiting Taylorville's new casino while we were in town for the day.

"They got the legend all wrong," Janell complained. "The Skookums were three evil sisters, not a bunch of gambling wood elves."

"The tribe spent $22 million to build this place. Let's at least look around, maybe put a few quarters in a slot machine."

She sighed, took out a quarter, and stopped in front of a shiny machine that flashed "25 cents." But there was no coin slot. Only after our eyes had adjusted to the dim room did I notice a black box beside the machine with the terse note, "Insert Bills: 1-5-10-20-100."

I opened my wallet. "All I've got is a ten."

"Let's just go," Janell said. "This doesn't look like our kind of place anyway."

Perhaps she was right. We were among the youngest people in the casino. Row after row of retirees with baseball caps and shopping bags sat punching the flashing buttons. In the middle of the room, atop a faux rock mountain with a waterfall, a bright yellow Humvee perched below a banner, "WIN A SKOOKUM RIG." In the shadows beyond, bored card dealers waited behind green felt tables.

We were on our way out, headed for the talking tree, when a voice stopped me. "Hey Bill, Janell!"

A blackjack dealer was waving at us. Although he wore the standard cowboy vest and bolo tie of the casino staff, I recognized his angular features and black ponytail at once.

"Butch?" I asked.

"Yeah, so can I deal you in?"

Janell and I came closer. She studied him. "This is where you work now?"

He laughed. "It's a gig. I gave up on butchering when folks like you started turning vegetarian. There was nothing left to slaughter, except at the casino. Two dollar minimum, straight blackjack. Two hands or one?"

I gave him my $10 bill. "Just one."

He pushed four chips across the table and left one in the pot. Then he laid two cards face down and two face up. "Wow. You show an ace. I've only got a seven. Look at me, I'm crying here."

Our hidden card was a five. "The casino seems pretty quiet for a grand opening," I commented.

"Boy, you two really did just crawl out of the woods. The grand opening was last month. We had ten thousand people to see Tammy Wynette. So do you want me to hit you?"

I looked at him uncertainly. I never knew if Butch meant what I thought.

"Hey, do you want another card or not?" he asked.

Janell shook her head. I would have risked another card, but I let it go.

Butch turned over his hidden card, revealing a king. "Dealer wins, seventeen to sixteen." He raked in our chip. "Are you in for another?"

I pushed out a chip. "You always said you wanted to take back

Skookum Rock for the tribe."

"Yeah, well a casino's not exactly a rock, but we'll take what we can get." He laid out the next set of cards, giving us a jack of spades and himself a two of hearts. "Gosh, you folks get all the breaks."

Our down card was a queen. That gave us twenty points. Janell pushed out the rest of our chips and said, "Don't hit us. And don't give us any cards either."

Butch raised his eyebrows. "Looks like the pioneers are circling the wagons. Let's see if the Injuns attack."

He flipped over his hidden card, a five. Then he dealt himself a seven, and then a three. By all the rules of casinos, he should have stopped there, with four cards showing seventeen points. But he drew another card anyway. It was a four.

"Twenty-one with five cards," he said, collecting our chips. "Dealer wins again, doggone it. You in for another hand?"

I looked at him evenly. "Butch, we're never going to win, gambling against you. But I've always wanted to ask you something."

"What's that?"

"Do you know who killed Clyde Moreland?"

Butch stacked the cards together and squinted up at a mirrored panel in the ceiling. Then he laid his hands on the table. "Sorry folks, game's over."

"Then you don't know who committed the murder?"

"No."

"You really don't?"

"I don't." He lowered his voice and leaned closer. "But I think I know who does. She's one of our regulars. Hey, maybe some dark night I'll bring her out to your log cabin. Then we'll all find out what happened."

We didn't have many visitors to the log cabin for the first half of that summer, so we had to come up with our own remedies for cabin fever. Karen, at fifteen, was now as tall as her mother. At the start of summer she had hit her head on the cabin's low doorway for the first time. She had dropped a box full of books and danced about, repeating words I didn't think she knew. Although I suspected the books might have been the source of her unexpected vocabulary, I knew they were also part of her antidote to cabin fever. An avid reader, she had brought a huge supply of books and rationed them carefully. To make sure she would not run out she put herself on a strict literature diet of no more than one a day.

Ian, thirteen years old, had planned to keep himself busy with whittling projects. But there's only so much whittling a boy can do. Before long he was trying to borrow Karen's five-volume *Hitchhiker's Guide to the Galaxy*.

"No way," Karen told him. Her lofty tone suggested that she enjoyed this power over her brother.

Finally I had to step in and pay Karen a dollar so Ian could have reading rights. A week later, after Ian had finished reading all five volumes and wanted to start over from the beginning, Karen told me I owed her another dollar.

Meanwhile, I had been working on the plywood cabin Pete left unfinished. Pete really hadn't returned since that day when he had stormed out, angry that he could not manage the Sahalie forest as he wanted. We had hardly spoken in the year since then. A hole had been torn in the family, a loss that somehow echoed the death of my mother. And yet, as much as it hurt, I still did not know how I could have avoided losing Pete.

At first, when I repaired the intercom he had built, I imagined it was a peacemaking gesture. Then I installed the oak paneling he had left stacked by a wall. The more I worked on Pete's unfinished cabin, the more I grew to like the place, with its large windows, its deck, its river view, and even its poignant memories. I built a dining-nook bench and mounted the kitchen cabinets so they lined up correctly. Janell pitched in by sewing curtains and seat cushions. Gradually the place became a cozy and welcoming guest cabin. Would Pete approve, I wondered? Would he ever see it? The summer dragged on, and despite our work on the guest cabin, we had no visitors.

In past years, our striped Siamese cat Kitsa had entertained us with mouse-chasing exploits. Now she was fifteen years old, with stiff, arthritic legs. She hobbled about like a wind-up toy that was running down. Kitsa began meowing mournfully to demand that we light the woodstove at whatever hour she chose, day and night. Heat was her god, and her altar was a shelf beside the stovepipe where she often sat.

By mid-summer we had become so desperate for entertainment that we actually looked forward to recounting our dreams at breakfast.

One morning Karen came down the ladder in her pajamas, sat at the table, and announced, "I dreamt that Cousin Mike has magic powers."

Ian looked up from his bowl of oatmeal. "What did Mike do?"

"Well, he told me the magic word for the empty guest cabin is *flamingo*."

"Flamingo," I repeated. "If we all say that, will visitors show up?"

"I don't know, but he said we have to be careful. The only other words that have meaning in that cabin start with a *p*. So all we can do there is pop popcorn, paint pictures, or peel potatoes."

I nodded. "That explains a lot."

"It does not," Ian said.

"I had a dream about Eugene," Janell volunteered, spooning cocoa mix into a mug. "The city fire department had gotten so tired of people ignoring their disaster emergency drills that they decided to blow up one house at random during each drill."

"I bet that got people's attention," I said.

"It sure did." Janell poured hot water into her cocoa mug. "The sirens went off one night and everybody rushed outside. I'd been sleeping in my underwear. On my way out the door I grabbed the only piece of clothing I could find."

Karen put her hand to the collar of her pajamas. "I've had dreams like that. You were lucky you found anything to wear at all. What was it?"

"It was a—" Janell hesitated. She set down her cocoa. "It was a pink Winnie-the-Pooh skirt. With little appliquéd bears."

I lifted a lid off the stove and dropped a piece of wood on the fire. "That's embarrassing, all right, but it's not as bad as my dream. I was back in college. Somehow the campus was so confusing I couldn't find the right classroom. When I finally got there they were already passing out the final exams."

"I think anybody who's been a student has had that dream," Janell said. "Did you try to take the test?"

"I did. I thought I had a chance because it was an open-book test. So I opened my book, but every page was blank. Somehow I'd been cheated at the bookstore."

Karen yawned. "What about you, Ian?"

Ian had started reading Volume One of the *Hitchhiker's Guide* yet again. "Huh?"

"Did you have a dream last night?"

"Oh." Ian marked his spot with a spoon. "I guess I had a few. In one of them, I dreamt I was asleep, maybe in a tent."

"You dreamt you were asleep?" Karen asked. "How boring!"

Ian looked a little hurt. "I don't always dream I'm asleep. Sometimes I dream I'm not sleeping."

"What do you mean?" Janell asked.

"You know, I dream that I'm lying awake and can't get to sleep."

"You dream you have insomnia?" Karen asked, amazed. "That's even more boring!"

Ian flushed. "But when I dream that, I usually wake up and realize it was all a dream. Then I can't get back to sleep, thinking about it."

We all thought about this for a while. I hazarded, "If dreaming about insomnia gives you insomnia, how can you be sure you were ever asleep?"

"Maybe it's the other way around," Janell suggested. "He might have been asleep the whole time and just dreamt that he woke up."

Karen rolled her eyes. "Maybe he's still in bed and the rest of us are having a nightmare."

"No, no," Ian objected, "Look, I had another dream last night too. A regular, real dream."

"And what happened in your regular, real dream?" Karen asked.

"I dreamt Mama sent me down to the corner store to buy a gallon of milk."

Karen groaned. "Ian! That's, like, the *third* most boring dream I've ever heard. How do you even know that was a real dream, and not just something you remembered?"

"Well," Ian said. "To get the milk I first had to find my passport. Then I had to pogo-stick through Prague for a week. When I finally got to the corner store I realized I'd had a half-full jug of milk in my backpack the whole time. Of course then I was afraid the clerk would think I'd stolen it, so I hid behind the dog food display and drank the rest of it."

We laughed so hard the cat meowed at us from her shelf. When Karen could talk again she said, "OK, Ian. That counts as a real dream."

Cabin fever wasn't so bad in the daylight hours. We took hikes, went on boat rides, and cut firewood. I spent several hours a day at the type-

writer in my little writing cabin, working on my latest book. It was in the dark hours of the evenings that our isolation felt intense.

When the dinner dishes were done I'd turn up the kerosene lantern as high as I dared and teach the kids to play card games. After a week of hearts, poker, and bridge, I had run out of new games. Finally one night

I shuffled a deck and said, "This time let's play brain-dead poker."

Janell looked up from her book. "What kind of game is that?" Although she never joined us at cards, she liked to watch us play.

"Regular poker, mostly. But whoever is dealer gets to add one new rule each hand."

"Any kind of rule?" Karen asked.

"Anything," I said. "As long as the dealer doesn't look at his own hand first."

"OK," Ian said. "You start, Papa."

From that point on, our card games were never the same. Suddenly, *how* you played the game made a real difference. The actual point total became less important than the untallied "cleverness points" a dealer could earn by creating a truly mind-boggling variant of the original game.

For our first hand of brain-dead poker, I decided that anyone who was dealt a pair had to stand up and say "Halleluja!" When Ian was dealer he decreed that anything with the letter *e* was wild—including ones, threes, fives, and sevens. For the next hand, Karen announced that anyone dealt an ace had to put a cooking pot on his head and run entirely around the outside of the cabin, banging himself on the head with a wooden spoon while repeating the words, "Oy oy oy oy, I am a weirdo."

After this madness had run its course for several nights, we decided to switch to brain-dead bridge. Bridge is a more refined game than poker, suitable to polished society where players do not bang pots on their heads, and so its brain-dead cousin was likewise more cerebral. Ian invented the rule that one-eyed jacks reversed the order of play. Karen said that queens and fours would switch places. I announced that sevens made the next card trump. Ian retaliated by insisting that we find an excuse to mutter "Excuse me" for every ace in our hands.

Finally Karen invented the mind-mangling rule that you could win back certain tricks with true-false questions. If you had narrowly lost a trick, you could triumph nonetheless by making a statement and challenging the other player to guess whether your statement was a lie. Following this rule, Karen managed to win a trick by announcing that she had put three handfuls of chocolate chips in the scones that morning—something none of us believed, but which proved to be true. Ian, on the other hand, lost a trick by declaring that his favorite species of animal was a cat, although we all knew he was partial to otters.

In the next trick, when Karen topped my queen with a king, I announced, "The statement I'm going to make is that I am going to win this trick."

This left Karen baffled. Was I lying or telling the truth? "I think you're lying," she said. "That means I'm going to win the trick."

In reply I took the cards and stacked them with my other tricks. "Look. This shows I told the truth about winning. So I win."

"Mama?" Karen asked, appealing to a higher authority. "What do you think?"

Janell put down her book. "I think it's a good thing visitors are coming tomorrow. We're going bonkers."

The next morning we awoke to the roar of a rainstorm. Heavy drops battered the roof's wooden shakes like marimba players gone mad. At the breakfast table, we stared out through the silver stream pouring from the eaves. The pasture beyond had vanished in a cold, gusty cloud. The world outside seemed to be dreaming it was January, not mid July.

Karen poked her mush with her spoon. "Lisa and Trevor will come visit anyway, won't they?"

"I hope so," Janell said, "Trevor's mother said she'd hike in with them at noon. She knows the way."

Our cat walked stiffly to the front door and gave a long, piteous meow. When I opened the door the cat took one step forward and stopped, staring at the wall of rain.

"Come on," I urged. "You need to go out to use the bathroom."

Kitsa meowed again, more mournfully than before. I carried her across the porch and set her under the cabin where it was dry.

Janell called after me, "Get an armload of firewood while you're out there."

"But it's raining."

"I know that. We're out of wood."

I took a breath, as if preparing to dive underwater. Then I dashed to the woodshed and grabbed some wood. By the time I got back I was drenched, with rain dripping from my hair. Janell looked at the wet wood and said, "I can't burn that. Put it on the stove to dry."

Noon came and went without any sign of our visitors. I tapped a pencil nervously as I waited, filling in crossword puzzles from old newspapers. Janell rearranged the bookshelves. Ian asked, "Maybe we could drive into town and telephone?"

I shook my head. "Either they're coming or they're not." I knew hikers could get through on the gas line track from Wilson Road in such weather, but I didn't want to try driving that route in our car. I would have to put on chains for the mud, and it still might get stuck before we reached the graveled county road. News at the log cabin would have to arrive on foot.

The kids took a plate of cookies and a board game of Clue upstairs. As the afternoon wore on, and the rain kept drumming on the roof, I could hear their voices gradually change in tone. First they grumbled. Then they bickered. Then they argued out loud. Finally, as daylight faded and our hopes of visitors dimmed, Karen and Ian began giggling.

Janell and I exchanged worried glances. "Are you two all right up there?" Janell asked.

The trapdoor at the top of the ladder opened. Karen's face appeared, wearing a strange grin. The shadows made our teenage daughter look possessed. "We're playing brain-dead Clue. It's a game for psychopaths. Want to join?"

"Um," I stalled. "Why don't you bring it down here where the light's better?"

Janell set a covered pan on the woodstove. "I think I'll just make popcorn. One of us has to stay sane."

I lit the kerosene lamp while the kids climbed down the ladder. They spread the Clue game on the kitchen table. The familiar board depicted the floor plan of an English manor house, with a pattern of squares separating rooms marked "Library," "Kitchen," "Conservatory," and the like. Tokens represented a variety of murder weapons, such as a knife and a rope, while colored pawns represented potential murderers, including Colonel Mustard, Mrs. White, and Miss Scarlet.

"I've been reading a lot of murder mysteries this summer," Karen explained. "I decided we should make the game more accurate."

"What do you mean, more accurate?" I asked. "The game's already a lot like an Agatha Christie mystery. You've got six people trapped in a remote house with a dead man. They go around looking for clues to figure out which one of them murdered him."

A kernel of corn popped, and then another. Janell began shaking the pan.

"No, Karen's right," Ian said. "In a real mystery all the people in the house are crazy. You know, because they've been cooped up together with a dead body?"

"Right," Karen agreed. "And before the book ends, almost all of them end up being murdered too. So here's how we've changed the rules."

In the brain-dead version of Clue that Karen described, the characters were no longer amateur sleuths, but rather homicidal psychopaths in a gothic demolition derby. All of the characters were murderers. The last one left alive was the winner. In this war of attrition, success involved lurking about the manor, hoping to trap somebody else alone in a room. If a suitable weapon was also in the room, the victim was a goner.

To make the game more "realistic," Karen and Ian had given each of the standard characters idiosyncratic strengths and weaknesses that affected the play. They showed me a list they had started:

Mr. Green—American plumber. Green gains a point when he attacks with his favorite weapon, the wrench. But because he is overweight, he loses one square of movement for each roll of the dice.

Mrs. Peacock—séance medium. Peacock excels at channeling, so she can sense hidden murder weapons.

Professor Plum—boring teacher. Plum puts his victims to sleep with history lessons, causing them to lose a turn.

Colonel Mustard—retired British soldier. His special ability, Boy Scout knowledge, makes him unstoppable with the rope.

"Sounds like most players won't last very long," I commented.

"Uh uh," Ian replied, grinning. "Dead people stay in the game."

"How does that work?" Janell brought a large bowl of popcorn. She dribbled melted butter over it and sprinkled on salt.

"If you're murdered, your spirit still haunts the house," Karen explained, her mouth so full of popcorn that she was hard to understand. "All you have to do is find one of the dead bodies and turn it into a zombie."

"Then you can use the weapons again," Ian added, scooping up another handful of popcorn. "Zombies can't win, but they can make other people lose."

"Yeah!" Karen agreed. "This is going to be such a cool game to play when Lisa and Trevor come."

The names of our absent visitors made everyone stop. We all looked out the window at the dark, rainy pasture.

Had I really hoped to see a flashlight bobbing among the wet grass? No one in his right mind would hike to our cabin in such a storm. And the rain looked like it could go on forever.

"Maybe we need a Sahalie Clue game," I mused.

Janell wiped her hands on a towel. "Do you suppose that would tell us who killed Clyde Moreland?"

I still stared out the window. "The weapons are about right, and we've got six suspects: Butch, Barry Bartola, Mrs. Nelson's husband, George Niemi, Lucas Hamilton, and Valerie Boucher."

"What would you guess happened?" she asked.

I sighed. "Maybe that Mr. Bartola did it in the pasture with a revolver?"

28

The Flood

(February 1996)

> Rivers ran to the sea, brown and flat with the clots of swirling yellow foam clinging to their surfaces, running to the sea like lathered animals.
>
> —Ken Kesey, *Sometimes a Great Notion*, 1963

When I asked our eighty-year-old pioneer neighbor, Mrs. Nelson, how high the Sahalie had crested in the flood of 1921, she pointed up into the treetops. Such things challenge the imagination.

When I asked George Niemi about the flood of 1964, he shook his head. "The water came across the pasture with my tractor still parked on the field below the house," he told me. "I didn't want to wade, so I thought I'd wait to get it until the water was lower. When the river reached the wheel hubs, I didn't want to try swimming out to it, so I thought I'd wait some more. As long as I could see the exhaust pipe still poking above the floodwater, I knew she'd be OK. That pipe stood ten feet high. But then even the pipe disappeared."

I myself remembered the flood of 1977. It was the first winter after we had started work on the log cabin, when the walls still stood unfinished. The river spread a quarter mile from its bank, filling the entire pasture to the foot of our construction site. Waves crested at the second slat of the fence gate, just eight feet below the cabin.

But since then the Sahalie had slept for eighteen years. It was easy to forget those murky green waters hid dragon teeth.

The rains that started in the summer of 1995 were not always hard, but they were insistent, like a chest cold you can't shake. By November the ground was so saturated that every shower made the river jumpy. As Jack Niemi later told us, he woke up one morning to see twenty of his cows standing on a hummock near the riverbank, with water already up to their knees. A deep, swift current had cut them off from the rest of the farm. For days the trapped cows held out, unable to sleep or even to lie down amid the muddy floodwaters. Desperate for food, they ate tree bark and thorny blackberry vines. When the river finally sank back, Jack managed to rescue all twenty cows and bring them to the safety of his barn.

Jack thought he had weathered the worst of that dark winter. But the next month brought winds. In January a big Southwester blew up from California and snapped the five-foot-diameter "bear tree" that had been a landmark behind our cabin. Moments later the lights went out at the Niemi farm. Soon the mail carrier was banging on their farmhouse door. He told them he was stranded. Fifty fallen trees had barricaded the Sahalie River Road in either direction. Jack threw a chainsaw in his pickup and spent the day cutting a swath through the logs for a dozen miles, reopening the road to town. But then, with the power out, the Niemi milking machines were silent. For the next week Jack worked night and day, struggling with the impossible task of milking eighty-five cows by hand. By the time the lights flickered back on, his hands were raw, half his herd was sick with mastitis, and he had lost $10,000 of milk.

Two weeks later, in February, a wall of rain slammed into the Coast, dumping twenty inches of rain in three days. The Sahalie roared up from its banks, a hundred times its normal size, and swallowed the valley from hill to hill. MaryLou telephoned nervously to report that water was lapping at the bottom log of our cabin. But what could we do?

Each morning we read frightening newspaper reports. Six feet of water swirled through the streets of Tillamook, where the Niemi milk is processed to cheese. The rain triggered landslides that closed every highway to the Coast. Entire counties were cut off from the outside world. Although the Niemi herd survived, five hundred cows in Tillamook drowned.

A month passed before the roads were repaired and the river had retreated enough that it was possible to check on the log cabin. We took along tall rubber boots and a chainsaw, not knowing what we might find.

I hiked in with Janell and the kids—now tall, serious high school students. We had to stop half a dozen times to clear fallen trees from the trail. When we reached the guest cabin we were relieved to see that it had weathered the storms in good shape. From its deck, however, I noticed several surprising changes to our property. A hundred feet of riverbank had disappeared, along with the large alders that had stood there. The entire pasture was covered with brown silt. And somehow the pasture fence looked like it was made of woven wicker. Only after

we hiked down for a closer look did I realize the barbed wire of the fence was entirely covered with a mat of dead grass carried by the flood.

"Look, the log in the field is gone!" Karen exclaimed, pointing. Sure enough, the seven-foot-diameter log that had dominated one end of our pasture for thirty years had vanished. Incredibly, the flood must have lifted this behemoth and sailed it *over* the fence.

"I hope the log cabin didn't float away too," Ian said. We hiked through the silt to the far end of the pasture. The cabin was still there, but the first logs of its walls were ominously dark. What damage had the river done inside?

"If it's ruined my stove, I don't know what I'll do," Janell said.

I prepared myself for the worst. The boards we had stored beneath the cabin had floated away. In the yard, one of the picnic table benches was gone. The other bench had lodged upside down beside the woodshed. I stepped onto the porch, fumbled with the locks, and pushed open the door.

With the windows still shuttered, it was too dark to see the extent of the damage for a moment. Janell groped her way into the kitchen and gasped.

"What is it?" I asked.

"Nothing!" she exclaimed.

"Nothing?"

"The water didn't get in! Everything's OK!" She started laughing with relief.

Ian called from outside, "It looks like the river crested about a foot below the floor, judging from the mud on the foundations. Waves must have splashed up against the first few logs."

I took Janell in my arms, and I started laughing too.

"I was so afraid the place would be a wreck," Janell said.

Karen said, "I was afraid it wouldn't be here at all."

"I guess we did it," I marveled.

"Did what?" she asked, no longer laughing.

"We beat the flood of the century. We built the cabin high enough."

"Don't say that." She rapped three times on the wooden table. "It's one thing to challenge ourselves. But don't ever challenge the Sahalie."

The river drifted back to sleep for two years. Then one morning, as I looked through the Eugene newspaper, I noticed what appeared to be a typographical error in the fine print of the weather page. A snappy little rainstorm had waded in off the Pacific, bringing an inch or so of rain to Western Oregon. In the newspaper's chart of river levels the Sahalie typically ranged from 2 feet to 6 feet. That morning, however, the listing read, "26 feet." Surely they had meant to print "2.6 feet." Still, I dialed the Niemi farm.

"Hello?" MaryLou answered.

"Hi, this is Bill Sullivan. I just thought I'd call to make sure everything was OK."

"Well, we've still got power, if that's what you mean, but the road to town's washed out. I don't know how the milk truck's gonna get through."

I frowned. "Then you really have had high water? It didn't rain much."

She laughed nervously. "It must have rained somewhere. Yesterday the river came up so fast everyone ran for high ground. For half an hour there was just a sheet of water from our yard to your cabin."

"How high on the cabin?"

"I'm sorry, Bill. The river was up to the window sills this time."

It was 1998, our last year together as a family before Karen left for college. Ian was almost sixteen, already thinking about a driver's license and a summer job.

Janell and I had wanted everything to be just the same at our retreat on the Sahalie one last time. Perhaps we had imagined that our little log cabin would forever appear from the mists each summer, magically unchanged in its own Brigadoon. Of course we knew that in the real world Karen had grown into a young woman with lofty career goals. Ian was suddenly man-sized, with a deep, earnest man's voice. But in the timeless log cabin of our imagination, they would always be children.

The four of us spent the week of spring vacation at the log cabin, cleaning out memories. Each discovery seemed more painful than the last. The table in the yard, where we had held so many picnics and played so many games, had sailed on to different seas. Inside the cabin, a quarter inch of muddy silt covered the floor, the throw rug, the wall logs, and everything else. The chairs, benches, and woodbox had floated about, coming to rest in haphazard poses. Kettles and pans stood brimful of stagnant river water. All the books on the first three shelves were a soggy loss—so swollen from the flood that I needed a crowbar to pry them loose. And of course the toys and supplies in the lower cupboards were ruined. Janell nearly wrenched her back trying to lift a wet twelve-pack of toilet paper that weighed thirty pounds.

Numb, I filled wheelbarrow after wheelbarrow with waterlogged detritus that had once been treasures: Ian's science fiction books, Janell's plant list, my binoculars, Karen's notebook of drawings. On our knees, we scraped up mud with putty knives and dustpans. Then we scrubbed and scrubbed and scrubbed.

By the end of the week, I had come to the conclusion that log walls survive floods better than plywood and plaster. Even Janell's chrome-plated woodstove had suffered no permanent damage. We drew a mental line beneath our losses and made a list of things to do when summer came: Refinish the floor. Buy a new rug. Sew new curtains. Restock the shelves with fresh memories. Try to heal after our loss.

The unseen spiral birds were looping their calls through the sun-dappled alder woods when we returned to the Sahalie in June, hiking in along the river trail. Karen and Ian took turns carrying the box that held our newest family member, an orange kitten.

Our beloved striped Siamese cat Kitsa had passed away that spring. After nineteen years, she had stopped eating, even when we offered canned salmon. For three days she continued to sleep on our laps and on our beds, purring feebly. Then she curled up peacefully on a corner of the carpet, dreaming perhaps that she was nestled beside her sacred stovepipe one last time.

For a month Janell and the children had turned away in horror when I suggested looking for a kitten. Then they began discussing what color kitten we might get if we were going to get a kitten, although of course we weren't. Finally I got a call from Janell saying that she and Karen had stumbled onto a Humane Society office, entirely by chance, and would I mind coming by, just to look?

The peaches-and-cream kitten we adopted gnawed on our arms so eagerly that we named him Snorri Gore-Fang, after a cutthroat Viking from the Icelandic sagas.

"I don't want Snorri hunting mice," Janell announced as we hiked along.

"What if we have mice in the cabin?" I asked.

"We have a live trap for that. And I don't want Snorri getting lost outside. I've decided I'm only going to let him out of the cabin on a leash."

"A leash?" My voice rose skeptically.

"Shh!" Ian, who had been leading the way, suddenly held up his hand. He nodded ahead toward the guest cabin. For an instant I thought my brother Pete might have come back, at long last, to make peace with me here at the Sahalie, and my heart jumped.

Instead there was a small owl, about the size of a feathery football, perched on the gable above the cabin's deck. It rotated its head as if on a ball bearing swivel, aiming its big dark eyes and tiny ear tufts toward us.

"A screech owl," Janell whispered.

Suddenly the owl swiveled its eyes downward with robotic grace. It studied the deck a moment. Then it hopped lightly off the roof, spread its surprisingly broad wings, and spiraled silently downward, falling as slowly as a maple leaf on a windless day. It must have turned around two or three times. When it landed, talons splayed, its wings luffed a moment for balance. Then it flew off into the trees, a mouse dangling in its grip.

"I wonder why an owl would be hunting in daylight?" Janell asked quietly.

"No sympathy for the mouse?" I asked.

"Papa." Karen pronounced the word sternly. "That owl probably has a nest full of owlets to feed."

Snorri squirmed about in his carrier, impatiently biting at the gate. We walked on down to the deck where the owl had landed. The guest cabin was empty, of course. I don't know why I had thought Pete might be there. Perhaps because he had seemed so different when I last saw him, a few months ago at his wedding.

"The pasture sure has changed." Janell was looking out at the field. The silty brown plain left by the flood had sprouted with a tall stand of bright green grass, more lush than ever.

"It's a shame the Niemis don't have cattle on our side of the river anymore," Ian said.

Janell shook her head. "With the floods and all, I don't think they'll ever swim heifers over here again. We should take down the barbed wire."

"I worked hard to build that fence," I objected.

"Still, I'd be curious to see what happens without it. There were plenty of other animals on the Sahalie before cattle. Maybe they'll come back."

When we reached the log cabin, I opened the windows and Janell built a fire in the woodstove, hoping to dispel the damp river smell that lingered from the flood. Snorri raced around the cabin, sniffing and exploring. Meanwhile Karen set up a litter box for him under the stairs.

For the rest of day, Snorri entertained us by leaping about the cabin, pouncing on dust and flies and shoelaces. Despite his energy, I soon decided our new orange kitten wasn't as adaptable to country life as Kitsa had been. In fact, Snorri seemed to have a few wires crossed. After using the litter box, for example, he scratched at the floorboards *outside* his box, as if this would somehow hide the smelly residue he had left uncovered. Likewise, when he ran out of cat food he did not meow, but rather pawed the floor beside his empty bowl. As far as I could tell, scratching was Snorri's way of saying, "There's a problem here," or "I'm all done," or "Something stinks, and this is how I'm going to express myself."

After dinner we tried out a new solar-powered radio Janell had brought. The fading daylight in the kitchen window was enough to make the radio crackle to life with oldies from KSEA, the station in Seaview. Karen and Ian both searched for a different kind of music. The only other station, KSRF in Taylorville, was airing local want ads for used cars and washing machines. So we listened to a Beatles retrospective and read books until night darkened the window and the radio stopped.

In the quiet that followed I heard a faint, hooted call—a single note repeated faster and faster, like the tone of a hollow bouncing ball. I wondered aloud, "Could that be the owl we saw?"

We took flashlights and followed the hoots to an alder tree by the creek. When our light beams found the little owl sitting on a branch, it stopped hooting and swiveled its head toward us.

"Why are they called screech owls if they don't screech?" I asked.

"Maybe they only screech when they're mad," Ian suggested.

"Listen," Karen said. "There's something else out here too."

I could just make out a strange purring noise coming from the direction of the pasture. The sound came in bursts, like a small, repeated whimper. "What kind of animal is that?" I asked.

"I don't know." Janell cautiously led the way toward the dark field, her flashlight scanning the grass. We were almost to the fence when she raised her light and stopped. Sitting on a fencepost was a fuzzy owlet, about the size of feathered softball. The next two posts also had owlets. The three of them took turns emitting plaintive, purred whimpers.

"They're so cute!" Karen whispered.

"Why are they crying like that?" Ian asked.

"I think they're hungry," Janell said. "You saw their mom. She's worn out. She's been hunting all day, trying to keep them fed."

We watched for ten minutes, charmed by the baby owls. When a cold night breeze came up, we reluctantly returned to the cabin.

Even before I lit the kerosene lamp I could tell by the sound of leaping feet that Snorri had found a toy to play with in the dark. When the lamplight came up, Janell cried, "Oh! Bad kitten!"

Snorri was biting, kicking, and batting a lifeless deer mouse. He tossed it in the air. He was about to pounce on it again when Janell angrily chased him away. "Snorri!" She glanced at the dead mouse and turned aside. "I'd hoped he wouldn't kill anything."

"He's a cat," I said.

She closed her eyes. "Please, just bury the mouse."

"I think I'll leave it on a fencepost instead." I put on a glove and carried the mouse out by its tail. The owlets were gone, but I could hear the bouncing ball of the mother's call nearby. I hoped she would make use of Snorri's catch.

When I returned Janell was sitting at the head of the kitchen table with her arms crossed. "I know kittens have to play," she announced. "So I want Snorri to have more interesting toys."

"What could be more interesting than a mouse?" I asked.

She frowned at me and went on. "That's why I'm declaring a Cat Toy Competition. Each of us will have three days to invent a cat toy. All the toys will be tested Friday night, with Snorri as judge. The winner won't have to do dishes or carry firewood for a week."

Ian whistled. "That's a nice prize. Are there any other rules?"

"The toys can't include anything alive, and they can't be made out of animal material," Janell said.

"Even leather?" Karen grabbed Snorri and tried to hold him on her lap, but he wriggled loose.

"Even leather. You can do whatever you want to interest Snorri in your toy beforehand, but once the judging starts, you can't interfere. He gets ten minutes alone with each toy. Whichever he plays with most, wins."

"Sounds fair," I said. "When do we start?"

Janell raised her finger like a starting flag. "Tomorrow at dawn."

At dawn the next morning I was jolted awake by a loud crackling noise downstairs. A voice I didn't recognize exclaimed, "There they go! Forty-seven of the fastest drivers in the world, competing for a million dollar prize!"

Janell sat straight up in bed. "What on earth?"

I ran downstairs in my underwear. When I saw sunshine streaming across the kitchen, however, I burst out laughing.

"What is it?" Janell called down the stairs. "Are you OK?"

"Yeah, I'm fine. We just forgot to turn off the solar radio last night."

As soon as breakfast was over, Karen went to work on her entry for the Cat Toy Competition. She filled a hollow hazelnut shell with tiny pebbles and wrapped the whole thing in a ragged ball of denim and string. About the size of a golf ball, Karen's toy was ugly but effective. The kitten could snag his claws in it, carry it in his mouth, and bat it easily across the floor.

All that day Ian and I worried about Karen's toy. But by evening Snorri had played with it so much that he became bored and ignored it.

"You've blown your lead, Karen," Ian smirked.

"Just wait," she replied. "I've got a secret weapon that will reactivate my toy for the competition."

The word "reactivate" gave me an idea. The next day I set to work constructing a wind-up toy I had seen in my youth. It consisted of a wooden spool of thread, a rubber band, and a pencil-sized stick. Because we didn't have any wooden spools, I had to manufacture one with a drill, a saw, and a pocketknife. When I finished the spool I tacked the rubber band on one end, stretched the rubber band through the spool's hole so a loop stuck out the other side, and poked the stick through the loop. For added flair, I tied a string with a bottle cap to the end of the stick. Then I wound up the rubber band and set the whole contraption on the floor beside the kitten. Janell and the kids gathered round to watch my toy's trial run.

I had set the spool upright on its end, so as the rubber band slowly unwound, the stick dragged the bottlecap around in a circle like a merry-go-round. Then the spool tipped over. With the stick trying to unwind against the floor, the toy started rolling away. Because the surface of the spool was not perfectly smooth, the rubber band unwound by fits and starts, jerking the bottle cap behind it crazily. The kitten put out a cautious paw, but the toy bopped him with the bottle cap and he jumped back.

By this time we were all laughing. Janell said, "If the object had been to amuse people, you'd win for sure."

Ian grew serious. "Snorri likes it too. Both Karen and Papa are real contenders. What about you, Mama? What are you going to do?"

Janell smiled. "I'm not worried. I've got a plan."

Ian frowned. "It looks like I'm going to have to do some research." He put the kitten in the harness and took him outside on the leash. They were out there for most of the afternoon, experimenting.

The day of the great Cat Toy Competition came at last. The kids took the kitten for a walk in the morning and let him sleep most of the day so he would be ready to go that evening. When he finally woke up he was eager to play. We lit the lantern in the front room, cleared the floor of anything Snorri might mistake for a toy, and closed all the doors.

"Ian, you go first," Janell said.

Ian proudly unveiled his entry: a handful of straw tied with a rubber band.

"That's your toy?" Karen scoffed. "A bunch of straw? You've got to be kidding."

Ian lifted his head. "I did my research, and I found out he likes to play with dead grass. After I made the toy I teased him a little, but he hasn't been allowed to play with it yet."

"If you say so." Karen shrugged.

Janell set the timer for ten minutes. "Go ahead."

Ian rustled the straw and tossed it on the floor. The cat went gaga, rolling with the toy, batting it about, and flinging it in the air. The timer showed that three minutes had passed when Snorri finally wandered off to eat some cat food. Ian watched tensely. The final seven minutes elapsed while the kitten chased a bug. He returned to the straw several times, but only for a few seconds each. The timer's buzzer rang.

I held out my hand to Ian as if I had a microphone for a radio interview. "Well, Ian, how do you feel about your effort today?"

Ian shook his head. "I had some problems with the bug and the cat food, but on the whole I feel pretty good. We had a good run, three minutes of intense play. Now we'll have to see how the other toys stack up."

Karen brought out her rag ball. Her secret weapon was an extra loop of string. She tied the string to the end of a table so the rag ball hung suspended four inches above the floor. Then she gave the ball a swing and said, "Start the timer."

The cat went into action at once. Every time he batted the ball, it swung around and hit him from a different angle. Seven full minutes passed before the kitten spotted a bug flying around the lantern and got distracted.

When the buzzer rang I held the "microphone" to Karen for her reaction.

"The bugs are bad," she said, "But my toy's looking like a winner. It's the toy to beat, and that's going to be hard."

I had to agree, especially because Snorri appeared to be getting a little tired. I wound up my spool toy and let it go. It sprinted past the cat, jerked on a crack in the floorboards, and wagged its stick in the air, dangling a scrap of string before the cat. Then it jerked onwards. Snorri watched this show condescendingly, with the strained patience of a cat that had seen it all before. He yawned and glanced back at us to see if we didn't have some other toy for him.

Karen held her hand in front of me as if she had a microphone in it. "Well, Papa," she said earnestly. "How are you feeling at this moment?"

I grabbed the "microphone" out of her hand. "Folks, this is incredible!"

I exclaimed. "The cat's going nuts, leaping into the air, batting this phenomenal toy all over. I've never seen an animal so captivated!"

Meanwhile, the actual cat had flopped on his side and was looking up at the lantern, apparently hoping for more bugs.

"Will he ever stop?" I raved. At this point the wind-up toy gave one final jerk before running out of rubber band power. To my surprise, the toy's lack of motion actually got Snorri interested. He dragged himself wearily to his feet, idled over to the dead spool, and sniffed it. I said nothing, not wanting to break the spell. The kitten touched the toy with a paw, and it actually crawled forward another few inches. But then Snorri jumped up to stare out the window. He watched bats fluttering outside until the timer ran out.

Everyone looked to Janell.

"So what's this secret toy you've been hiding?" I demanded.

Without saying a word she walked to the cupboard, opened the door, and took out a full roll of toilet paper. Then she tossed it up the spiral staircase and let it unroll as it bumped back down.

"Start the timer," Janell said.

The cat played with the roll for a while, biting and kicking it simultaneously until the paper on the outside was shredded. But his enthusiasm lasted less than a minute. He wandered off to sit on the rug.

Janell coaxed him from a distance, trying to remind him of his abandoned toy. "Listen, cat," she said, "This is the first, last, and only time I'm going to let you play with toilet paper. Enjoy it while you can, buster."

When the timer dinged we settled down to argue about the results. Karen claimed that she had won outright.

I hedged, "Yes, but my wind-up toy should win the People's Choice Award."

"People's Choice?" Karen laughed. "Who cares if it was interesting to people? This is supposed to be a game for cats."

"Well, if it's a cat's game," I retorted, "That means we've all tied."

Karen gave me a sideways glance. "Sheesh."

Ian started winding up the unraveled toilet paper. "I think Mama's toy wins the Multiple Use Award."

Meanwhile, the cat had rediscovered Ian's straw bundle behind the cupboard door and had begun batting it about in a frenzy.

"Yeah, right," Ian said sarcastically. "Now that my time's over, he loves it."

Janell took us all into the kitchen, where she opened a tin of cookies and began making tea. "Of course Karen did win," she said. "But I think everyone played very well. And the real winner is Snorri, who now has enough interesting toys that he doesn't have to catch mice."

Perhaps because I feared this would be our last summer together, the weeks seemed to melt away. I took down the fence wire and typed in my writing cabin, working on a book about Oregon history. In July Karen had to leave for several weeks to attend an introductory session for her college. Then it was August, and the maple trees along the river began yellowing for fall.

One evening Janell and I strolled to the creek in the twilight, hoping to see the screech owl family one last time. We had watched week by week as the owlets grew and explored farther afield. They had even learned to screech when they argued. But now the only call we heard in the creekside alders was the spiral song of the mysterious Sahalie bird we had never seen.

Janell tilted her head. "Have you noticed how the spiral call has gotten shorter?"

"No. Has it?"

"When we came in June, the spiral bird sang four complete loops. Later it was three, and then two. Now the song is a single measure."

"What will happen if the song vanishes altogether?"

"I don't want to know."

We walked in silence back to the log cabin, where a lamp in the window cast a dim orange keystone of light onto the yard. We could faintly hear Karen and Ian laughing inside. But a full moon was rising over the spruces along the river, and I was not yet ready to go inside. I put my arm about Janell's shoulder. Together we watched the evening mist creep across the pasture. Like a flood of silver, the moonlit fog spread slowly toward the log cabin.

"Look!" Janell whispered. "Under the trees at the edge of the field."

Dark shapes were massing along the former fenceline. Giant shadows, moving among the mist. "What are they?" I whispered.

Gradually the spectral shapes began gliding through the pasture in a long line—too silent for cattle, too massive for deer. I held Janell's shoulder tighter.

When the moonlit procession was almost in front of us the giant, antlered head of a bull elk rose up from the mist. He looked our way, snorted once, and walked on.

29

Open House

(August 2002)

> I went to the woods because I wished to live deliberately, to front only the essential facts of life, and see if I could not learn what it had to teach, and not, when I came to die, discover that I had not lived.
>
> —Henry David Thoreau, Walden, 1854

Janell and I decided to hold an open house for the log cabin's twenty-fifth anniversary. We had no idea how many people would be willing to hike a mile for a potluck picnic at our rainforest retreat. Still, we chose a Saturday in August—a month when it almost never rains—and started putting out the word.

Somehow, one step at a time, the scale of this picnic got out of hand. We began simply by mailing invitations to people on our Christmas card list. Then, since Janell wanted to invite the staff of her preschool, it made sense that I invite my writers' group and the local hiking club as well. We reasoned that very few of the club's 600 members would actually show up. At that point my father asked if this really was a come-one-come-all event. After we agreed that it probably was, he printed an open invitation in his newspaper column—an article read by more than 60,000 people.

The enormity of our proposed party began sinking in when acquaintances from as far away as Italy started sending word that they hoped to drop by. Then we moved to the Sahalie for the summer, and of course it became impossible to keep track of who might come, because we had no telephone or mail service there. We simply had to wait to see what would happen.

Janell and I sat nervously at the breakfast table on the morning of that August day, watching a steady rain dampen the trees, the grass, and our hopes for the open house. Against all odds it had poured for three days in a row.

Janell sighed. "Think of all the people we invited—our families, our friends, our neighbors. I wish there was some way we could cancel the whole thing."

I shook my head. "If they have any sense, they'll look out the window and stay home."

"In this weather, hiking through the tall grass along the trail will be like walking through a car wash. Except muddier." Janell shoved her breakfast aside. "We'll be lucky if our own children make it."

"Then maybe our luck's improving." I nodded out the window. A pair of bedraggled hikers in raincoats and rubber boots were slogging through the grass. Even at this distance I could tell it was Ian and his girlfriend Gwen. Ian was now nineteen years old, majoring in physics at the University of Oregon. Gwen, a tall, long-haired music major, seemed to share his enthusiasm for outdoor adventure.

"Wow, you really picked a day for a picnic," Ian said, shaking the rain from his coat on the cabin porch.

Gwen set down her backpack in the cabin's front room. "Actually, it was sunny in Eugene. When we reached Seaview we suddenly drove into this wall of wet fog. It's only raining here on the Coast."

I groaned. "That means people are going to show up in short sleeves and sneakers."

Ian opened his backpack. "We've brought enough apple juice and paper plates for an army. What you're really going to need, though, is hot coffee and umbrellas."

Just then the intercom buzzer rang. We all turned to look at the handset phone on the bookshelf. "That intercom hasn't worked for years," I marveled. The line my brother Pete had installed between the cabins was hard to keep operational.

"It must be Karen," Ian suggested. "She said she'd come early. She probably hiked in behind us and stopped at the guest cabin."

I picked up the phone. "Hello?" There was only static.

Janell shrugged. "If Karen's trying to call, she must want help with something."

"I'd better go check." I pulled on my high-topped rubber boots and took an umbrella.

Janell called after me, "And make sure people can find the trail from Wilson Road."

As I hiked to the guest cabin I found myself thinking about my brother Pete. Eight years ago he had walked angrily away from the cabin he had built. For most of that time we had hardly seen each other. When we did speak, our stiff conversations stepped awkwardly around the gap between us.

But then in March I had attended Pete's wedding. At the age of fifty, my brother had married a woman he met in a scuba diving class. Vivacious and gregarious, Melinda brought with her half a dozen grown children from a previous marriage. She even had several grandchildren. Pete had drifted through the wedding ceremony with the goofy grin of a man who had just won the lottery.

Now, as I climbed the hill to the guest cabin, I was astonished to see Pete himself standing behind the sliding glass door. He slid it open, smiling in the same sort of blissful daze I remembered from his wedding.

"Pete!" I groped for words, afraid that I might say something wrong and break this spell. This was my chance to win back my brother.

While I stood there speechless, Melinda appeared beside him and waved me inside. She was nearly as tall as Pete, with brown hair and pretty, smooth-skinned features that looked much too young for a grandmother. "Come on out of the rain, Bill," she said. "I was just trying to light a fire. You know, this cabin is a lot nicer than Pete said."

"I'm glad you like it." I was growing more fond of Melinda all the time.

"We came early to help out," she continued, kneeling down beside the woodstove. "I brought potato salad for the picnic. Pete's been doing something with the phone."

"I guess the contacts had gotten a little rusty," Pete said with a sheepish shrug. He looked about the cabin at the cupboards, the counters, and the paneling. "You did a nice job of finishing this place, Bill."

"I tried to do it the way you would have wanted," I said. "You're always welcome here, you know."

He raised his eyebrows mischievously. "Even if I chainsaw the forest?"

"Pete!" Melinda had been laying kindling in the stove, but now she stopped to give my brother a warning glance. Then she struck a match and held it to the crumpled newspaper beneath the kindling. "Pete bought two hundred acres of cutover timberland on the other side of Coast Range, so he's going to be plenty busy doing his forestry work elsewhere. He's not going to upset anyone here at the Sahalie. Isn't that right, Pete?"

"That's right," Pete said. But as soon as she turned away he raised his eyebrows mischievously again.

I couldn't help smiling. Obviously Melinda was a powerful socializing influence on my brother. But he would never be entirely tamed, and I decided I was glad. "If this new land of yours is cut over, maybe I could come help you plant trees."

"Sure," Pete said. "I'd appreciate it. I guess it's about time we worked together again."

With the fire crackling, Melinda closed the stove door and stood up. "People will be arriving soon for the open house. Pete and I should go help Janell get ready."

"Thanks, both of you," I said, and I meant it. I opened the sliding door and picked up the umbrella I had left on the deck. The rain had nearly stopped. Trees dripped rings into the river. A spiral bird sang out for all it was worth. Even if no one came to our open house but Pete and Melinda, I would count the day a success.

"I'll catch up with you later," I told my brother. "First I have to hike out to the road to make sure everyone finds the right trail."

Five minutes down the path I heard voices in the woods ahead. When I rounded a corner I found Karen leading a troop of perhaps twenty dripping hikers.

"Hi, Papa," Karen said, smiling. "I ran into your hiking club at the gate, so I'm showing them the way."

My friends from the hiking club waved and exchanged greetings. They had come prepared with raincoats, but I was dismayed that Karen herself stood there like a tenderfoot, in a wet, hooded sweatshirt and soaked tennis shoes. Her hair was cut as short as a boy's, and I thought I noticed a new silver ring on her ear. She was twenty-one, and although

I was embarrassed by her lack of raingear, I was proud of her independence. She had graduated from the University of Oregon that June and had been accepted for graduate study in linguistics at Berkeley. She would be leaving for California soon to look for an apartment.

"What's in the box?" I asked, pointing to a plastic carrier in her hand.

"Oh, I brought my rabbit and guinea pig. It was easier than finding someone to watch them."

"Ah. All right, just don't let them get underfoot in the cabin. And try to keep dry." I offered her my umbrella. "Here, at least take this."

"Why?" She shrugged and walked on. "It's not really raining, Papa."

I sighed at my daughter's independence. When the troop had hiked past I continued onward to the gate. Fortunately, the hiking club had beaten down the tall grass, making the route easy to follow. Unfortunately, they had also churned parts of the path to mud.

An astonishingly large crowd had gathered at Wilson Road. Cars jammed the shoulder for a hundred yards in either direction. My sister Susan was trying to herd people across the roadway to the gate. I recognized dozens of friends and acquaintances. Some were changing their shoes or putting food dishes in backpacks. Others were looking uncertainly at the sky or trying in vain to use their cell phones. My brother Mark and his wife Kim had brought several colleagues from the high-tech company where they worked in Beaverton. They were joking with each other as they put on identical, clear plastic ponchos.

Rather than serving as a guide, I wound up being swept up in the tide of visitors marching in along the river trail. At some point I was jostled next to our friends from Italy. I hailed them and asked if they were enjoying their trip.

"It is very nice," Carlo told me, "But I have a question. My guidebook for America says that moss grows only on the north side of trees. This helps people who are lost. Here, why does the moss grow on all sides?"

"It's a rainforest," I explained. "There's a lot of moss."

One of the women from my writer's group added gaily, "If moss is growing on all sides of the trees, it must mean we're on the North Pole!"

My brother Mark objected, "Actually, that would mean we're on the South Pole."

"Ah," Carlo said, laughing. "Then at least we know where we are."

We paused long enough at the guest cabin for everyone to peer through the sliding glass window. Then the stream of hikers surged across the pasture to the log cabin.

Fortunately the rain had stopped altogether when we reached the cabin. Janell quickly moved tables for the buffet out into the front yard to accommodate the crowds. Pete and Ian put boards on stumps to serve as benches outside. Still, so many visitors jammed into the cabin itself that I feared it might lurch loose from its stone foundations. Everyone wanted to see Janell's chrome-plated woodstove in the old part of the cabin. Children climbed the loft ladder and ran up the spiral staircase. Our cat Snorri leapt out the window and cowered in a box under the cabin.

And the food! Susan and Nick had brought Greek rice dolmas, hand-wrapped in grape leaves. Mark and Kim unveiled a jellyfish salad. Others had brought gorp, wine, hot dogs, and goat cheese. Casseroles and salads of all descriptions loaded the tables. Within half an hour, the crowds had reduced most of the repast to empty plates.

I led a group up along the creek to visit my "office" in the woods, the little

log cabin where I wrote my books. When we returned I heard voices whooping and squealing from the direction of the outhouse. Apparently a heavyset hiker had broken the floor of the "husicka" and nearly slipped through. A group of men had rescued the hiker and patched the damage with a piece of plywood. Already the line for the repaired outhouse stretched to the woodshed.

"Hi, remember me?" A tall, bearded young man stepped in front of me. He held a plate of desserts from the picnic table.

I searched his face, but could only stammer apologetically.

He smiled. "I'm Trevor. Remember, Ian's friend?"

"Of course! You've sure changed a lot." I shook his hand warmly. Now I could recognize, behind the beard, the skinny teenager who had visited us years ago. "What are you up to these days? Still building thistlewhackers?"

"No, I fight fires for the Forest Service in the summers. In the winters I'm studying to be a mechanic."

Trevor nodded to a young

woman beside him. "I drove here with Lisa."

"Lisa, what a surprise!" Karen's friend had cut her hair, but I recognized her more easily than Trevor. "I remember when you and Karen played Limited Vocabulary. What are you doing now?"

She had just taken a bite of chocolate pecan cake. She waved her fingers until she had swallowed. "I'm doing grad work for Dartmouth. We're studying the vocalizations of bats in Costa Rican caves."

"Wow," I said. "That sounds fascinating."

At that point Karen arrived with her own plate of desserts, and Janell waved me over to greet other guests.

By mid-afternoon the crowds began to thin as our visitors, one after the other, thanked us for the picnic and said their farewells. To my surprise, no one complained about the mud or the rain or the primitive facilities. It had been a wilderness adventure to remember, they told us.

Finally only Sullivans remained. There were a dozen of us, with Mark, Susan, Pete, and our families. It was Susan who asked, "Where's Dad?"

As if in reply, the buzzer rang. I lifted the intercom handset. "Hello?"

The static was as thick as before, but in the distance I could hear a faint voice, as if from another world. "We're at the other cabin, on the other side of the pasture. The fire's going nicely. Can you come over?"

"Dad! Hello?" I shouted into the intercom, but the line had gone dead. I looked up at the others. "I guess he wants us at the other cabin."

Mark and Susan packed up their dishes from the potluck. Karen corralled her guinea pig and rabbit. Then we all hiked across the pasture.

My father was waving to us from the deck, side by side with his new wife Nell. At eighty-one, my father still stood tall, with a full head of white hair. He had married Nell two years after my mother passed away. At first I had resented his decision to remarry. No one could replace my mother. But Nell had gradually won me over. Although she was several years older than my father and looked frail, she had surprising reserves of wit, grace, and inner strength.

"Look at this! The whole family's here," Grandpa Wes exclaimed, ushering us inside. It was so crowded in the guest cabin that several of us had to stand. "I'm sorry Nell and I missed so much of the party. We got a late start, and I didn't want Nell to walk any farther than this. How did things go?"

Janell sank into a chair by the woodstove and blew out a long breath. "Hectic. Crazy. I'm not doing it again for the cabin's next anniversary."

Nell took a kettle off the stove and poured herself a cup of tea. "We had a chance to talk with almost everyone on their way out. There were so many nice people, and they were all so pleased. How many do you think there were in all?"

Pete said, "I counted ninety at lunch."

"Ninety?" Janell said. "It seemed like a thousand."

"Ninety is quite a lot," Nell said, with the air of someone who had hosted many a luncheon. "Was there anyone who couldn't make it?"

I thought at once of my mother. With a lump in my throat, I turned to look out the window. From the silence in the room, I guessed I wasn't the only one who missed her. Mom would have been proud that her family had gathered here at the Sahalie. This had been her favorite place.

"What about the dairy farmers across the river?" Susan asked.

"We sent Jack and MaryLou an invitation," Janell said. "I guess they were too busy with farm work to come."

"I didn't see any of your other Sahalie neighbors either." Pete put a piece of wood in the stove. "Maybe mob scenes don't suit the country lifestyle."

I sighed. "I'm afraid a lot of the neighbors we used to know have died. There was Mrs. Nelson, the woman who had the farm downriver. And Lucas Hamilton, the lawyer who sold us the property. He must have been a hundred years old. And then last winter, George Niemi." George's death had hit me particularly hard. For years we had visited him every week in summer to get milk and to talk. The patriarch of the Niemi dairy had been found on the seat of his tractor, slumped against the wheel after a heart attack.

"Wait a minute." Susan's son Mike raised his hand as if he were in a school class. "Those three people were all suspects in the big murder mystery. If they're dead, what are you going to do for ghost stories?"

"That's right," Pete said. "How are we going to find out who killed Clyde Moreland?"

"Maybe Lucas Hamilton really did do it." My father was rocking slowly in his favorite chair. "He inherited Moreland's property, so he had a motive."

"A lot of people have suspected him," Janell said. "It haunted his career. Once I think he tried to donate money to have a Portland park renamed Hamilton Square, and the city refused."

"Wait a minute," I said. "I thought Hamilton had an alibi. When he found Moreland's body, Moreland had already been dead for a couple of hours."

Janell shook her head. "We're not going to solve anything like this. I'm not sure we ever will."

"Listen!" Mike pointed melodramatically out the window. A spiral bird was looping its weird call up through the trees. "In one of Bill's stories he said that's the call of the Skookums. Maybe demon spirits got the old homesteader after all."

"That's just a bird," Janell said. "Bill only made up stories about it because we've never seen it."

"Maybe I can spot it. Birding is my new hobby." Susan's husband Nick opened his backpack and took out an enormous pair of binoculars. He aimed them out the window and fiddled with the adjustments. "This cabin makes a nice blind for—sure, there it is."

"You're kidding." Janell borrowed his binoculars. "I don't see anything. Or wait. You're right, it's just camouflaged. Sort of like a brown, speckled robin."

"With an eye ring. That's the key identifier." Nick took a guidebook from his backpack and flipped pages. Then he tapped a picture. "A Swainson's thrush. The song is an upward rising *preee-reee-ree* and the call is a single, short *whit*."

I slapped my forehead. "You mean the 'spiral bird' and the 'what bird' are the same thing?"

"Looks like it," Nick said.

"All right." My father stood up. " If we've settled your ornithological questions, I'm afraid Nell and I need to start heading back."

"Already?" I asked. My father's visits to the Sahalie had become shorter as he grew older. But this hour-long stay was a new record.

Nell smiled and reached for her coat. "I'm a lot slower at hiking than you kids."

For the next few minutes people bustled about, organizing coats and packs and goodbyes. Kim lined everyone up on the deck for a family portrait with a self-timer. Then she and Mark waved farewell and hiked out the trail. Melinda and Pete left next, walking slowly so Pete could give Nell an arm. Nell had said she wanted a head start on Wes.

Susan's family was about to leave when Janell stopped Nick for one more question. "About the spiral bird—you know, the thrush. Why does its song gets shorter at the end of summer?"

Nick cinched down his backpack's straps. "Probably because it's getting ready to leave. According to the guidebook, your 'spiral bird' ranges across North America in the summer, but it winters in the tropics, as far south as Argentina."

"In other words," I commented, "They're practically invisible, but they're everywhere."

"Oooh," Mike moaned like a ghost as he hiked up the trail with Karen and Ian. "The spirits of the Skookums are all around us."

My father was the last to leave. He carried his rocking chair out of the cabin and set it on the deck. Then he put his hand on my shoulder. "When my time comes, I want you to scatter my ashes here at the Sahalie."

I was taken aback by the suddenness of this request. "I hope that won't be for years."

"I hope not too." He sat down in the chair facing the pasture, as if he had all the time in the world.

Janell and I looked at each other, puzzled. Earlier my father had seemed eager to head home. She asked him, "Don't you have to catch up with Nell on the trail?"

My father did not turn around. He rocked slowly, gazing out through the trees. "I just need a minute here first. To be with Elsie."

The log cabin seemed eerily silent after the hubbub of our open house. That evening Janell and I sat by the kitchen window and opened a left-over bottle of wine. We watched the stars come out, one by one. They danced above the pasture shyly, as if they were afraid it might not yet be safe to celebrate the return of clear skies.

I had almost nodded off in my chair when I noticed an odd hum outside. The sound grew louder and louder, until I looked up in alarm. Finally it resembled the engine growl of an airplane about to crash. I opened the window. Twin searchlights lit stripes across the pasture, aiming straight for the cabin.

"What the hell is it?" I asked.

Janell calmly set her wine glass aside. "I can guess. Can't you?"

The searchlights roared up to the old fenceposts beneath our window and swerved to one side. Below us stood a gigantic yellow Humvee. In the dim light I could just make out the logo of the Skookum Rock Casino on the truck's hood.

"It's the butcher," I said. Somehow our old acquaintance must have driven the casino's Humvee over the abandoned, impossibly muddy gas line track.

The driver's door opened and a familiar voice called, "Hey friends, so is it too late for the party? I brought a special guest."

Janell and I exchanged glances. When we had last met Butch he had been dealing blackjack in the casino. He had hinted there might be someone who knew about the case of Clyde Moreland.

"Come on up," Janell called out the window. "We've still got jellyfish salad left."

"Dead meat, my favorite," Butch called back.

I lit an extra lantern while Janell cleared the table. Soon Butch ducked in through the front door. He had cut his ponytail, and his black hair now had streaks of silver, but I was struck by how little his sharply chiseled features had changed over the years. He held out a large flashlight to light the step for his guest, an elderly woman in a teal overcoat.

"Allow me to introduce you all," Butch said with a slight bow. "Bill and Janell, this is Mrs. Geraldine Moreland."

For an instant I thought he was introducing us to Clyde Moreland's wife, and my mind reeled. But then I remembered that the old homesteader had died a bachelor. We had only invented a fictitious wife for him in our ghost stories. And besides, this woman was named Geraldine, not Josephine.

"What a tiny house," Mrs. Moreland said, looking about. "It's even smaller than the place my uncle had here."

"Would you like some coffee? Or apple juice?" Janell asked, taking her coat.

"Juice would be fine, thank you," she replied.

Butch had already found our half-full bottle of wine on the kitchen counter. He poured himself a mug and sat down, smiling.

I brought an extra chair and offered Mrs. Moreland a place at the kitchen table. "Then Clyde Moreland was your uncle?"

She sat down and folded her thin, wrinkled hands in her lap. She had quick eyes and white hair that was so neatly coifed I assumed it must be a wig. "Actually, Clyde was my late husband's uncle. We lived in Seaview then. Clyde was always trying to invite us out here to his farm, I suppose because Philip was his only relative. He even offered to give us free land if we'd move near him."

Janell handed her a glass of apple juice. "Why didn't you accept?"

Mrs. Moreland fingered a silver necklace that hung among the ruffles of her blouse's collar. "You may like it here on the Sahalie, but it was simply too dreary for me. We had a lovely house in the city, with a picket fence and a piano." She sighed. "Of course my husband later blamed himself when Clyde was shot. If we had moved closer, he probably wouldn't have been killed."

"By who?" Butch set down his mug of wine and leaned closer. "Who murdered your uncle?"

Janell and I held our breath. We had waited twenty-five years to hear the answer to this question.

"I never talk about it," Mrs. Moreland said.

I sat back, disappointed.

"At least, I didn't used to," Mrs. Moreland went on. She took a sip of apple juice. "I suppose now that the murderer is dead, the danger is past."

She had our attention again. Butch asked, "Well? Who did kill him?"

"Why, Lucas Hamilton, of course. He was the only one who profited from Uncle Clyde's death."

"But I thought Hamilton had an alibi," I said. "Didn't a witness say he was somewhere else when Clyde was shot?"

Mrs. Moreland wrinkled her nose. "The witness was Barry Bartola. That scoundrel was in cahoots with Hamilton. The two of them had planned the whole thing, trying to make it look like a suicide."

"I've always wondered why Hamilton inherited Clyde Moreland's property," Janell said. "He told us he was in the will because they'd been friends together in law school."

"Friends?" Mrs. Moreland shook her head. "They ended up hating each other. Clyde was too honest to be a lawyer. Hamilton only cared about power and fame. He kept saying he'd loaned Clyde money long ago. Of course that must have been nonsense."

"Hamilton told us that Clyde didn't have any family," I said. "If your husband was Clyde's nephew, shouldn't he have been the heir instead?"

"Yes, and at first the judge said so too," Mrs. Moreland said, her quick eyes flashing. "Then Lucas Hamilton showed up with a signed will. We took it to court because Clyde's signature looked suspicious. But Hamilton found an expert who said the signature was probably authentic, and of course the will had two witnesses, so we lost the case."

"Let me guess," I said. "The witnesses were Lucas Hamilton and Barry Bartola."

She nodded.

"Bartola ended up with a lot of Clyde's land," I noted. "How did he get it if he wasn't in the will?"

Mrs. Moreland wagged a finger. "That's where Hamilton got in trouble. After we lost the case, Philip and I drove over to Uncle Clyde's house to pick up a few of our things. It was a dark, rainy night, just like the one when Clyde was shot. We stopped on the porch because we could hear voices inside. I wanted to leave right then, but Philip insisted that we stay on the porch and listen."

I leaned forward. "What did you hear?"

"Bartola and Hamilton were arguing. First we heard Hamilton complaining that everyone still suspected him. Then Bartola got angry because he wanted to split Clyde's land fifty-fifty. That was supposed to be his payback for giving Hamilton an alibi. Hamilton said he'd sell Bartola some of the land cheap, but he wasn't going fifty-fifty. Then we heard them fighting, and a gunshot broke the window."

Mrs. Moreland held her hand to her forehead. "That's when I ran for the car. Philip and I drove away and never came back. I figured there's no point trying to deal with murderers. They'd already killed Clyde. Unless we dropped the whole thing, we might have been the next to die."

I sat back in my chair and mulled her words. "I guess I still don't understand why Hamilton thought he had to shoot your uncle. If Clyde was dying of cancer anyway, why didn't Hamilton just wait?"

"Cancer?" Mrs. Moreland scoffed. "Clyde had weak lungs, but he never told us anything about cancer. No, he probably would have lived another twenty years. By then who knows what he would have done with his land?"

"What about Barry Bartola's death?" Janell asked. She had obviously been thinking along different lines. "Was that murder related to your uncle's?"

Mrs. Moreland shrugged. "Not directly. But it shows what kind of person Bartola was. After he'd blackmailed Hamilton into giving him Uncle Clyde's best land, Bartola tried to get even richer by subdividing it. Of course it turned out he was a fool as a land developer. He forgot to leave himself a right-of-way to his property at Skookum Rock. When he tried to force the Bouchers into giving him road access, they shot him."

Butch shook his head. "Man. What a godawful mess. First the white men take the reservation away from the tribe. Then they kill each other fighting over it. Looks like the curse of the Skookums to me."

"If greed is a curse, then you're right," Janell mused.

Butch grinned. "And now the tribe gets revenge by dealing greed back to the white men at the casino every day."

"Wait a minute," I objected. "It sounds to me like the whole case is closed. Bartola and Hamilton are both dead. What's left to argue about?"

"That's right." Janell looked to Mrs. Moreland. "The only one left who was involved is you. For that matter, if you and your husband had been treated fairly, this log cabin might have been your house, not ours."

The elderly woman glanced about at the woodstove, the log walls, and the cast iron cookware. She shook her head. "No, I didn't want Clyde's land then and I don't want it now. Pioneering sounds all romantic, but I never was fond of roughing it."

Butch looked at his wristwatch and whistled. "Listen folks, it's been a wild party, but I'm going to miss my shift unless we hustle." He pulled out his car keys. "You ready to roll, Mrs. M?"

She stood up and sighed. "I suppose so, Butch."

I helped her put on her overcoat. "Thanks for coming. I feel like we've gotten to know your uncle over the years. Thanks for telling us what happened."

Mrs. Moreland smiled. She took Butch's flashlight and made her way out onto the porch.

Janell offered Butch a Tupperware container. "Do you really want the jellyfish salad? It's pickled, so it should keep."

"Yum. Better than raccoon." Butch took the container, but he didn't yet leave. He whispered, "By the way, Mrs. M doesn't know the whole story."

"What do you mean?" I asked.

"Hamilton didn't have to murder the old homesteader at all."

"Why?" Janell asked.

"Because Clyde really did have cancer. He had about a month to live. He just didn't want anyone to know. Not even his niece."

"Are you sure?" I asked. "How did you find out?"

Butch smiled. "Back then half the farms in this valley had their phones on the same party line. The morning before Clyde was shot my stepmother picked up her phone and overheard him talking to a doctor in Taylorville. Clyde told him to cancel his appointments and his pain medicine prescription. He said he wanted to die on his own farm with all his marbles intact."

"So the murder was pointless," Janell said.

"Aren't they all?" Butch winked and closed the door behind him.

Janell and I sat back at the kitchen table, shaking our heads. When Butch and Mrs. Moreland reached the Humvee I called, "Hey Butch, won't you get in trouble for taking the casino's truck? I thought it was supposed to be a prize."

"Yeah, they give one away each summer," Butch called back. He slammed the driver's door. "Guess who won it this year?"

Mrs. Moreland's thin voice laughed in the dark. Then the engine roared, and the truck jolted into the night.

30

A Meander Tour

(August 2002)

To learn humility, a man must stand in the midst of the Oregon forest.
—Don Berry, To Build a Ship, 1963

The next morning dawned so seductively sunny that the whole hectic open house seemed like a strange, fuzzy dream. Janell and I lay in bed watching out the window as the alders flashed their leaves in the breeze.

"Do you want to go for a meander tour today?" I asked.

"What's a meander tour?"

"It's where you set up lawn chairs in the boat. You take along books and snacks, of course. Then you just drift, and you find out where the river takes you."

Janell rolled over and looked at me skeptically. "You just made that up, didn't you?"

"Maybe." I kissed her nose. "Want to try it anyway?"

She smiled. "Why not?"

And so we drifted that day with the tide, eddying slowly upstream as the lazy green Sahalie reeled away from the rising sea. By turns the backwards river would spin Janell or me to the fore. She poured coffee from a thermos and reread *Jane Eyre*. I rested my feet on the edge of the boat and opened a mystery novel.

But I couldn't get far in the book without thinking about our own murder mystery on the Sahalie. There had been something unsatisfying about Mrs. Moreland's explanation the night before. Her story suited her just a little too well. It was as tidy as her ruffled blouse, white wig, and teal overcoat.

"You know what struck me about Mrs. Moreland?" I asked.

Janell marked her spot in the book with a leaf. "You've been thinking about her too?"

"Yes. It struck me that she never liked her uncle's farm. It's almost as if she'd been looking for a villain to steal her inheritance, so she could wash her hands of the whole dirty business."

Janell nodded. "I'm having trouble with the picture she painted of Lucas Hamilton. Remember when he hiked over to see us that first summer?"

"Yes." I thought back to a misty day when the log cabin stood half built. "He was old but well dressed, with a fancy cane and hat. He wanted us to find Moreland's murderer so he could clear his name. He said he was keeping a piece of Moreland's old farm for its memories, but I suspected he was just waiting for the right price."

"Exactly. He seemed like a man who could cut your throat in court. What I can't picture is Hamilton chasing down Clyde Moreland with a rifle. It's simply too messy for a city lawyer."

"Besides, I remember Hamilton specifically telling us that Moreland had cancer. According to Butch, he was right. That means Hamilton didn't have a reason for murder."

"That's right. Then someone else must have shot Clyde Moreland after all."

We drifted a while, lost in thought. A blue jay followed our boat, watching curiously from the mossy branches of the maple trees that overhung the bank. The jay hopped to a branch directly overhead and screamed, imitating a hawk. Then, when that didn't seem to frighten us, the jay squawked and flew away.

"I've got it," I said.

Janell looked at me. "Well, I have an idea about it too. You go first."

"All right, let's say Hamilton was telling the truth about loaning Clyde Moreland money—but it was a long time ago, when they were still friends."

"I'll believe that. Moreland couldn't have had much income from his farm, and yet he managed to buy quite a bit of Sahalie land in the Depression. Mrs. Nelson told us about it."

"Well, by the 1960s Clyde's property had gotten valuable, right? So Hamilton demands his money back, with interest, knowing Clyde can't pay. When Clyde gets frantic, Hamilton suggests an alternative: Write up a will with him as heir."

Janell tilted her head. "That sounds like Hamilton, especially if he had somehow found out that Clyde had cancer. But I can't imagine Clyde cutting his nephew out of the will altogether."

I considered this setback for a moment. "OK. So Hamilton was already

planning to alter the will once he got the signature. What a slimeball! He lets Barry Bartola in on the plan because he needs a witness who will vouch that the will is genuine, even after he's switched a couple of crucial pages."

"Maybe."

"No, this is it! I've got it. Bartola was just shifty enough that he would have done it this way. Remember that first summer, when we bought a rowboat from him and he kept trying to raise the price?"

Janell nodded. "Even Mrs. Nelson thought he was a thief."

"OK, here's the trick: Hamilton knew about Clyde's cancer, *but Bartola didn't.*"

"So?"

I put my feet down and diagrammed the plot in the air with my hands as I spoke. "So Hamilton must have promised Bartola a bonus when Clyde died, as a thank-you for witnessing the altered will. But Bartola didn't know about the cancer. He figured, 'Why should I wait until Clyde dies of old age to get my bonus?' He picked a day when he knew Hamilton was coming to visit, got Clyde's rifle, shot him, and went back home. Then when Hamilton showed up and found the body, there were only two options: Either people would think Hamilton killed Clyde, or they'd think Clyde committed suicide. Of course the suicide story only worked if Bartola gave Hamilton an alibi for the time when the shooting took place."

"Why didn't Hamilton just tell the police that Bartola murdered Clyde?"

"Because then Bartola would tell how Hamilton altered the will. That's how he blackmailed Hamilton into giving him so much of Clyde's land."

I thought I had tied things together nicely. Surely it was a more credible explanation than the one Mrs. Moreland had given us the night before.

Janell, however, was shaking her head. "Barry Bartola might have been a scoundrel, but I don't think he was a cold-blooded murderer. And he wasn't shrewd enough to orchestrate a blackmailing scheme like that."

I put my feet back up on the side of the boat. "All right. You've heard my idea. Now it's your turn. Who shot Clyde Moreland?"

She looked out across the broad green river. "Well, if Lucas Hamilton didn't do it, and Barry Bartola didn't do it, I think the answer's pretty obvious."

I laughed. "Obvious? What's obvious?"

"That Clyde Moreland planned his own suicide."

"What! Clyde wasn't a quitter. The man was a pioneer. No one really believes he shot himself with his own rifle. Even Hamilton thought it was impossible."

"Exactly." She smiled. "Clyde knew no one would believe it. Remember Butch told us Clyde called his doctor to cancel his pain medication? That's pretty strange behavior for a cancer patient with a month to live."

"You're saying he already knew he was going to commit suicide later that day? But why?"

"To get revenge on Lucas Hamilton. They started out as friends, but Clyde had watched him go from bad to worse. Finally, Hamilton was so obsessed with power and fame that he didn't care about his old friends. Clyde must have suspected Hamilton was planning to manipulate Clyde's will to get his land—and soon, because they both knew Clyde was dying."

"How did Hamilton find out about the cancer?"

"Who knows? Lawyers have their ways. Anyway, Clyde waited for a dark, rainy night when Hamilton was coming to visit. Then just before Hamilton arrived, Clyde walked out into his yard, held his own rifle at arm's length, and pushed the trigger."

"Wow," I whispered. "If you're right, Hamilton must have been frightened out of his mind. There he was with a dead body, a motive, and an opportunity. Everything pointed to Hamilton as the murderer."

Janell nodded. "He panicked, went straight to Bartola's house, and told him what happened. That's when Bartola's shiftiness came into play. It was simple, really. All he had to do was give Hamilton an alibi for the time of the shooting. Then, when the courts declared Clyde's death a suicide, Bartola could demand anything he wanted."

I closed my eyes and sighed. "Of course there's no proof. There never will be proof. Still, that makes a lot more sense than any other explanation."

"Hamilton was a clever enough lawyer that he didn't go to jail. But suspicion hung around him all his life. It left a pall over his career. Clyde's revenge was taking away the two things Hamilton wanted most, fame and power."

By this time our rowboat had drifted upstream beyond the landmarks we knew. "It all seems so petty now, doesn't it?"

"What do you mean?"

"All the arguing over who owns what. No one owns anything out here. People come and they go. Even the Skookums turn into birds and fly south. But the river's always here. The Sahalie's taking us wherever it wants."

I picked up my mystery book and tried to read another chapter. Finally I gave up and set it aside. "What happens next?" I asked Janell.

She looked up, and the sun shone through her hair like spilled honey. "What do you mean?"

"Well, we've spent twenty-five summers here. We finished the cabin and the kids grew up. We found out as much about Clyde Moreland as we're likely ever to know. This coming year Karen and Ian are both moving out. Then it's just you and me. What's going to happen next?"

She smiled and looked out across the river. The tide had slowed somewhat, but the Sahalie was still pulling our boat upstream, around a bend we did not know.

Also by William L. Sullivan

The Cart Book
Listening for Coyote
Exploring Oregon's Wild Areas
Desktop Publishing
100 Hikes in the Central Oregon Cascades
100 Hikes in Northwest Oregon & South-
west Washington
100 Hikes/Travel Guide: Oregon Coast &
Coast Range
100 Hikes in Southern Oregon
Hiking Oregon's History
A Deeper Wild
100 Hikes/Travel Guide: Eastern Oregon
Oregon Trips & Trails
The Case of Einstein's Violin
Oregon's Greatest Natural Disasters
Atlas of Oregon Wilderness
The Ship in the Hill

About the Author

A native of Salem, Oregon, William L. Sullivan studied at Deep Springs College, a remote school in the California desert where his duties included milking cows by hand. After transferring to Cornell University and completing a bachelor's degree in English, he studied linguistics for two years at the University of Heidelberg, Germany. In 1979 he earned an M.A. in German literature at the University of Oregon.

In 1985 Sullivan backpacked more than a thousand miles across Oregon to research the state's wilderness areas. His journal of that adventure, *Listening for Coyote,* was chosen by the Oregon Cultural Heritage Commission as one of Oregon's "100 Books." Since then he has authored three novels, two books on Oregon history, and many Oregon guidebooks. He also writes a monthly "Oregon Trails" column for the Eugene *Register-Guard*.

When he's not writing, Sullivan plays the pipe organ, reads books in seven languages, and undertakes backcountry ski expeditions. He and his wife, Janell Sorensen, live in Eugene during the winter. They spend about six weeks each summer far from roads, mail, and telephones at their log cabin in the Oregon Coast Range, where he continues to write his books with a typewriter.